pentawards

THE PACKAGE DESIGN BOOK

VOLUME 2

TASCHEN

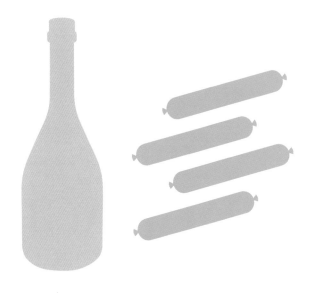

beverages food

18 **188**

INTRODUCTION
by Julius Wiedemann

6

body

366

luxury

446

other markets

562

AN ODE TO PACKAGE DESIGN AND ITS PROMISING FUTURE

by Julius Wiedemann

The field of package design never ceases to expand and innovate. It is probably the most dynamic field of design today. Pentawards has capitalized on this to create the most dynamic and diverse award in the field, and has been around now for 15 years. In our highly digitalized world, everything we can touch has become even more precious. Package design encompasses so many different areas, from branding to materials, from typography to color, from 3D to storytelling, from logistics to unboxing. It has become a universe in itself, and designers have had to make great efforts to specialize within it, though maybe not intuitively in the beginning. But when companies need designers that understand packaging, they will look for those who already have experience in the field. Pentawards understands that designers must go to great lengths to study, understand, interpret, and deliver new experiences, and they award the professionals and studios that do this, as well as the companies who hire them.

Every other year Pentawards produces a publication featuring the awarded projects. This second compilation, which includes volumes four to six, presents not only the stunning developments, but also a clear vision of the evolution of the entire industry, especially in the areas of new materials and sustainability. Even though the biyearly publications are more complete, feature projects with more details, such as project descriptions, this smaller publication is fundamental for the accessibility that Pentawards has always strived for. Such compilations provide the reader with a broader sense of development in the field, which you can't see by looking only at one year or another. This is crucial for designers who aim to keep up with the trends and innovations happening across the globe.

There are three factors that should be the focus in a publication like this. The first factor is the professionals and the studios, both those with recurring appearances on the awards list and also the newcomers. These latter designers are just getting the opportunity to join this tier of excellence, and they bring new ideas every time they are challenged with a briefing from a client. Secondly are the clients themselves. Pressured by market competition, environmental policies, logistical nightmares, and marketing demands, they are now taking every single project to the next level and understand that this is the only way they will make a difference at the end of the earnings report every quarter. They understand how serious the business of packaging is, so kudos to them. Thirdly and also very important are the suppliers. Challenged by both designers and clients, service providers, material suppliers, printers, and every company that is involved in the process of making a package a reality need to be involved from the beginning and are an integral part of the success of a project. They dedicate R&D facilities, feedback loop channels, and their best professionals to meet the challenges set by their clients. And many times over, they will be the one to come up with ideas and offer solutions.

The challenge for package design projects is enormous. On the one hand, they have to pass muster at supermarkets and on the shelves. On the other hand, they have to comply with the growing online market. And that second part comes with a little twist. With the pandemic, delivery has become the only source of revenue for many companies, and making sure food and groceries arrive in customers' hands in impeccable shape and with aesthetic appeal has driven designers to take every project to the next level. On top of that, ESG compliance norms are representing a new challenge in every project. The environment is not just a marketing strategy anymore. It has become a major pillar for the success of enforcing broad environmental policies, whether coming from companies or from legislation. Not to mention customers themselves: they are either making or are going to make such demands. With this in mind, companies and designers need to make the jump to producing designs that are oriented toward the future.

Much of the beauty of designing packages is in the context of cultural aspects, diversity, local suppliers, how users interact with that product in a specific country, and so many other parameters. The web of studios, clients, and suppliers needs to be aligned not only to their creative ambitions but also especially to externalities. Every project exhibits the creativity of one's own niche—sometimes with a more universal aesthetic approach and in other cases with a more local language. But this is the real beauty of creativity: to adapt and rethink every single aspect of a project, so that its success is based on collaboration and understanding rather than a greater mission.

When creating compilations like this, one might think that the most challenging part is the curation. On the one hand, for this book, there is the technical side. Pentawards gives out platinum, gold, silver, and bronze awards. We do not always show the selection from top to bottom, but we want to make sure that the reader experiences the selection as a whole. It is important that the curation takes into account the main subjects, the fields of expertise, the diversity of approaches, and also the most challenging projects. On the other hand, we want this book to be joyful and beautiful to look at. To that point, the sequence and layout of the book is done in a way that it will never bore the reader. This last part sounds like a little detail, but it's not. The balance between these two criteria is fundamental to its success. This being the second volume, we want to make it even more exciting than the first. We are very confident that you will be inspired and that this book can help you take your next project, whatever it might be, to the next level.

BIONIC BOTTLE

Concept: Uwe Melichar
Structural Packaging, Design Factor Concept and Visualizations: Heiko Nietzky, Deluma
Company: Factor Design
Country: Germany
Category: Packaging concept (beverages)

SILVER PENTAWARD 2017

EINE ODE AN DAS VERPACKUNGSDESIGN UND SEINE VIELVERSPRECHENDE ZUKUNFT

von Julius Wiedemann

Der Bereich des Verpackungsdesigns wird immer größer und innovativer – er ist vermutlich der dynamischste Bereich im Design heutzutage. Pentawards hat sich das zunutze gemacht, um den vielseitigsten Preis in diesem Bereich zu schaffen, den es nun schon seit 15 Jahren gibt. In unserer stark digitalisierten Welt ist alles, was man anfassen kann, mittlerweile umso wertvoller geworden. Verpackungsdesign umfasst so viele verschiedene Bereiche, von der Markenentwicklung zu Materialien, von der Typografie zur Farbe, von 3D zum Geschichtenerzählen, von der Logistik zum Auspacken. Es hat sich zu einem eigenen Universum entwickelt und Designer mussten sich sehr bemühen, um sich innerhalb dieses Universums zu spezialisieren, wenn auch zu Beginn vielleicht nicht unbedingt instinktiv. Wenn Unternehmen allerdings Designer brauchen, die Verpackung verstehen, suchen sie diejenigen, die bereits Erfahrung auf dem Gebiet haben. Pentawards versteht, dass Designer große Anstrengungen unternehmen müssen, um zu beobachten, zu verstehen, zu interpretieren und neue Erfahrungen zu ermöglichen, und sie zeichnen die Profis und Studios aus, die das schaffen, ebenso wie die Unternehmen, die sie anstellen.

Alle zwei Jahre veröffentlicht Pentawards ein Buch, in dem die ausgezeichneten Projekte dargestellt werden. In diesem zweiten Sammelwerk – einer Auswahl aus den Originalbänden 4 bis 6 – werden nicht nur die herausragenden Entwicklungen, sondern auch eine klare Vision der Weiterentwicklung der ganzen Industrie vorgestellt, vor allem im Bereich neuer Materialien und Nachhaltigkeit. Auch wenn die Publikation, die alle zwei Jahre erscheint, vollständiger ist und die Projekte mit mehr Details wie Projektbeschreibungen darstellt, so ist diese kleinere Edition grundlegend für die Zugänglichkeit, um die sich Pentawards so bemüht. Solche Sammelwerke geben dem Leser einen umfassenderen Blick auf die Entwicklung in diesem Bereich, die man nicht erkennt, wenn man nur den Vergleich zwischen zwei Jahren hat. Das ist essenziell für Designer, die mit den Trends und Neuerungen auf der ganzen Welt mithalten wollen.

Es gibt drei Faktoren, die in einer solchen Publikation wie dieser im Mittelpunkt stehen sollten. Der erste Faktor betrifft die Profis und die Studios – sowohl solche, die regelmäßig Preise gewinnen, als auch die Newcomer. Letztere Designer bekommen erstmals die Möglichkeit, sich in die Riege der Besten einzureihen und sie bringen jedes Mal neue Ideen ein, wenn ein Kunde sie mit Anweisungen herausfordert. Als Zweites sind die Unternehmen selbst zu nennen. Unter dem Druck des Wettbewerbs auf dem Markt, der Umweltpolitik, logistischer Albträume und Forderungen des Marketings bringen sie jetzt jedes einzelne Projekt auf eine neue Ebene und verstehen, dass das der einzige Weg ist, am Ende jedes Quartals im Geschäftsbericht einen Unterschied zu machen. Sie verstehen, wie ernst das Geschäft um die Verpackung ist – deswegen gebührt auch ihnen Lob. Zuletzt und auch sehr wichtig sind die Lieferbetriebe. Unter dem Druck, sowohl von Designern als auch Kunden, müssen Dienstleister, Materiallieferanten, Druckereien und jedes Unternehmen, das am Prozess der Verpackungsherstellung beteiligt ist, von Anfang an involviert sein und sind daher ein integraler Bestandteil des Erfolgs eines Projekts. Sie kümmern sich um Forschung und Entwicklung, Feedbackschleifen und setzen die besten Fachkräfte ein, um den Anforderungen ihrer Kunden gerecht zu werden. Sehr oft haben sie dabei Ideen und bieten Lösungsansätze.

Die Herausforderung für Verpackungsdesignprojekte ist riesig. Zum einen müssen sie in den Supermärkten und Regalen bestehen. Zum anderen müssen sie auch zum wachsenden Online-Handel passen. Und dieser zweite Teil hat eine kleine Besonderheit. Durch die Corona-Pandemie wurde die Lieferung zur einzigen Einnahmequelle für viele Unternehmen. Um sicherzugehen, dass Lebensmittel und Einkäufe in tadellosem Zustand und optisch ansprechend bei den Kunden ankommen, mussten Designer jedes Projekt auf eine neue Stufe bringen. Dazu kommt, dass die Berücksichtigung der ESG-Kriterien in jedem Projekt eine neue Herausforderung darstellt. Die Umwelt ist nicht mehr nur eine Marketingstrategie. Sie ist zu einem großen Pfeiler für den Erfolg der Durchsetzung von Umweltpolitik geworden, ob durch die Unternehmen oder die Gesetzgebung. Nicht zu sprechen von den Kunden selbst: Entweder stellen sie bereits solche Forderungen oder sie werden das in Zukunft tun. In diesem Sinne müssen Unternehmen und Designer den Sprung wagen, Designs zu kreieren, die sich an der Zukunft orientieren.

Die Schönheit im Designen von Verpackungen steht zu großen Teilen im Zusammenhang mit kulturellen Aspekten, Vielfalt, lokalen Anbietern, der Nutzung des Produkts von Kunden in bestimmten Länder und so vielen anderen Dingen. Das Netzwerk, bestehend aus Studios, Kunden und Lieferbetrieben muss nicht nur im Bereich ihrer kreativen Ambitionen aufeinander abgestimmt sein, sondern auch wenn es um externe Einflüsse geht. Jedes Projekt stellt die Kreativität der eigenen Marktnische dar, manchmal durch eine universellere ästhetische Herangehensweise und in anderen Fällen durch eine eher regionale Ausdrucksweise. Aber das ist die wahre Schönheit der Kreativität: sich anzupassen und jeden einzelnen Aspekt eines Projekts zu überdenken, sodass dessen Erfolg auf Zusammenarbeit und Verständnis basiert statt auf einer größeren Mission.

Man könnte denken, das Kuratieren sei bei Sammelwerken wie diesem die größte Herausforderung. Dieses Buch hat jedoch auch eine fachliche Seite. Pentawards vergibt Auszeichnungen in Platin, Gold, Silber und Bronze. Wir zeigen die Auswahl nicht zwangsläufig von „oben nach unten". Stattdessen möchten wir sichergehen, dass der Leser die Gewinner als Ganzes wahrnimmt. Es ist wichtig, dass die Hauptthemen, die Fachgebiete, die Vielfalt an Herangehensweisen und auch die herausforderndsten Projekte bei der Kuratierung in Betracht gezogen werden. Gleichzeitig wollen wir, dass dieses Buch voller Freude und schön anzusehen ist. Daher sind die Reihenfolge und das Layout des Buches so gestaltet, dass der Leser sich nie langweilt. Das mag wie ein unwichtiges Detail klingen, das ist es aber nicht. Das Gleichgewicht zwischen diesen beiden Aspekten ist grundlegend für den Erfolg des Buches. Da dies der zweite Band ist, möchten wir ihn noch aufregender gestalten als den ersten. Wir sind davon überzeugt, dass Sie inspiriert sein werden und dass dieses Buch Ihnen helfen kann, Ihr nächstes Projekt, was auch immer es sein mag, auf eine neue Stufe zu bringen.

PEPSI PRESTIGE BOTTLE
Design: PepsiCo Design & Innovation team, Karim Rashid
Company: PepsiCo Design & Innovation
Country: USA
Category: Soft drinks and juices
SILVER PENTAWARD 2017

UNE ODE AU DESIGN DE PACKAGING ET À SON AVENIR PROMETTEUR

par Julius Wiedemann

Le domaine du design de packaging ne cesse de prendre de l'ampleur et d'innover, s'inscrivant probablement comme la branche la plus active du design. Fondée il y a maintenant 15 ans, Pentawards a su tirer parti de cette évolution pour créer le prix le plus dynamique et varié en la matière. Dans notre monde hautement numérisé, tout ce que nous pouvons toucher est devenu encore plus précieux. Le design de packaging englobe une foule de spécialités, de l'image de marque aux matériaux, de la typographie à la couleur, du 3D à la narration, de la logistique au déballage, au point d'être devenu tout un univers en soi. Les concepteurs ont dû déployer de grands efforts pour se spécialiser, et les débuts ne se sont pas forcément faits de façon intuitive. Mais lorsque les entreprises ont besoin de concepteurs qui comprennent le concept d'emballage, elles font appel à ceux déjà dotés d'expérience dans le domaine. Consciente que les concepteurs doivent investir beaucoup de leur temps à étudier, assimiler, interpréter et offrir de nouvelles expériences, Pentawards récompense les professionnels et les studios qui se prêtent à cette démarche, ainsi que les entreprises qui les embauchent.

Tous les deux ans, Pentawards lance une publication présentant les projets récompensés. Cette seconde compilation, qui inclut les volumes quatre à six, ne s'en tient pas aux brillantes conceptions : elle apporte aussi une idée claire de l'évolution de l'ensemble du secteur, en particulier concernant les nouveaux matériaux et la durabilité. Les publications semestrielles sont certes plus complètes et présentent des projets avec plus de détails et des descriptions, mais cette publication plus succincte est fondamentale pour l'accessibilité que Pentawards a toujours recherchée. De telles compilations donnent au lecteur un sens plus large des avancées dans le domaine, imperceptibles s'il ne se penche que sur une année ou une autre. Cette approche est cruciale pour les concepteurs qui visent à rester au fait des tendances et des innovations qui se produisent à travers le monde.

Trois facteurs doivent être au cœur d'une publication du genre. Le premier relève des professionnels et des studios, tant ceux aux apparitions récurrentes dans la liste des prix que les nouveaux venus. Ces derniers se voient offrir l'occasion de rejoindre ce niveau d'excellence, et ils apportent des idées nouvelles chaque fois qu'ils sont confrontés au briefing d'un client. Le deuxième facteur a trait aux clients à proprement parler. Sous la pression de la concurrence du marché, des politiques environnementales, des cauchemars logistiques et des exigences marketing, ils repoussent les limites pour chaque projet, conscients que c'est pour eux la seule façon de faire la différence au terme du rapport d'activité trimestriel. Ils comprennent toute l'importance des emballages et méritent en cela d'être félicités. Troisième facteur non moins essentiel : les fournisseurs. Mis à l'épreuve par les concepteurs et les clients, les fournisseurs de services, les fournisseurs de matériaux, les imprimeurs et toutes les entreprises prenant part au processus d'élaboration d'un emballage doivent être impliqués dès le début et font partie intégrante de la réussite d'un projet. Ils dédient des installations de R&D, des canaux de boucle de rétroaction et leurs meilleurs professionnels pour relever les défis posés par leurs clients. Bien souvent, ils contribuent en apportant des idées et en proposant des solutions.

Le défi est énorme pour les projets de design de packaging. D'une part, ils doivent convenir pour les supermarchés et les rayonnages. D'autre part, ils doivent se conformer au marché en ligne en pleine croissance, et ce second point suppose une nuance. Avec la pandémie, la livraison est devenue la seule source de revenus pour de nombreuses entreprises. Pour garantir que les aliments et les provisions parviennent aux clients dans un état impeccable et avec un attrait esthétique, les concepteurs ont dû aborder chaque projet de façon plus ambitieuse. Sans compter les normes de conformité ESG, autre défi au sein de chaque projet. L'environnement n'est plus seulement une stratégie marketing : il est devenu un pilier majeur pour la réussite des politiques environnementales à grande échelle, qu'elles émanent des entreprises ou de la législation. Ne pas oublier par ailleurs que les propres clients font ou feront aussi de telles demandes. Dans cet esprit, les entreprises et les concepteurs doivent s'orienter vers la production de designs tournés vers l'avenir.

La beauté du design de packaging réside grandement dans les aspects culturels, la diversité, les fournisseurs locaux, la façon dont les utilisateurs interagissent avec ce produit dans un pays donné, et bien d'autres paramètres. Le réseau de studios, de clients et de fournisseurs doit être en phase avec leurs ambitions créatives, mais aussi avec les externalités. Chaque projet reflète la créativité de son propre créneau, parfois avec une approche esthétique plus universelle, d'autres fois avec un langage plus local. Mais c'est bien là toute la beauté de la créativité : adapter et repenser chaque aspect d'un projet, afin que son succès repose sur la collaboration et la compréhension, plutôt que de servir une mission plus vaste.

La curation peut sembler l'aspect le plus complexe au moment d'élaborer des compilations de ce genre. Pour le présent ouvrage existe d'une part le plan technique. Pentawards décerne des prix de platine, d'or, d'argent et de bronze. Nous ne présentons pas la sélection de haut en bas – nous voulons nous assurer que le lecteur découvre la sélection dans son ensemble. Il est important que la curation prenne en compte les principaux sujets, les domaines d'expertise, la diversité des approches, mais aussi les projets les plus exigeants. D'autre part, nous voulons que ce livre soit agréable et beau à regarder. En ce sens, l'ordre et la mise en page sont pensés pour ne jamais ennuyer le lecteur. Cet aspect semble un simple détail, mais il n'en n'est rien. L'équilibre entre ces deux critères est fondamental pour son succès. S'agissant du second volume, nous le voulons encore plus captivant que le premier. Nous sommes convaincus que vous serez inspiré et que cet ouvrage peut vous aider à faire passer votre prochain projet, de toute nature, au cran supérieur.

MUTTI

Creative Direction: Davide Mosconi
Design: Davide Mosconi, Giovanni Stillittano
Company: Auge Design
Country: Italy
Category: Best of show
DIAMOND PENTAWARD 2018

Best of the category
Water
Soft drinks and juices
Tea and coffee
Functional beverages
Beer
Ciders and low-alcohol drinks

beverages

Wines
Wine as bag-in-box
Spirits
Milk and chocolate
Limited editions, limited series, event creations
Self-promotion
Distributors'/retailers' own brands, private labels
Packaging concept

GUOCUI WUDU

Design: Xiongbo Deng
Company: Shenzhen Lingyun Creative
Packaging Design
Country: China
Category: Best of the category

PLATINUM PENTAWARD 2018

LIFEWTR: SERIES 1

Design: PepsiCo Design & Innovation team
Company: PepsiCo Design & Innovation
Country: USA
Category: Water

GOLD PENTAWARD 2017

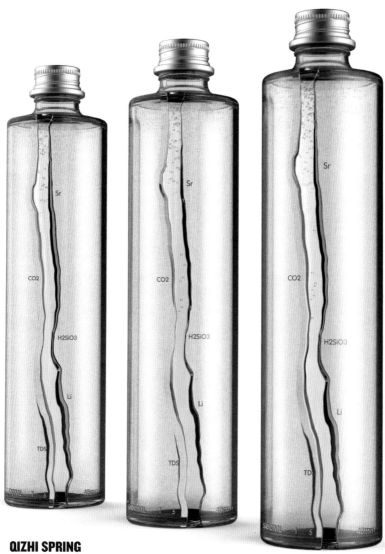

QIZHI SPRING

Design: Xiong Hao, Kong Chengxiang, Wang Yingxin,
Liu Ping, Zhong Qiuyan, Dong Yugang
Company: Kurz Kurz Design China
Country: China
Category: Water

SILVER PENTAWARD 2017

VELLAMO

Design: Aki Vänni, Markus Heinonen,
Sami Fiander
Companies: Vännin paja, Creactive
Country: Finland
Category: Water

SILVER PENTAWARD 2018

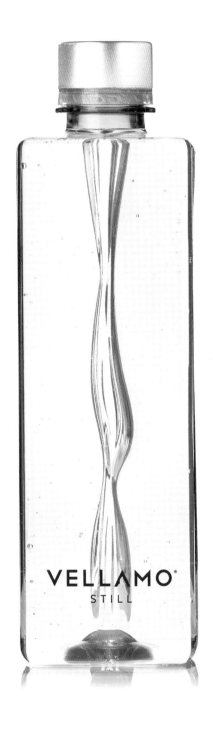

DEEP ORIGIN

Design: Stephan Jelich
Company: Grenache Bottle Design
Country: New Zealand
Category: Water

GOLD PENTAWARD 2010

Deep Origin is a tear-drop-shaped, crystal-clear glass bottle, with dimple recesses positioned in parallel. These two 9 mm-deep indentations on opposite sides of the bottle, resembling the bowl of a spoon in shape, not only function as an inviting grip for the hand, but also feature Deep Origin's company logo. To create a unique and functional package with low environmental impact Grenache Bottle Design chose packaging elements that used fewer resources and lent themselves to multiple re-use, or composting. The bottle's main label is in raised letters on the glass itself, reducing waste. The small biodegradable cellulose neck-label has water-soluble adhesive and is printed using vegetable-based inks.

Deep Origin ist eine kristallklare Glasflasche in Tropfenform mit parallelen Einkerbungen. Sie ist an zwei gegenüberliegenden Stellen 9 mm tief eingebuchtet. Diese Vertiefungen ähneln in der Form einem Löffel und dienen nicht nur als einladender Griff für die Hand, sondern tragen auch das Firmenlogo von Deep Origin. Um eine unverwechselbare und funktionale Verpackung möglichst ohne Umweltbelastungen zu schaffen, entschied sich Grenache Bottle bei der Verpackung für Elemente, die weniger Ressourcen verbrauchen und sich für Mehrfachverwendung oder Kompostierung eignen. Der Namenszug wird mit erhabenen Buchstaben auf das Glas selbst aufgebracht, was Abfall vermeidet. Das kleine Etikett, dessen Aufdruck aus pflanzlicher Druckfarbe besteht, ist biologisch abbaubar und wird mit wasserlöslichem Klebstoff befestigt.

Deep Origin est une bouteille en verre transparent comme le cristal, en forme de goutte, avec des creux en forme de fossettes placés face à face. Ces deux renfoncements profonds de 9 mm de chaque côté de la bouteille prennent la forme de la partie concave d'une petite cuiller, et invitent à y placer les doigts pour saisir la bouteille, mais servent aussi à mettre en valeur le logo de Deep Origin. Pour créer un emballage original et fonctionnel tout en minimisant l'impact sur l'environnement, Grenache Bottle Design a choisi des matériaux qui consomment moins de ressources et qui se prêtent à être réutilisés plusieurs fois, ou à être compostés. Le texte principal de la bouteille est inscrit en relief directement sur le verre, pour réduire les déchets. La petite étiquette biodégradable en cellulose placée sur le col est collée avec de l'adhésif soluble dans l'eau, et est imprimée avec des encres végétales.

ACQUA PANNA
S. PELLEGRINO
Design: Paolo Rossetti
Company: Rossetti Design
Country: Italy
Category: Water
BRONZE PENTAWARD 2011

PARIS BAGUETTE
EAU

Design: Karim Rashid
Company: Karim Rashid Inc.
Country: USA
Category: Water

SILVER PENTAWARD 2010

NONGFU SPRING
MINERAL WATER FOR KIDS
Design: Ian Firth, Sarah Pidgeon
Illustration: Brett Ryder
Production Management: Spencer Forster
Company: Horse
Country: UK
Category: Water
GOLD PENTAWARD 2016

This new mineral water from **Nongfu Spring**, which comes with a leak-free cap, is aimed specifically at young people. Since the water is from Moya Spring, a dense coniferous region on the northern edge of the Changbai Mountains, it was important to communicate its natural source in a way that would engage the target market. The label design brings this imaginatively to life in an accessible style, using a set of fantastical illustrations that were commissioned to represent the four seasons and the great diversity of wild species that inhabit the nature reserve where the water is found.

Dieses neue Mineralwasser von **Nongfu Spring** mit absolut dichtem Flaschenverschluss richtet sich speziell an junge Leute. Das Wasser stammt aus der Moya-Quelle aus einer dicht mit Nadelwäldern bewachsenen Gegend am nördlichen Rand der Changbai-Berge. Der natürliche Ursprung des Wassers sollte entsprechend der jungen Zielgruppe kommuniziert werden. Die Etiketten wurden dafür fantasievoll und lebendig in einem zugänglichen Stil gestaltet: Fantastische Illustrationen repräsentieren die vier Jahreszeiten und die große Vielfalt der Natur in diesem Reservat, in dem sich die Quelle befindet.

Cette nouvelle eau minérale de **Nongfu Spring**, dotée d'un bouchon antifuite, cible particulièrement les plus jeunes consommateurs. Comme l'eau provient de la source Moya, dans une région conifère dense au nord du massif de Changbai, il était important d'exprimer son origine naturelle. L'étiquette donne vie à cette idée dans un style accessible, à l'aide d'illustrations féériques représentant les quatre saisons et la grande diversité des espèces sauvages qui peuplent la réserve naturelle dont l'eau est issue.

SPRING AQUA PREMIUM

Design: Minna Ali-Haapala, Iida Nylander
Company: Finn Spring
Country: Finland
Category: Water

GOLD PENTAWARD 2015

FENG SHAN HU

Design: Shen Hai Jun
Company: D + Creative Design (Shenzhen)
Country: China
Category: Water

BRONZE PENTAWARD 2016

HANSHUIXIGU

Creative Direction and Design: Xiongbo Deng
Illustration: Zhijie Liu
Client: Shaanxi Selenium Valley Industry Development
Company: ShenZhen Lingyun Creative Packaging Design
Country: China
Category: Water

GOLD PENTAWARD 2019

This limited edition of **HanShuiXiGu** mineral water was launched in 2018 with packaging inspired by its water source, the Qinling Mountains. The main features of the design are the drawings of four rare animals that live in these mountains: the panda, the crested ibis, the golden monkey and the antelope. Within the outline of these the local landscape of the mountains is visible. Furthermore, to help promote the importance of environmental protection, the conventional plastic water bottles were swapped with "Ooho", an edible water blob widely promoted in 2017.

Diese limitierte Edition des **HanShuiXiGu**-Mineralwassers wurde 2018 auf den Markt gebracht. Die Verpackung ist von der Quelle des Wassers, den Qinling-Bergen, inspiriert. Die Hauptmerkmale des Designs sind die Zeichnungen von vier seltenen Tieren, die in diesen Bergen leben: der Panda, der japanische Ibis, die Goldmeerkatze und die Antilope. Im Umriss der Tiere ist die Gebirgslandschaft sichtbar. Um die Wichtigkeit des Umweltschutzes zu unterstreichen, wurde eine konventionelle Plastikflasche durch essbare „Ooho"-Wasserkugeln ersetzt, die seit 2017 für Aufsehen sorgen.

Cette édition limitée de l'eau minérale **HanShuiXiGu** a été lancée en 2018 avec un packaging inspiré de sa source naturelle, les monts Qinling. Le design se caractérise principalement par les dessins de quatre animaux rares qui vivent dans ces montagnes : le panda, l'ibis nippon, le singe doré et l'antilope. Le paysage montagneux sert de remplissage à ces illustrations. En outre, pour promouvoir la protection de l'environnement, le plastique habituel des bouteilles d'eau a été substitué par Ooho, un emballage comestible qui a connu une large diffusion en 2017.

QIZHI SPRING

Design: Xiong Hao, Kong Chengxiang, Liu Ping,
He Weisheng, Huang Weiwen, Li Jiabao
Manufacturing: Huang Qiqi
Company: Kurz Kurz Design
Country: China
Category: Water

SILVER PENTAWARD 2019

LUZHUOQUAN MINERAL WATER

Design: KL&K Design
Creative Direction: Hong Ko
Design Direction: Dayong Zhang
Design: Yu Cao, Yongsheng Lu
Company: Luzhuoquan Mineral Water
Country: China
Category: Water

BRONZE PENTAWARD 2019

RISHI TEA & BOTANICALS

Creative Direction: Dan Olson
Art Direction and Senior Design:
Christina Fischer
Photography: Brent Schoepf
Project Management: Ian Gerstl
Company: Studio MPLS
Country: USA
Category: Water
BRONZE PENTAWARD 2020

SOURCY

Design Direction: Thea Bakker, John Comitis
Account Management: Aart Brandsma
Company: VBAT
Country: Netherlands
Category: Water
SILVER PENTAWARD 2015

LIFEWTR SERIES 6: DIVERSITY IN DESIGN

Design: PepsiCo Design & Innovation team
Artwork: Ji Won Choi, Jamall Osterholm, Daniel Cloke
Company: PepsiCo Design & Innovation
Country: USA
Category: Water

SILVER PENTAWARD 2019

SEPOY&CO

Creative Direction: Erika Barbieri
Brand and Bottle Design: Erika Barbieri,
Henrik Olsson
Client: Sepoy&Co
CAD Development: Hansson Design
Company: OlssønBarbieri
Country: Norway
Category: Soft drinks and juices
SILVER PENTAWARD 2019

Sepoy&Co Tonic Water makes a nod to Indian history with a name inspired by the legacy of the Sepoy warriors who have deep roots in Indian culture and are an integral part of the story of gin and tonic itself. The visual strategy is based on colour codes and patterns that communicate the different taste profiles, whilst the typography is a combination of sans serif and script creating a contrast between heritage and contemporary brand identity. The structured vertical pattern of the bottle design borrows inspiration from spirits and soda water bottles from the 19th century and is another nod to the brotherhood of the Sepoys and their mantra "stronger together".

Das Design von **Sepoy&Co Tonic Water** ist eine Hommage an die indische Geschichte. Mit einem Namen, der von dem Vermächtnis der Sepoy-Krieger inspiriert ist, die tief in der indischen Kultur verwurzelt und ein bedeutender Teil der Geschichte von Gin und Tonic selbst sind. Die visuelle Strategie basiert auf einem Farbsystem und Mustern, die die verschiedenen Geschmackssorten widerspiegeln, während die Typografie, eine Kombination aus Sans Serif und Script, einen Kontrast zwischen Erbe und zeitgemäßer Markenidentität schafft. Das vertikale Muster des Flaschendesigns zieht seine Inspiration von Spirituosen- und Sodaflaschen des 19. Jahrhunderts und verweist außerdem auf die Bruderschaft der Sepoy und deren Mantra: „Gemeinsam sind wir stärker".

L'eau tonique **Sepoy&Co Tonic Water** fait un clin d'œil à l'histoire de l'Inde avec un nom inspiré de l'héritage des soldats cipayes, dont les racines sont profondément ancrées dans la culture indienne et qui font partie intégrante de l'histoire du gin et de l'eau tonique à proprement parler. La stratégie visuelle repose sur des codes chromatiques et des motifs distinguant différents goûts. Pour sa part, la combinaison typographique Sans serif et Script crée un contraste entre cet héritage et l'identité contemporaine de la marque. Le motif vertical du design de la bouteille puise son inspiration dans les bouteilles de spiritueux et de sodas du XIXe siècle, avec une claire référence à la confraternité des cipayes et à leur devise « Plus forts ensemble ».

HOOGESTEGER

Creative Direction: Claire Parker
Design Direction: Denise Faraco
Design: Luke Morreau
Direction: Melinda Szentpetery
Company: Design Bridge London
Country: UK
Category: Soft drinks and juices
GOLD PENTAWARD 2011

PEPSI
RAW

Design: Stuart Lelsie, Taek Kim (4sight);
Robert Lebras-Brown (Pepsi)
Company: 4sight Inc.
Country: USA
Category: Soft drinks and juices

BRONZE PENTAWARD 2009

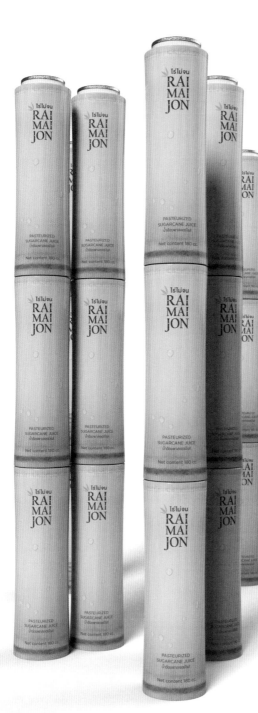

RAIMAIJON
Design: Prompt Design X CORdesign team
Company: Prompt Design
Country: Thailand
Category: Soft drinks and juices
BRONZE PENTAWARD 2018

NONGFU SPRING

Design: Mousegraphics team
Company: Mousegraphics
Country: Greece
Category: Soft drinks and juices
SILVER PENTAWARD 2017

WORKAHOLIC

Strategy and Copywriting: Aleksandr Bozhko, Ivan Dergachev
Art Direction: Lidiya Kapysh
Design: Anna Pazyuk, Albert Safin, Alexandra Chushkina
Illustration: Viktor Khomenko, Alexandra Chushkina
3D: Albert Safin
Motion: Alexandra Chushkina
Company: The Clients
Country: Russia
Category: Tea and coffee (ready-to-drink)
GOLD PENTAWARD 2020

A coffee for workaholics, designed by workaholics. The **Workaholic** cold coffee brew packaging design project begun with just one wine bottle and one beer can. But this quickly evolved into a true workaholics project with the team developing 10 logos and 10 label design variations based on the 'workaholics' concept, to use across multiple containers and items including coffee bean bags, coasters, stickers, wine bottles, beer cans, gift boxes, flasks, posters and even Telegram sticker packs.

Ein Kaffee für Workaholics, entworfen von Workaholics. Das Designprojekt für den Cold Brew **Workaholic**-Kaffee begann mit einer Flasche Wein und einer Bierdose. Daraus entwickelte sich sehr schnell ein wahres Workaholic-Projekt, im Zuge dessen das Team auf Grundlage des Konzepts „Arbeitsmensch" zehn Logos und zehn Etiketten entwarf, die auf verschiedenen Behältern und Artikeln zum Einsatz kommen sollten, darunter Kaffeebohnensäcke, Untersetzer, Weinflaschen, Bierdosen, Geschenkboxen, Flachmänner, Poster und sogar Sticker für den Messengerdienst Telegram.

Un café pour accros du travail conçu par des accros du travail. Le projet de design du packaging pour **Workaholic**, qui propose un café à consommer froid, se limitait au début à une bouteille de vin et une cannette de bière. Le projet s'est toutefois vite intensifié et l'équipe a mis au point 10 logos et 10 variantes d'étiquettes à partir du concept « accros du travail ». On les retrouve sur divers emballages et articles, tels que paquets de café en grains, sous-verres, adhésifs, bouteilles de vin, cannettes de bière, coffrets-cadeaux, gourdes, posters, et même des packs d'autocollants Telegram.

TYPE-FACES PROJECT

Art Direction: Jimmi Tuan
Design: Si Tran, Alex Dang, Nguyễn X. Hoàng
Account Direction: Hien Nguyen
Company: Bratus Agency
Country: Vietnam
Category: Tea and coffee (ready-to-drink)
SILVER PENTAWARD 2020

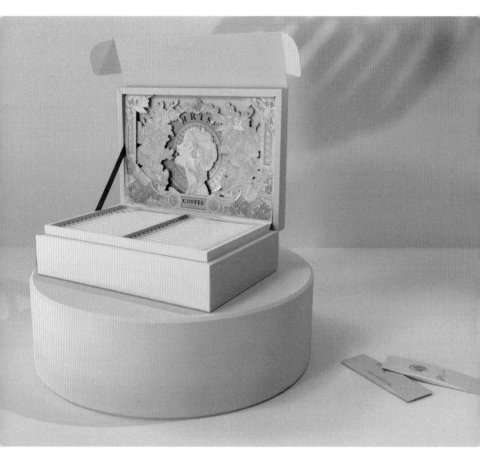

BALLE IRIS COFFEE

Project Direction: Haishan Li
Project Management: Chi Zou
General Design Guidance: Ji Chen
Design: Ji Chen, Zhiguang Huang
Company: Shenzhen Jinye Wannyuan R&D
Country: China
Category: Tea and coffee (ready-to-drink)

SILVER PENTAWARD 2020

SONG CHINESE CUISINE

Design: Shaobin Lin
Client: Haiyang Song
Photography: Yanpeng Chen
Company: Lin Shaobin Design
Country: China
GOLD PENTAWARD 2019

The three colours of packaging for **Song Chinese Cuisine Mountain Tea** reflect the different concentrations of the charcoal-baked tea and the mountainous area in which the tea is grown. The burn mark effect on the packaging was copied from real burnt paper and folded to highlight the charcoal-baked nature of the tea, and to create the effect of layer upon layer of mountains. The products are placed in a gift box, which when opened shows abstract paintings of flying cranes, high mountains and the moon.

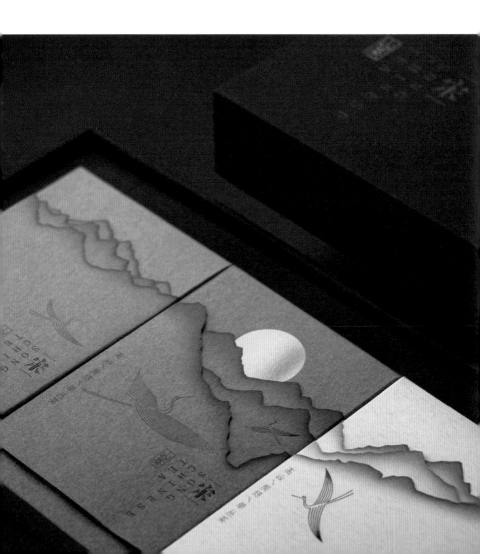

Die drei Farbtöne der Verpackung des **Song Chinese Cuisine Mountain Tea** spiegeln die Nuancen des über Holzkohle gerösteten Tees und der Gebirgsgegend, in der er angebaut wurde, wider. Die Brandspuren wurden echtem verbranntem Papier nachempfunden, das gefaltet wurde, um die Charakteristik des gerösteten Tees darzustellen. So entsteht ein Effekt, der den vielschichtigen Bergen gleicht. Die Produkte befinden sich in einer Geschenkbox, die beim Öffnen abstrakte Bilder von fliegenden Kranichen, hohen Bergen und dem Mond zeigt.

Les trois couleurs du packaging de **Song Chinese Cuisine Mountain Tea** sont à l'image des différentes concentrations de ce thé cuit au charbon, et de la région montagneuse où il est cultivé. L'effet de trace de brûlure sur l'emballage est la reproduction d'un véritable papier brûlé et plié pour évoquer la cuisson au charbon du thé et créer l'effet de superposition de couches de montagnes. Les produits sont logés dans un coffret-cadeau : à son ouverture, il révèle des peintures abstraites de grues en vol, de hauts massifs et de la lune.

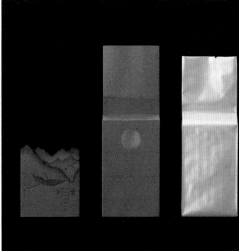

L.A BREWERY

Management Partners: Kate Marlow,
Tess Wicksteed
Design: Josh Williams
Company: Here Design
Country: UK
Category: Tea and coffee (ready-to-drink)
GOLD PENTAWARD 2018

XIAOXIAOHUO

Design: Xiongbo Deng
Company: Shenzhen Lingyun Creative
Packaging Design
Country: China
Category: Tea and coffee (ready-to-drink)
SILVER PENTAWARD 2017

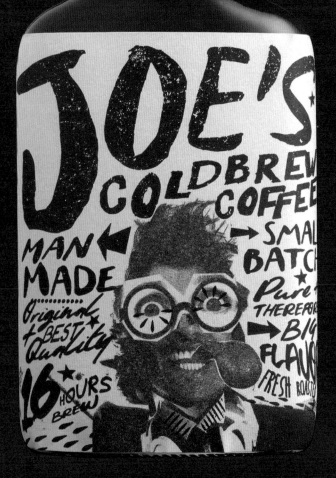

JOE'S COLDBREW
Design: Stranger & Stranger team
Company: Stranger & Stranger
Country: UK
Category: Tea and coffee (ready-to-drink)
SILVER PENTAWARD 2017

**UNI PRESIDENT ENTERPRISES
AHA DEAR**

Design: Mousegraphics team
Company: Mousegraphics
Country: Greece
Category: Tea and coffee (ready-to-drink)
BRONZE PENTAWARD 2017

MING MING SHI CHA

3D Design: In Spirit Design
Creative Direction: Christophe Blin
Brand/Graphic Design: Bravis International
Creative Direction: Yoshito Watanabe
Companies: In Spirit Design, Bravis International
Country: Spain, Japan
Category: Tea and coffee (ready-to-drink)

SILVER PENTAWARD 2014

**SUNTORY
GREEN TEA IYEMON**

Creative Direction: Akiko Kirimoto
Art Direction: Kei Nishikawa
Design: Keiko Genkaku, Kei Nishikawa
Bottle Design: Yoji Minakuchi
Company: Suntory
Country: Japan
Category: Tea and coffee (ready-to-drink)
BRONZE PENTAWARD 2017

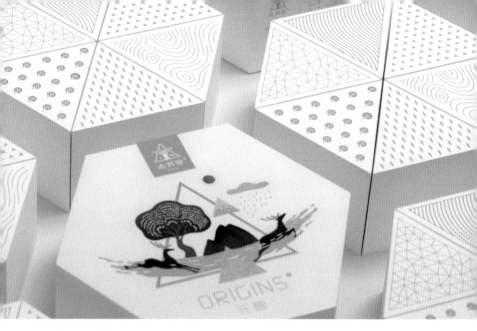

ANCIENT FOG PAVILION TEA

Creative Direction: Shi Changhong
Art Direction: Li Mingdeng
Design: Wang Zhong
Illustration: Wang Zhong
Company: Guizhou Uplink Creative Brand Design
Country: China
Category: Tea and coffee (ready-to-drink)
GOLD PENTAWARD 2020

Ancient Fog Pavilion Tea comes from deep in the mountains, picked from ancient trees surrounded by clouds and mist. On the outer packaging, illustrations of ancient trees and forest foothills are used, whilst on the inside, the container is made up of six separate triangular boxes that are imprinted with the words "viewing the clouds, hunting the mountains, guarding the trees, moistening the soil, habitat water, and tea". These concepts highlight the product's key selling points, a belief in environmental protection and respect for the ancient trees that are the source of the tea.

Ancient Fog Pavilion Tea kommt tief aus dem Gebirge und wurde von alten Bäumen gepflückt, die von Wolken und Nebel umgeben sind. Auf der äußeren Verpackung wurden Illustrationen von Bäumen, Wäldern und dem Fuß des Gebirges verwendet, während der Innenbehälter aus sechs separaten dreieckigen Schachteln besteht, auf denen die Worte „Die Wolken sehend, die Berge jagend, die Bäume bewachend, den Boden befeuchtend, Lebensraum Wasser und Tee" zu lesen sind. Diese Konzepte unterstreichen die wichtigsten Verkaufsargumente des Produkts, den Glauben an den Umweltschutz und den Respekt für die alten Bäume, von denen der Tee stammt.

Au creux des montagnes, le thé **Ancient Fog Pavilion Tea** est cueilli d'arbres séculaires baignés par les nuages et la brume. L'extérieur du packaging affiche des illustrations de ces arbres anciens et des contreforts de forêts, alors que l'intérieur compte six boîtes triangulaires sur lesquelles on peut lire « observer les nuages, arpenter les montagnes, protéger les arbres, humidifier le sol, préserver l'habitat, l'eau et le thé ». Ces concepts mettent en valeur les arguments de vente du produit, à savoir la protection de l'environnement et le respect des arbres séculaires produisant le thé.

**IYEMON CHA
GREEN ESPRESSO**

Creative Direction: Yoji Minakuchi
Art Direction/Design: Keiko Genkaku
Design: IFF Company Inc.
Company: Suntory
Country: Japan
Category: Tea and coffee (ready-to-drink)

BRONZE PENTAWARD 2012

RUBRA

Graphic Design/Photography: Geoff Bickford
Graphic Design: Esther Lee
Company: Dessein
Country: Australia
Category: Tea and coffee (dry and capsules)
SILVER PENTAWARD 2010

JINGYANG BRICK TEA

Creative Direction: Langcer Lee
Design: Jie Yang, Linwei Guo, Riso Guo, Limo Pan
Illustration: Fan Zhang
Photography: Tao Jiang
Company: Litete Brand Design
Country: China
Category: Tea and coffee (dry and capsules)
SILVER PENTAWARD 2019

CHATEAU ROUGE

Design: David Beard, Bronwen Edwards,
Mel Beeson
Company: Brandhouse
Country: UK
Category: Tea and coffee (dry)

GOLD PENTAWARD 2009

The Parisian **Chateau Rouge** brand created
a line of premium teas from around the world,
with Brandhouse using the name to imagine a real
mansion somewhere in Paris filled with the finest
art collection. Each package features the image
of an antique item found and shot in the imaginary
chateau's richly sumptuous interior, with each item
carefully echoing a particular tea in origin, taste
or name.

Die Pariser Marke **Chateau Rouge** schuf eine
Produktlinie mit Premium-Tees aus aller Welt.
Brandhouse nutzte den Markennamen, um sich
irgendwo in Paris eine echtes Herrenhaus aus-
zumalen, das mit einer ausgezeichneten Kunst-
sammlung gefüllt ist. Auf jeder Packung wird das
Bild eines antiken Gegenstandes gezeigt, der in
der opulenten Innenausstattung des imaginären
Herrensitzes gefunden und fotografiert wurde.
Jeder Gegenstand bezieht sich hinsichtlich
Ursprung, Geschmack oder Name wohlüberlegt
auf einen bestimmten Tee.

La marque parisienne **Château Rouge** a créé
une ligne de thés haut de gamme issus des quatre
coins du globe. En partant de ce nom, l'agence
Brandhouse a imaginé un vrai manoir quelque part
dans Paris, décoré d'une exquise collection d'art.
Chaque emballage est illustré par une antiquité
trouvée et photographiée dans le décor somptueux
de ce château imaginaire, qui fait écho à l'origine,
au goût ou au nom du thé concerné.

CHATEAU ROUGE

FORMOSA
POUCHONG
GREEN OOLONG

CHATEAU ROUGE

JASMINE
DOWNY PEARLS
GREEN TEA

CHATEAU ROUGE

WIEDOUW
LONG CUT
ROOIBOS
TISANE

CHATEAU ROUGE

WILD HARVEST
HONEYBUSH
TISANE

CHATEAU ROUGE

ILAM
FIKKAL
[1ST FLUSH] [EUROPE]
BLACK TEA

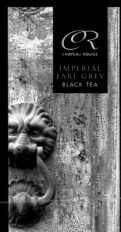

CHATEAU ROUGE

IMPERIAL
EARL GREY
BLACK TEA

CHATEAU ROUGE

WHITE
MONKEY
GREEN TEA

CHATEAU ROUGE

SIKKIM
TEMI
[1ST FLUSH] [EUROPE]
BLACK TEA

ESSELON

Executive Creative Direction: Kristen Modestow
Design: Steve Oparowski
Project Management: Jessica Dawson
Company: Brigade
Country: USA
Category: Tea and coffee (dry and capsules)

GOLD PENTAWARD 2018

When **Esselon**, the award-winning coffee producer and café, decided it was time for a rebrand, their brief to the designers was "elegance without being elegant." They opted for a clean, refined look, designed to stand out on the shelf and encourage local grassroots brand growth while also aiming for a presence in national chains. Clean linework, plenty of negative space, and flowing horizon lines combine with a suite of graphic elements tied to the local scene, rendering a landscape that captures the brand's unique vigor. The locally iconic cafe is featured front and center, with an ascending set of stairs creating a welcome to attract coffee lovers.

Esselon, preisgekrönter Kaffee-Erzeuger mit Café, entschied, es wäre Zeit für einen Imagewechsel. Der Auftrag an die Designer lautete: „Eleganz ohne elegant zu sein." Der Entwurf setzt auf einen klaren, edlen Look, der im Regal herausstechen und lokale Marken fördern soll, während zugleich die Präsenz in landesweiten Handelsketten angestrebt wird. Klare Linien, viel Negativraum und fließende Horizontlinien verbinden sich hier mit einer Folge grafischer Elemente. Die Einbindung der lokalen Szenerie unterstreicht die besondere Lebendigkeit der Marke. Das Kultcafé selbst ist zentriert auf der Vorderseite zu sehen, und die ansteigenden Stufen davor wirken wie ein Willkommensgruß an alle Kaffeeliebhaber.

Lorsque **Esselon**, producteur de café et bar à café primé, a décidé qu'il était temps de moderniser son identité de marque, les designers devaient trouver une solution « élégante sans être élégante ». Le choix s'est porté sur un look épuré et raffiné, conçu pour se distinguer dans les rayons et encourager la croissance de cette marque à l'échelle locale, mais aussi avec une présence dans les chaînes nationales. Des dessins aux traits purs, une abondance d'espace négatif et des lignes d'horizon gracieuses se combinent à une série d'éléments graphiques associés à l'environnement local pour créer un paysage qui exprime la vigueur unique de la marque. Le bâtiment emblématique à l'échelle locale est placé sur le devant de la scène, avec des escaliers qui accueillent et invitent les amateurs de café.

YOUNG AND BEAUTIFOOD
THE BEAUTEA

Creative Direction: Paco Adin
Account Management: Lourdes Morillas
Company: Supperstudio
Country: Spain
Category: Tea and coffee (dry and capsules)

SILVER PENTAWARD 2017

MEDOVYI DOM

Design: Maria Ponomareva
Country: USA
Category: Tea and coffee (dry and capsules)
BRONZE PENTAWARD 2018

CAFÉ DA CONDESSA

Design Direction: Gustavo Piqueira
Design: Gustavo Piqueira, Samia Jacintho
Team: Marcela Souza
Company: Casa Rex
Country: Brazil
Category: Tea and coffee (dry and capsules)
BRONZE PENTAWARD 2018

TASTEFUL TEA

Design: Victor Branding Design
Company: Victor Branding
Design Corp.
Country: Taiwan
Category: Tea and coffee
(dry and capsules)
BRONZE PENTAWARD 2014

SILK ROAD
PU-ERH TEA

Design: Pu Wei-Ping,
Yang Tzu-Hsing, Chen Kuei-Lan
Company: PH7 Creative Lab
Country: Taiwan
Category: Tea and coffee
(dry and capsules)

GOLD PENTAWARD 2017

PEEZE

Design: Sogood creative team
Company: Sogood
Country: Netherlands
Category: Tea and coffee (dry and capsules)
SILVER PENTAWARD 2011

NOA POTIONS
RELAXATION

Creative Direction: Yashar Niknam
Client Direction: Simon Kamras
Senior Design: Yashar Niknam
Design: Carl Du RietzI
Illustration: Negare Emdadian
Photography: Tomas Monka
Structural Design: Urban Ahlgren (No Picnic)
Company: Super Tuesday & No Picnic
Country: Sweden
Category: Functional beverages

GOLD PENTAWARD 2015

SENSER SPIRITS:
LIFT YOUR MIND & MOOD

Creative Direction: David Azurdia
Creative Direction: Ben Christie
Design: Heidi Shepherd, John Randall
Project Management: Alice Thompson
Illustration: Jessica Benhar, David Azurdia, Heidi Shepherd
Copywriting: Joe Coleman, David Azurdia,
We All Need Words
Client: Vanessa Jacoby, James Jacoby
Company: Magpie Studio
Country: UK
Category: Functional beverages
GOLD PENTAWARD 2020

The producers of **Flyte**, a new energy drink, are committed to using natural ingredients and planet-protective practices. Their logo is designed as an open structure of powerful lines generating the brand name. The hummingbird graphic is a key brand characteristic. This tiny nectarivore is full of energy and strength, with a uniquely high metabolism and the uncanny ability to hover, fly, and dive at speeds that are disproportionate to its size. The color of each flavored drink is matched by the color of the birds. The back of the packaging offers dynamic infographics in the same colors, giving useful information in short, clean lines.

Die Hersteller von **Flyte**, einem neuen Energy-Drink, haben sich der Verwendung natürlicher Inhaltsstoffe und umweltfreundlicher Verfahren verschrieben. Das Logo wurde als offene Struktur aus kräftigen Linien konzipiert, die sich zum Markennamen zusammenfügen. Die Kolibri-Grafik ist ein typisches Erkennungszeichen der Marke. Dieser kleine Nektarfresser steckt voller Kraft und Energie, besitzt einen einzigartig hohen Stoffwechsel und die unheimliche Fähigkeit, zu schweben, zu fliegen und herabzustürzen – in einem Tempo, das in krassem Widerspruch zu seiner geringen Größe steht. Die Farbe des Vogels passt zur Farbe der jeweiligen Geschmacksrichtung des Drinks. Die Rückseite der Flasche enthält dynamische Infografiken in der gleichen Farbe. Sie liefern kurz und bündig nützliche Informationen.

Les fabricants de **Flyte**, une nouvelle boisson énergisante, s'engagent à utiliser des ingrédients naturels et des pratiques qui protègent la planète. Leur logo est conçu comme une structure ouverte avec des lignes audacieuses qui composent le nom de la marque. Le colibri est une caractéristique clé de la marque. Ce minuscule nectarivore plein d'énergie et de force possède un métabolisme extrêmement élevé, ainsi que la capacité extraordinaire de faire du surplace, voler et plonger à des vitesses tout à fait disproportionnées par rapport à sa taille. La couleur de chaque boisson aromatisée correspond à la couleur des oiseaux. Au dos, le packaging présente des infographies dynamiques dans les mêmes couleurs, avec des lignes courtes et épurées.

FLYTE
Design: Mousegraphics team
Company: Mousegraphics
Country: Greece
Category: Functional beverages
GOLD PENTAWARD 2018

FLYTE
clean energy

orange clementine

caffeine from green coffee
100% from natural sources
low calorie

FLYTE™
clean energy

energy

mango

purple kola

citrus lemon

green coffee
atural sources
alorie

caffeine from green coffee
100% from natural sources
low calorie

caffeine from green coffee
100% from natural sources
low calorie

UNI-PRESIDENT ENTERPRISES

Design: Mousegraphics team
Company: Mousegraphics
Country: Greece
Category: Functional beverages

GOLD PENTAWARD 2017

HEALTHY FOOD BRANDS
SWITCHLE

Art Direction: Adrian Whitefoord
Company: Pemberton & Whitefoord
Country: UK
Category: Functional beverages

SILVER PENTAWARD 2018

ANCIENT & BRAVE

Creative Direction: Scott Wotherspoon,
Jem Egerton
Design: Ranulph Horne, Harry Ives
Artwork: Steve Morphy
Company: Liquid Studio
Country: UK
Category: Functional beverages

SILVER PENTAWARD 2020

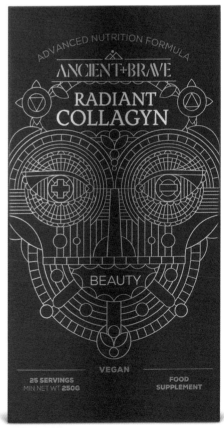

OCTA
SMART FOOD

Art Direction: Lidiya Kapysh
Design: Irina Kosheleva
Strategy: Nikita Podlipskiy
Project Management: Janna Gitelson
Company: Insight Agency
Country: Russia
Category: Functional beverages
BRONZE PENTAWARD 2017

KRONE
Lead Design: Marc Ligeti
Design: Kristina Nyjordet
Contributor and Concept: Thor Erik Ramleth
Company: Creuna
Country: Norway
Category: Beer

GOLD PENTAWARD 2017

HEINEKEN
FOBO, FORWARDABLE BOTTLE

Concept: VBAT & Heineken Design
Design Direction: Erik Wadman
Brand Direction: Elseline Ploem
Senior Design: Peter Eisen
Design: Stephane Castets
Account: Kim Hogenbirk en Marisca Wood
Model Maker: NPK
Client Liaison: Mark van Iterson, Ramses Dingenouts
Company: VBAT
Country: Netherlands
Category: Beer

SILVER PENTAWARD 2017

HEINEKEN
Design Direction: Erik Wadman
Brand Direction: Elseline Ploem
Company: VBAT
Country: Netherlands
Category: Beer
BRONZE PENTAWARD 2018

POESIAT & KATER
V. VOLLENHOVEN & CO.
Design: Kyanne Bückmann, Kevin Davis
Company: Bowler & Kimchi
Country: Netherlands
Category: Beer

SILVER PENTAWARD 2018

Wanting to harmonise their visual identity across their global portfolio, **Carlsberg** revisited all elements of their product, from the 100-year-old logo to the colour of the glass bottle. As part of the rebrand, each element was redrawn by hand, a new typeface was created and a more eco-friendly "greener green" signature colour was developed, inspired by the natural green of the buds and the mature leaves of the hop plant. The team were guided by three design principles from the founder's devotion to "the constant pursuit of better beer": Crafted Authenticity, Danish By Nature and Progressive Ingenuity, all of which were reflected in the packaging redesign.

Weil **Carlsberg** die visuelle Identität seines globalen Portfolios harmonischer gestalten wollte, wurden alle Elemente des Produkts überarbeitet – von dem 100 Jahre alten Logo bis hin zur Farbe der Glasflasche. Als Teil des Rebrandings wurde jedes Element neu von Hand entworfen, eine Schriftype wurde konzipiert und ein umweltfreundliches „grüneres Grün" entwickelt, inspiriert von der natürlichen Farbe der Knospen und den reifen Blättern der Hopfenpflanze. Das Team ließ sich dabei von den drei Designprinzipien des Gründers und seiner Hingabe für ein „konstantes Streben nach dem besseren Bier" leiten: handgemachte Authentizität, „Danish by nature" und fortschrittlicher Einfallsreichtum. All das spiegelte sich im Verpackungsdesign wider.

Dans l'optique d'harmoniser son identité visuelle pour l'ensemble de sa gamme, **Carlsberg** a repensé tous les éléments de son produit, du logo centenaire à la couleur de la bouteille en verre. Pour cette nouvelle image, chaque élément a été dessiné à la main, une nouvelle police a été créée et une couleur de signature d'un « vert plus vert » a été conçue à partir de la couleur naturelle des boutons et des feuilles matures du houblon. L'équipe de design a obéi à trois principes basés sur l'attachement du fondateur de la marque à « la quête incessante d'une bière meilleure » : authenticité artisanale, nature danoise et ingéniosité. La refonte du packaging reflète parfaitement ces lignes directrices.

CARLSBERG

Creative Partner: Spencer Buck
Associate Creative Direction: Jonathan Rogers
Senior Creative Strategy: Rob Wynn-Jones
Account Direction: Laura Lancaster, Hannah Bartholomew
Design Direction: Jonathan Ferriday
Senior Account Management: Lottie Pettinger
Senior Design: Ali Bartlett, Dave Badock
Design: Jasmine Rees
Junior Design: Liv Beresford-Evans
Client: Carlsberg
Chief Commercial Officer: Jessica Spence (Carlsberg)
Global Design Direction: Jessica Felby (Carlsberg)
Head of Marketing: Richard Whitty (Carlsberg)
Global Brand Direction: Julian Marsili (Carlsberg)
VP Marketing: Russell Jones (Carlsberg)
Design-to-print Management: Rob Martin (Carlsberg)
Design Management: Benjamin Hoffmann (Carlsberg)
Company: Taxi Studio
Country: UK
Category: Beer
GOLD PENTAWARD 2019

DONG YOU JI

Design: Wen Liu, Weijie Kang, Shuanglong Wang
Company: Shenzhen Oracle Creative Design
Country: China
Category: Beer

GOLD PENTAWARD 2020

MATEO & BERNABÉ AND FRIENDS

Design: Javier Euba, Daniel Morales
Company: Moruba
Country: Spain
Category: Beer

SILVER PENTAWARD 2012

SWEDISH TONIC

Client Direction: Johanna Augustin
Production Management: Niclas Hemlin
Senior Design: Viktoria Hamberger
Design: Robin Boström
Final Art: Anna Johansson
Copywriting: Malin Strinnhed
Company: Pond Design
Country: Sweden
Category: Ciders and low-alcohol drinks

GOLD PENTAWARD 2020

Drawing on the strategic brand essence of "the art of nature," the design for the **Seedlip Range** was inspired by botanical illustrations. For Spice 94, the illustration takes the form of a subtle "S" which reveals itself as the profile of the native red fox – a creature indigenous to the English countryside. Garden 108 and Grove 42 follow suit, leading with illustrations of a hare and a squirrel on the face of each bottle as a nod to the disruptive nature of these non-alcoholic spirits and acknowledgement of the power of the ingredients within. A pharmaceutical-style bottle reinforces the spirit's medicinal roots, while a copper cap and copper detailing elevate the brand and reference the copper stills used to create it.

Basierend auf dem strategischen Markenkern „die Kunst der Natur", wurde das Design der **Seedlip Range** von botanischen Zeichnungen inspiriert. Für Spice 94 nimmt die Illustration die Form eines einfachen „S" an, das sich als das Profil eines Rotfuchses – einer einheimischen Tierart der englischen Landschaft – herausstellt. Garden 108 und Grove 42 tun es ihm gleich mit Illustrationen eines Hasen und eines Eichhörnchens auf dem Etikett der Flasche, als Hinweis auf die disruptive Natur dieser alkoholfreien Spirituosen und als Anerkennung der Kraft der Inhaltsstoffe. Die pharmazeutische Flasche bestärkt die medizinischen Wurzeln, während der Kupferdeckel und kupferfarbene Details die Marke hervorheben und eine Referenz auf die Kolben sind, die für die Herstellung der Spirituose verwendet wurden.

S'appuyant sur l'essence de la marque de « l'art de la nature », le design pour **Seedlip Range** s'est inspiré d'illustrations botaniques. Pour Spice 94, l'illustration a la forme d'un subtil « S » qui se devine dans le profil du renard roux, espèce indigène dans la campagne anglaise. L'approche est identique pour Garden 108 et Grove 42, avec des illustrations de lièvre et d'écureuil à l'avant de chaque bouteille, en référence au caractère décalé de ces spiritueux non alcoolisés et en reconnaissance du pouvoir de leurs ingrédients. D'allure pharmaceutique, la bouteille vient consolider les racines médicinales du spiritueux, alors que le bouchon et les détails cuivrés évoquent les alambics de cuivre employés pour son élaboration.

SEEDLIP RANGE

Founder and CCO: Jonathan Ford
Founder and CEO: Mike Branson
Creative Direction: Hamish Campbell
Head of Realization: Brandi Parker
Senior Digital Artwork: Stephen Kwartler
Senior Visualization: Liviu Dimulescu
Company: Pearlfisher
Country: USA
Category: Ciders and low-alcohol drinks

SILVER PENTAWARD 2019

SEEDLIP
DISTILLED NON-ALCOHOLIC SPIRITS
GARDEN 108
HERBAL

SEEDLIP
DISTILLED NON-ALCOHOLIC SPIRITS
GROVE 42
CITRUS

SEEDLIP
DISTILLED NON-ALCOHOLIC SPIRITS
SPICE 94
AROMATIC

NIIGATA SAKE
WITH FURUMACHI GEIGI

Art Direction: Ryuta Ishikawa
Design: Kiyokazu Shimizu
Company: Niigata Chamber of Commerce
& Industry
Country: Japan
Category: Ciders and low-alcohol drinks

BRONZE PENTAWARD 2020

EL TAMAL

Design: Gonzalo Jaen
3D Rendering: Marco Silva
Company: Digital Fish
Country: Spain
Category: Ciders and low-alcohol drinks

SILVER PENTAWARD 2019

ABROGATTO 18

3D: Oscar Gómez
Company: Alejandro Gavancho
Country: Peru
Category: Ciders and low-alcohol drinks

SILVER PENTAWARD 2020

Abrogatto 18 is a brand of premium, ready-to-drink bottled cocktails. As a small company, they chose to create collections of small batches of classic cocktails, the first one being Negroni. The visual identity of Abrogatto 18 is versatile and neutral so that it can adapt to each of the collections without losing the essence of the brand, whilst the design was inspired by the name of the brand and history of alcoholic drinks around the world. It's sophisticated and classic but contemporary, and in line with the values of the brand: premium and meticulous.

Abrogatto 18 ist eine Marke trinkfertiger Premium-Cocktails in der Flasche. Als kleines Unternehmen entschieden sie sich, Kollektionen mit kleinen Chargen klassischer Cocktails herzustellen, der erste war ein Negroni. Die visuelle Identität von Abrogatto 18 ist vielseitig und neutral sodass sie sich an jede Flasche der Kollektion anpassen kann, ohne die Essenz der Marke zu verlieren. Das Design wurde dabei von dem Namen der Marke und der Geschichte von alkoholischen Getränken aus der ganzen Welt inspiriert. Es ist raffiniert und klassisch, aber zeitgemäß und auf einer Linie mit den Werten der Marke: hochwertig und akribisch.

Abrogatto 18 est une marque de cocktails en bouteille prêts à boire. De petite taille, l'entreprise a opté pour lancer des collections limitées de cocktails classiques, en commençant par le Negroni. L'identité visuelle d'Abrogatto 18 est à la fois neutre et versatile, s'adaptant ainsi à chaque collection sans perdre l'essence de la marque. Le design s'est inspiré quant à lui du nom de la marque et de l'histoire des boissons alcoolisées du monde entier. Il est sophistiqué, classique mais aussi contemporain, en phase avec les valeurs de cette marque haut de gamme et soignée.

ABSOLUT/PERNOD RICARD
THE FINE COCKTAIL COMPANY

Client Direction: Anna-Karin Trydegård
Creative Direction and Senior Design: Cecilia Bjare
Illustration: Anna Blomberg
Production Management: Niclas Hemlin
Art: Anna Johansson
Company: Pond Innovation & Design
Country: Sweden
Category: Ciders and low-alcohol drinks
BRONZE PENTAWARD 2016

SHIVOO

Creative Direction: Arthur van Hamersveld
Concept & Design: Heather Svoboda
Photography: Twenty Ten, Amsterdam
Client Services Direction: Pryscilla Amijo
Company: Brandnew
Country: Netherlands
Category: Ciders and low-alcohol drinks

GOLD PENTAWARD 2018

Shivoo cocktails come in a smoothly designed bottle within a handy pocket-sized pouch. The classic matte black of the packaging contrasts with the powdery colors of the labels printed on shiny paper, giving the design elegance and refinement. Designed with a modern stripe effect, the double 'O' in the logo is a symbol of friendship and infinity.

Shivoo-Cocktails sind in weich geschwungenen Flaschen im praktischen Taschenformat-Beutel erhältlich. Das klassische Mattschwarz der Umverpackung steht im Kontrast zu den glänzenden Etiketten in Pastellfarben, was dem Design Eleganz und Finesse verleiht. Der Streifeneffekt ist modern, und das doppelte „O" im Logo symbolisiert Freundschaft und Ewigkeit.

Les cocktails **Shivoo** sont présentés dans une bouteille lisse accompagnée d'une petite pochette pratique. Le noir mat classique du packaging contraste avec les couleurs poudrées des étiquettes imprimées sur papier brillant, et confère élégance et raffinement au design. Les rayures donnent un effet moderne, et le double « O » est un symbole d'amitié et d'infini.

SHICHI HON YARI

Art Direction: Yoshiki Uchida
Design: Yoshiki Uchida, Shohei Onodera
Client: Tomita Shuzo
Company: Cosmos
Country: Japan
Category: Ciders and low-alcohol drinks

BRONZE PENTAWARD 2015

KIRIN KAWA GOKOCHI
Creative Direction: Zenji Hashimoto
Art Direction: Zenji Hashimoto
Design: Midori Hirai
Account Management: Koichi Furusawa
Company: Cloud8
Country: Japan
Category: Ciders and low-alcohol drinks
BRONZE PENTAWARD 2017

SHICHIHONYARI

Design: Yoshiki Uchida, Shohei Onodera
Creative/Art Direction: Yoshiki Uchida
Company: Cosmos
Country: Japan
Category: Ciders and low-alcohol drinks

SILVER PENTAWARD 2014

RASURADO

Creative Direction/Design:
Daniel Morales, Javier Euba
Copywriting: Albert Martinez
Lopez-Amor
Company: Moruba
Country: Spain
Category: Wines

GOLD PENTAWARD 2013

SYDNEY ST
08/10/15

LONDON CRU
LDN SW6

Design Direction: Kath Tudball
Design: Oli Bussell
Junior Design: Charlie Alford, Sam Chapman
Artwork: Phillippe Rondeau
Company: The Partners
Country: UK
Category: Wines

GOLD PENTAWARD 2017

London Cru is the capital's first winery, producing
limited stocks of fine wine in Southwest London. The
range is called **LDN SW6**, referencing the winery's
location. The distinct visual signature of a vine leaf and
stem was inspired by the map of London with the River
Thames running through it. Each wine is named after
a London street with a phonetic or semantic link to
the grape, including Charlotte St Chardonnay, King's
Cross Red Blend and Barbican Barbera. The bottle uses
different leaf shapes, making the product stand out on
the shelf.

London Cru ist die erste Weinkellerei der englischen Hauptstadt und erzeugt in Südwest-London
eine limitierte Menge erlesener Weine. Der Sortimenten-
name **LDN SW6** nimmt Bezug auf die Lage der Kellerei.
Das auffällige Weinblatt mit Stiel erinnert an den Stadt-
plan von London mit der durch die Stadt fließenden
Themse. Jeder Wein wurde nach einer Londoner Straße
benannt, deren Name eine phonetische oder semantische
Ähnlichkeit mit dem Namen der Traube aufweist, zum
Beispiel Charlotte St Chardonnay, King's Cross Red
Blend oder Barbican Barbera. Zur Unterscheidung setzt
man auf unterschiedliche Blattformen, wodurch das
Produkt im Regal heraussticht.

London Cru est la première cave vinicole de la capi-
tale anglaise, et produit un stock limité de vins fins dans
le sud-ouest de Londres. La gamme est baptisée **LDN
SW6** en référence à la situation géographique de la cave.
La signature visuelle distinctive, une feuille de vigne et
sa tige, a été inspirée par le plan du métro de Londres,
traversé par la Tamise. Chaque vin est baptisé d'après
une rue de Londres dont le nom a un lien phonétique
ou sémantique avec le raisin, comme Charlotte
St Chardonnay, King's Cross Red Blend et Barbican
Barbera. La bouteille est ornée de différentes formes de
feuille, ce qui fait ressortir le produit dans les rayons.

Lés-a-lés was the dream of a Portuguese wine-maker, who decided to recover old grape varieties and styles that had almost disappeared in Portugal. For more than ten years he traveled across the country and the result is a collection of exclusive wines produced in limited editions; *lés-a-lés* is a Portuguese expression meaning "from one end to the other." From the "Medieval de Ourém" to the "Arinto de Pedra e Cal" and the "L'imigrant Sauvignon Blanc," each wine is a journey, each wine label a ticket to the unknown.

Lés-a-lés war der Traum eines portugiesischen Winzers, der sich entschlossen hatte, alte Rebsorten und Weinstile wiederzubeleben, die in Portugal fast verschwunden waren. Über zehn Jahre lang reiste er durchs Land, und herausgekommen ist eine Kollektion exklusiver Weine in limitierter Abfüllung; Lés-a-lés bedeutet auf Portugiesisch „von einem Ende zum anderen". Vom „Medieval de Ourém" bis zum „Arinto de Pedra e Cal" und „L'imigrant Sauvignon Blanc" steht jeder Wein für eine Reise, ist jedes Etikett eine Fahrkarte ins Unbekannte.

Lés-a-lés était le rêve d'un viticulteur portugais, qui décida de récupérer des variétés et styles de raisin anciens, qui avaient presque disparu au Portugal. Pendant plus de dix ans, il a voyagé dans tout le pays, et le résultat est une collection de vins exclusifs produits en édition limitée ; *lés-a-lés* est une expression portugaise qui signifie « d'un bout à l'autre ». De « Medieval de Ourém » à « Arinto de Pedra e Cal » ou « L'imigrant Sauvignon Blanc », chaque vin est un voyage, chaque étiquette un ticket pour l'inconnu.

LÉS-A-LÉS

Concept, Strategy and Naming: Rita Rivotti
Design: João R. Saúde
Creative Direction: Rita Rivotti, Pedro Roque
Company: Rita Rivotti Wine Branding & Design
Country: Portugal
Category: Wines

GOLD PENTAWARD 2018

CAIAFFA WINERY
Design: Mario Di Paolo
Company: Spazio Di Paolo
Country: Italy
Category: Wines
BRONZE PENTAWARD 2017

COQUILLE

Design: SeriesNemo team
Company: SeriesNemo
Country: Spain
Category: Wines

SILVER PENTAWARD 2017

LOS LOCOS DE LA BAHIA

Creative Direction: Paco Adín
Account Direction: Lourdes Morillas
Company: Supperstudio
Country: Spain
Category: Wines
BRONZE PENTAWARD 2018

VIGNETI RADICA

Design: Mario Di Paolo
Company: Spazio Di Paolo
Country: Italy
Category: Wines

SILVER PENTAWARD 2018

HARDIN

Creative Direction: David Schuemann
Design Direction and Design: Kevin Reeves
Company: CF Napa
Country: USA
Category: Wines

SILVER PENTAWARD 2018

UOVO

Creative Direction and Design: Margaret Nolan
Finished Artwork: Lloyd Richards
Company: Denomination
Country: Australia
Category: Wines
GOLD PENTAWARD 2019

The brand of wine **Uovo**, Italian for "egg", was born when Larry Cherubino imported individual special clay cement ovoid tanks – or giant "eggs" – to age his wines. The egg name was incorporated into the creative solution, from the shape of the label and paper stock with its eggshell-like texture, to the touch of the gift box with its egg-carton-like shape and feel. Similar to the stripped-back nature of the winemaking, the label for the wine was stripped of any branding, copy or graphics, letting the shape alone become the unique identifier of the brand.

Die Weinmarke **Uovo**, italienisch für „Ei", wurde ins Leben gerufen, als Larry Cherubino eiförmige Spezialtanks – oder gigantische „Eier" – aus Tonzement importierte, um darin seinen Wein altern zu lassen. Der Ei-Name wurde Teil der kreativen Lösung, von der Form des Etiketts über das Papier mit seiner ei-ähnlichen Textur bis hin zur Haptik der Geschenkbox, die die Form und Beschaffenheit eines Eierkartons hat. Der einfachen Art der Weinproduktion entsprechend, wurde das Etikett des Weins von jeglicher Markenerkennung, Schrift oder Grafik befreit und macht damit die Form zum einzigartigen Alleinstellungsmerkmal der Marke.

La marque de vin **Uovo**, mot italien signifiant « œuf », a vu le jour quand Larry Cherubino a importé des cuves ovoïdes en ciment d'argile, sorte d'œufs géants, pour faire vieillir ses vins. Le concept d'œuf a été intégré à la solution créative, de la forme de l'étiquette (dont la texture rappelle celle d'une coquille) à l'aspect et au toucher du coffret-cadeau, tel une boîte d'œufs. À l'image de la nature dépouillée de la vinification, l'étiquette a été débarrassée de tout inscription ou illustration, ce qui fait de la forme la seule identification de la marque.

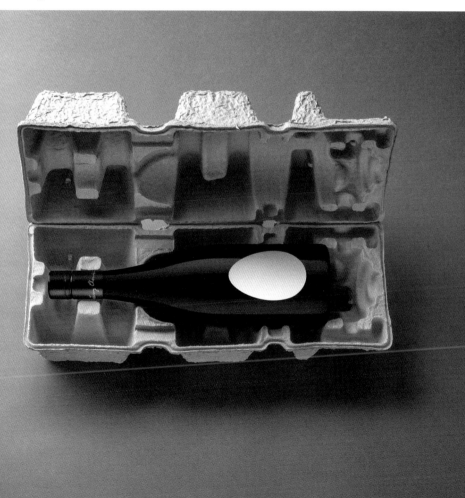

ADARAS
Art Direction: Miguel Ángel del Baño
Project Management: Beatriz Suárez
Company: Estudio Maba
Country: Spain
Category: Wines
BRONZE PENTAWARD 2019

PEACOCK

Creation Direction: Rui Niu
Design: Zhen Shen
Photography: Wei Hong
Manufacturing: Swan Wine Group
Company: I'mnext Communications
Country: China
Category: Wines

BRONZE PENTAWARD 2019

CÓDICE

Strategy Direction: Beatriz Suárez
Creative Direction: Miguel Ángel del Baño
Design: Miguel Ángel del Baño
Design Assistance: Manel Quílez, Jose Lorente
Illustration: Borja Torres
Company: Estudio Maba
Country: Spain
Category: Wines

GOLD PENTAWARD 2020

BOUQUET WINE

Design: Wei Peng
Company: LionPeng Packaging Design Studio
Country: China
Category: Wines

SILVER PENTAWARD 2019

WINEMAKER'S SELECTION
ALBERTO FENOCCHIO

Design: Henrik Olssøn, Erika Barbieri
Company: OlssønBarbieri
Country: Norway
Category: Wine as bag-in-box

GOLD PENTAWARD 2013

Winemaker's Selection is a range of wines picked by world-renowned winemakers to represent the industry's "state-of-the-art", beginning with Alberto Fenocchio from Italy. To involve the winemakers as closely as possible, making every wine unique but linked to the others by a common theme, they were asked to select a decorated ceramic plate from their home and tell a little story about it. Each plate gives a sense of place, and associations with food and culture, whilst their ordinary domestic usage is transformed as the story reveals facets of the winemaker's personality and thus of the wine as well. The personal touch is supported by a handwritten dedication and information about the winemaker, along with the grape and the terroir.

Winemaker's Selection ist ein von weltbekannten Winzern ausgewähltes Sortiment, um die aktuellen Erzeugnisse der Branche vorzustellen, beginnend mit Alberto Fenocchio aus Italien. Damit jeder Wein einzigartig bleibt, aber gleichzeitig mit den anderen über ein gemeinsames Thema verbunden ist, wurden die Winzer so eng wie möglich eingebunden: Sie sollten aus ihrem Zuhause einen dekorierten Keramikteller wählen und dazu eine kleine Geschichte erzählen. Jedes Keramikstück lässt ein Gespür für den Ort wach werden. Es schafft Assoziationen mit Essen und Kultur und transformiert gleichzeitig seine gewöhnliche Nutzung im Haushalt, während die Geschichte Aspekte der Winzerpersönlichkeit und damit auch des Weines enthüllt. Die persönliche Note wird durch eine handgeschriebene Widmung sowie durch Infos über Winzer neben denen über Traube und Terroir unterstützt.

Winemaker's Selection est une gamme de vins choisis par des viticulteurs de renommée mondiale pour représenter la « crème » du secteur, en commençant par l'Italien Alberto Fenocchio. L'idée était de faire des vins uniques partageant un thème commun et d'impliquer le plus possible les viticulteurs : ces derniers ont dû prendre chez eux une assiette en céramique et expliquer une anecdote la concernant. Chaque assiette évoque un lieu et les relations avec la nourriture et la culture ; son usage domestique s'efface pour révéler des facettes de la personnalité du viticulteur et donc du vin en soi. La touche personnelle est ajoutée par la dédicace à la main et des informations sur le professionnel, sur le cépage et sur le terroir.

Winemaker's
Selection ®

WINEMAKER'S SELECTION IS A SERIES
OF WINES SELECTED BY SOME OF THE MOST
RECOGNIZED WINEMAKERS IN THE WORLD.
THEY WISH TO SHARE THEIR PASSION AND
DEDICATION FOR WINE MAKING, AND HAVE
CAREFULLY CHOSEN SOME OF THEIR
FAVORITE BLENDS FOR YOU TO ENJOY.
WITH THIS SELECTION OF DIFFERENT WINES
FROM DIFFERENT ORIGINS, WE HOPE TO
BRING THESE GENEROUS WINE REGIONS AROUND
THE WORLD CLOSER TO YOUR HOME.
A WINE FROM WINEMAKER'S SELECTION AIMS
TO ENRICH YOUR MEAL AND CREATE REMARKABLE
MOMENTS FOR YOU AND YOUR FRIENDS.

PLATE BY RICHARD GINORI
COURTESY OF FONDAZIONE MUSEO DELLA
CERAMICA DI MONDOVÌ - ITALY

BARBERA
D'ALBA DOC

PRODUCT OF ITALY

Winemaker's Selection ©

ALBERTO
FENOCCHIO

Alberto Fenocchio

BARBERA D'ALBA

PRODUCT OF ITALY

FENOCCHIO

JUNMAI DAIGINJO
SOTO SAKE
Design: Joe Doucet & Partners
Companies: Sōtō Sake, Joe Doucet
Country: USA
Category: Spirits
BRONZE PENTAWARD 2017

BOZAL MEZCAL

Design: Kevin Roberson, Paul Morales
Company: Swig
Country: USA
Category: Spirits
GOLD PENTAWARD 2018

Bozal Mezcal is a new brand of mezcal sourced from a number of small family distillers in remote regions of Oaxaca and Guerrero. The word *bozal* means "wild" or "untamed." The color-coded series of custom ceramic bottles, which are hand-produced in Mexico, allude to the terracotta *copitas* traditionally used for drinking mezcal.

Bozal Mezcal ist eine neue Mezcal-Marke, die in mehreren kleinen Familienbetrieben in entlegenen Regionen von Oaxaca und Gurerrero gebrannt wird. Das Wort *bozal* bedeutet „wild" oder „ungezähmt". Die farbkodierte Serie von Keramikflaschen wird in Mexiko von Hand herge-stellt – eine Anspielung auf die Terrakotta-*copitas*, aus denen traditionell der Mezcal getrunken wird.

Bozal Mezcal est une nouvelle marque de mezcal qui provient de petits distillateurs fami-liaux dans les régions isolées de Oaxaca et de Guerrero. Le terme *bozal* signifie « sauvage » ou « indompté ». La série de bouteilles en céramique, dont la couleur obéit à un code, est fabriquée à la main au Mexique, et fait référence aux *copitas* en terre cuite traditionnelles pour boire le mezcal.

H-THEORIA

Design: Joël Caussimo, Samy Halim
(Almost Fabulous Studio)
Company: Pixelis
Country: France
Category: Spirits

GOLD PENTAWARD 2017

H-Theoria is a French liquor made from a complex mixture of roots, vegetables, fruits, herbs, and spices, which comes in three varieties: Perfidie, Hystérie and Procrastination. Each label has its own personality and each flavor is unique, with bottles inspired by old-fashioned perfume containers. The illustrations may look like pen and ink etchings, but were created on a modern drawing app, then assembled and produced on computer. The sublime finish of the bottle combined with the detailed illustrations and gold foil debossing makes this a sensational pack.

H-Theoria ist ein französisches alkoholisches Getränk aus einer komplexen Komposition von Wurzeln, Gemüse, Früchten, Kräutern und Gewürzen. Seine drei Varianten sind Perfidie, Hystérie und Procrastination. Jedes Etikett vermittelt einen eigenen Charakter, jede Geschmacksrichtung ist einzigartig. Die Flaschenform erinnert an altmodische Parfümflakons. Die Illustrationen sehen zwar aus wie mit Feder und Tinte gestaltet, tatsächlich wurden sie aber mittels einer modernen Zeichen-App erstellt. Das edle Finish der Flasche, kombiniert mit den detaillierten Illustrationen und der Goldfolienstanzung, macht diese Verpackung sensationell.

H-Theoria est une liqueur française faite à partir d'un mélange complexe de racines, légumes, fruits, herbes et épices. Elle est disponible en trois variantes : Hystérie, Procrastination et Perfidie. Chaque étiquette a sa propre personnalité, et chaque saveur est unique. Les bouteilles sont inspirées de flacons de parfum anciens. Les illustrations ressemblent à des gravures à l'encre, mais ont été créées avec une application de dessin moderne, puis assemblées et élaborées sur ordinateur. La finition sublime de la bouteille, associée aux illustrations détaillées et au dégaufrage à la feuille d'or, en font un packaging sensationnel.

CAPUCANA

Design: SeriesNemo team
Company: SeriesNemo
Country: Spain
Category: Spirits

BRONZE PENTAWARD 2018

YIJINGFANG

Design: Xiongbo Deng, Yao Xu
Company: Shenzhen Lingyun Creative
Packaging Design
Country: China
Category: Spirits
SILVER PENTAWARD 2018

**SUMMERISLE SPIRITS
BOUKMAN RHUM**
Design: Stranger & Stranger team
Company: Stranger & Stranger
Country: UK
Category: Spirits
BRONZE PENTAWARD 2018

ROE & CO
Design: Adam Ellis, Tom Probert
Company: The Cabinet
Country: UK
Category: Spirits
SILVER PENTAWARD 2017

LIND & LIME

Art Direction and Design: James Hartigan
Artwork: Chris McCluskie
Account Management: Lauren Baillie
Photography: Paul Hollingworth
Printing: CCL Labels
Bottle Production: Vetro Elite
Company: Contagious
Country: UK
Category: Spirits

PLATINUM PENTAWARD 2019

Inspiration for the **Lind & Lime Gin** bottle was drawn from the histories of the people and industries of Leith in Scotland, represented by the unique intricacies of the bespoke bottle, label and name. The outline of the Edinburgh and Leith Glass Works factory could once be seen rising above sea level, which is reflected in both the strong, elegant long neck of the bottle and in the embossed depiction stamped at its base. The design also takes inspiration from the bottle contents, with the translucent light green hue of the glass epitomising the citrus tones of the gin.

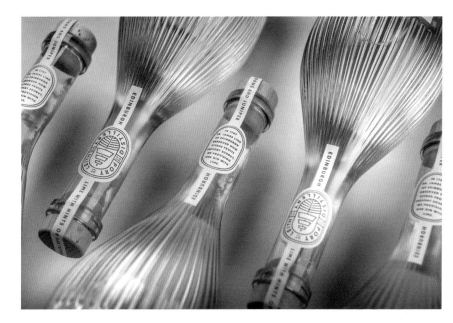

Die **Lind & Lime Gin**-Flasche ist von der Geschichte der Menschen im schottischen Leith und ihrer Industrie inspiriert, die in den einzigartigen Feinheiten besagter Flasche dargestellt werden. Die Umrisse der trichterförmigen Glasbrennöfen der Edinburgh und Leith Glass Works Fabrik erhoben sich einst über dem Meeresspiegel. Die Form findet sich in dem starken, eleganten langen Hals der Flasche und in dem eingravierten Bild auf deren Boden wieder. Vom Inhalt der Flasche inspiriert, verkörpert der durchscheinende hellgrüne Farbton des Glases die Zitrusnuancen des Gins.

L'inspiration à l'origine de la bouteille **Lind & Lime Gin** se trouve dans les histoires des habitants et des industries de la ville écossaise de Leith, évoquées par les subtilités du nom, de l'étiquette et de la bouteille sur mesure. Il fut un temps où la silhouette de la fabrique de verre Edinburgh and Leith Glass Works se dressait au-dessus du niveau de la mer : le long col, à la fois robuste et élégant, et l'inscription en relief sur le culot de la bouteille font référence à ce passé. Le design s'inspire également du contenu, avec une teinte vert clair translucide qui symbolise parfaitement les notes citronnées du gin.

AIR VODKA

Co-Founder and CEO: Gregory Constantine
(Air Company)
Co-Founder and CTO: Dr. Stafford Sheehan
(Air Company)
Graphic and Packaging Design: Joe Doucet,
Chris Thorpe (Joe Doucet x Partners)
Logo Design: Mythology
Company: Air Company
Country: USA
Category: Spirits

DIAMOND PENTAWARD 2020

With a mission to be the most sustainable alcohol brand in the world, the packaging for **Air Company**, the world's first carbon negative vodka brand, is both reusable and 100% sustainable. Keeping the vodka as the star, the label is split in two parts, with one placed at the neck of the bottle and the other at the bottom, giving ample space to display the spirit. The label itself is simple, custom-made, natural and non-toxic and can be removed easily so the bottle can be used for other purposes, such as a water bottle, flower vase or candle holder. This packaging and design is as forward-thinking, modern and transformative as the approach to creating the Air Company brand.

Mit der Mission, der nachhaltigste Alkohol-hersteller der Welt zu sein, entwirft die erste emissionsfreie Wodka-Marke **Air Company** eine Flasche, die sowohl wiederverwendbar als auch 100 % nachhaltig ist. Damit der Wodka der Star bleibt, ist das Etikett in zwei Teile geteilt, eine Hälfte ist auf dem Flaschenhals platziert, die andere auf dem Boden. So bleibt genügend Platz, um die Spirituose zu präsentieren. Das Etikett selbst ist schlicht, handgefertigt, schadstofffrei und kann leicht entfernt werden. So kann die Flasche für andere Zwecke genutzt werden, etwa als Blumenvase oder Kerzenhalter. Diese Verpackung ist zukunftsorientiert, modern und wandelbar, genau wie die Marke.

Servant l'objectif d'être la marque d'alcool la plus écoresponsable de la planète, l'emballage pour **Air Company**, première marque de vodka au monde à bilan carbone négatif, est à la fois réutilisable et 100 % durable. La vodka reste la vedette et l'étiquette compte deux parties : l'une sur le goulot et l'autre au bas de la bouteille, laissant un grand espace pour exhiber le spiritueux. L'étiquette en soi est simple, sur mesure, non toxique mais aussi amovible, ce qui permet d'utiliser ensuite la bouteille comme récipient à eau, vase ou bougeoir. Packaging et design s'avèrent être aussi visionnaires, modernes et transformateurs que l'approche créative de la marque Air Company.

SLAMSEYS FRUIT GINS

Creative Direction: Shaun Bowen
Design: George Hartley
Account Direction: Kerry Plummer
Company: B&B Studio
Country: UK
Category: Spirits
SILVER PENTAWARD 2013

KANSAS CLEAN
DISTILLED WHISKEY

Creative Design: Paul Goldman
Bottle Design: O-I NA product
development team
Company: O-I
Country: USA
Category: Spirits

BRONZE PENTAWARD 2012

HEGAN

Creative Direction: Xiongbo Deng
Design: Xiongbo Deng, Min Lin
Client: Shaanxi Tianmu Industry
Company: Shenzhen Lingyun Creative
Packaging Design
Country: China
Category: Spirits

GOLD PENTAWARD 2020

HUANG DI NEI JING

Creative Direction: Zhang Xiaoming
Design Direction: Chen Yue
Design: Liu Danhua, Huang Renqiang, Xie Shijun,
Liao Fenfen, Xu Hanxin
Company: Unidea Bank
Country: China
Category: Spirits

GOLD PENTAWARD 2019

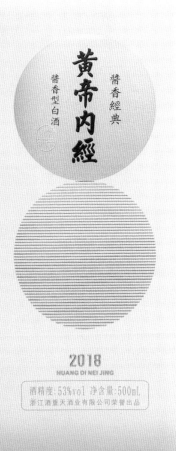

ISLAND GIN

Bottle Design: Andi Ross (Island Gin),
Tanja Ledwich (Tanja Ledwich Design),
Gavin Wong (OI NPD & Innovation Management)
Branding and Label Design: David Macdonald,
Rachel Doherty, Casey King (One Design)
Manufacturing: O-I APAC
Strategic Marketing Direction: Bayard Sinemma
Asia Pacific (O-I APAC)
Company: Madame Distiller Limited
Country: New Zealand
Category: Spirits

SILVER PENTAWARD 2020

YUXINLONG

Creative Direction and Design: Xiongbo Deng
Company: Shenzhen Lingyun Creative
Packaging Design
Country: China
Category: Spirits
SILVER PENTAWARD 2020

N.º 2
REPOSADO

100% TEQUILA AGAVE

EL RAYO®

DESDE ¡HA VUELTO! MÉXICO

EL RAYO TEQUILA

Art Direction: Mario Hgno
Design: Mario Hgno, Nubia Fernández
Copywriting: Olga Villegas, Karen Vizcarra,
Jack Vereker
Photography: Fredy "el gato" Morfín,
The Clerkenwell Brothers, Elliott Lacey
Company: Toro Pinto
Country: Mexico
Category: Spirits

SILVER PENTAWARD 2020

El Rayo, 'The Lightning', is designed to challenge traditional perceptions of tequila. Gone are the days of lime, salt and lazy stereotypes of sombreros – this identity does nothing to reflect the incredible vibrancy and depth of Mexico. The idea of the brand is to reinvent how you think about tequila by opening up the idea of a more modern, tasteful Mexican culture. The intention is to create a balance between heritage, progress and endless possibility - something that speaks about Mexico today. It's a twist on a classic product, to attract a new generation of drinkers.

El Rayo, „der Blitz", wurde entworfen, um die traditionelle Wahrnehmung von Tequila in Frage zu stellen. Die Tage von Limette und Salz und dem Klischee Sombreros sind vorüber – diese Zuschreibung wird der unglaublichen Lebendigkeit und Tiefe Mexikos nicht gerecht. Die Absicht der Marke ist es, Tequila neu zu erfinden, indem eine moderne, anspruchsvolle mexikanische Kultur erschlossen wird. So soll ein Gleichgewicht zwischen Erbe, Fortschritt und unendlichen Möglichkeiten geschaffen werden – etwas, das vom heutigen Mexiko erzählt. Es ist ein klassisches Produkt mit modernem Twist, um eine neue Generation von Kunden anzuziehen.

La bouteille **El Rayo**, « L'éclair », est pensée pour révolutionner l'image traditionnelle de la tequila. Fuyant les citrons verts, le sel et les clichés de sombreros, l'identité visuelle ne cherche en rien à refléter la vitalité et l'intensité du Mexique. L'idée de la marque est de réinventer la perception de la tequila en révélant une culture mexicaine plus moderne et sophistiquée. Son objectif est de trouver l'équilibre entre héritage, progrès et possibilités infinies pour parler du Mexique actuel. Cette remise au goût d'un produit classique vise à séduire une nouvelle génération d'amateurs de cette boisson.

HEGAN

Creative Direction: Xiongbo Deng
Design: Xiongbo Deng
Client: Shanxi Tianmu Industrial
Company: ShenZhen Lingyun Creative
Packaging Design
Country: China
Category: Spirits

SILVER PENTAWARD 2019

TOISON

Creative Direction, Graphic Design and
Structural Design: Juraj Demovic
Technical Support: Anton Bendis, Vojtech Varga
Photography: Marco Balaz
Company: Pergamen s.r.o.
Country: Slovakia
Category: Spirits

BRONZE PENTAWARD 2020

GOJI WINE

Creative Direction: Guozheng Jiang, Dan Chen
Graphic Design: Qiurong Ji, Sijie Pei
Illustration: Jing Peng
Industrial Design: Zilei Jiao
Company: Shanghai Nianxiang Brand Design & Consulting
Country: China
Category: Spirits
BRONZE PENTAWARD 2019

Goji Wine is a trendy "health" wine for young Chinese people which uses goji berries as its main ingredient. As goji is recognised for its strong health-giving effects, one of the challenges was to make a healthy drink seem more exciting. For this, the brand image of a "health care punk" was created. This is embodied in the external packaging of the wine which features characters from Chinese culture in trendy illustrations, as well as the small goji-coloured block-like containers which can be piled one on top of the other.

Goji Wine ist ein trendiger „gesunder" Wein für junge Chinesen mit Goji-Beeren als Hauptzutat. Da die Goji-Beere für ihre starken gesundheitsfördernden Effekte bekannt ist, war es eine der größten Herausforderungen, aus dem gesunden Getränk etwas Aufregendes zu machen. Dafür wurde das Markenimage des „Gesundheitspunks" entworfen. Das spiegelt sich auch in der Verpackung wider, die Charaktere aus der chinesischen Kultur in trendigen Illustrationen zeigt sowie in den kleinen gojifarbenen blockartigen Behältern, die übereinander gestapelt werden können.

Goji Wine est un vin « santé » en vogue chez les jeunes Chinois et dont les baies de goji sont le principal ingrédient. Les bienfaits du goji pour la santé sont reconnus, mais tout le défi était de créer une boisson saine plus attrayante. Pour ce faire, l'image de la marque s'est basée sur une sorte de « punk sanitaire » qui se matérialise dans le packaging externe du vin : des personnages de la culture chinoise y sont représentés dans des illustrations sophistiquées, et les petits flacons cubiques couleur goji sont empilables.

WE LOVE

Design: Onfire Design
Creative Direction: Matt Grantham
Design and Illustration: Georgina Brothers
Design: Michelle Maude
Company: Onfire Design
Country: New Zealand
Category: Spirits

BRONZE PENTAWARD 2019

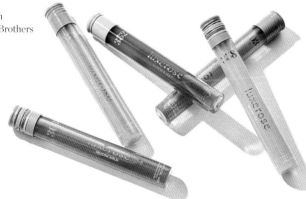

ZUI JIN JIU

Design: Shenzhen Excel Brand
Design Consultant team
Company: Shenzhen Excel Brand
Design Consultant
Country: China
Category: Spirits
BRONZE PENTAWARD 2020

LE LAIT DE LA FORET

Director/Producer: Shigeki Kunimatsu
Design: Shigeki Kunimatsu, Makiko Sato
Company: Hinomoto Design
Country: Japan
Category: Milk and chocolate (ready-to-drink)

GOLD PENTAWARD 2010

Mariestads is one of Sweden's oldest brands of beer. To strengthen its premium position in the market, two limited-edition craft brews were created to inspire pub-owners, restaurant managers and consumers. Bottled in small batches of fewer than 2,000 each, these beers retrace the routes of boats such as the *Juno* on Sweden's beloved Göta Canal and the sailing-ship *Götheborg*, which established trade between Sweden and Asia during the 1700s. The comprehensive design features hand-numbered labels on bottles dipped in wax, carefully packed in hand-crafted wooden boxes, with the overall package signifying the attention to detail the master brewers have put into creating this special experience.

Mariestads gehört zu den ältesten schwedischen Biermarken. Um die Premiumposition auf dem Markt zu stärken, braute man als Inspiration für Kneipenbesitzer, Restaurantmanager und Verbraucher zwei Craft-Biere. Diese Biere werden in kleinen Margen unter 2 000 Flaschen abgefüllt. Sie folgen den Strecken von Booten wie der *Juno* auf Schwedens geliebtem Göta-Kanal und des Segelschiffs *Götheborg*, das im 17. Jahrhundert den Handel zwischen Schweden und Asien eröffnete. Das Design umfasst handnummerierte Etiketten auf in Wachs getauchten Flaschen sorgfältig verpackt in handgefertigten Holzkästen. Die Verpackung spricht den Blick fürs Detail an, den die Braumeister diesem speziellen Erlebnis angedeihen ließen.

Mariestads est l'une des plus vieilles marques de bière suédoises. Pour renforcer son positionnement haut de gamme sur le marché, deux bières artisanales en édition limitée ont été créées à l'intention des pubs, restaurants et consommateurs. Embouteillées en petits lots de moins de 2 000 unités, ces bières retracent les itinéraires de bateaux tels que le *Juno* sur le canal Göta, et le bateau à voiles *Götheborg*, qui a initié le commerce entre la Suède et l'Asie vers 1700. Le concept comprend des étiquettes numérotées à la main sur des bouteilles fermées à la cire, soigneusement emballées dans des boîtes en bois faites à la main, et l'ensemble souligne le sens du détail des maîtres brasseurs.

MARIESTADS LIMITED EDITION

Creative Direction: Henrik Hallberg
Design: Lachlan Bullock
Production Management: Maria Florell
Company: Neumeister Strategic Design
Country: Sweden
Category: Limited editions, limited series, event creations

BRONZE PENTAWARD 2016

ABSOLUT.
ORIGINAL VODKA
IMPORTED — VODKA
40% ALC./VOL. (80 PROOF) 750ML
PRODUCED AND BOTTLED IN ÅHUS, SWEDEN
LIMITED EDITION

Something extra is needed for spirits to stand out in the busy October-December holiday season, and for **Absolut** this new limited-edition design turned to the thriving culture around electronic dance music. Inspired by the minimalism of repetitive beats, the graphics are kept purposely low-key and to the bottom of the bottle so that the mirrored surface can radiate and reflect the different images playing across it. This specially developed semi-transparent coating emphasizes the silhouette of the bottle but also allows the contents to be seen through the glass, so that vodka, glass and coating together pick up and reflect surrounding light, creating an 'Electrik' effect of subtle hues of blue.

Damit Spirituosen in der umsatzstarken Zeit der Feiertage zwischen Oktober und Dezember besonders hervorstechen, braucht es Extras. Für **Absolut** bezieht sich das neue Design der Limited Edition auf die florierende Kultur der elektronischen Tanzmusik. Inspiriert vom Minimalismus repetitiver Beats, ist die Grafik absichtlich zurückhaltend gestaltet und auf den unteren Rand der Flasche gesetzt, damit die spiegelnde Oberfläche strahlen und die darüber gespielten Bilder reflektieren kann. Die speziell entwickelte, semitransparente Beschichtung betont die Silhouette der Flasche, doch der Inhalt wird durchs Glas sichtbar, damit Wodka, Glas und Beschichtung gemeinsam das Licht der Umgebung aufnehmen und reflektieren. Dies sorgt für einen ‚Electrik'-Effekt der subtilen Blautöne.

Pour qu'un alcool puisse se démarquer lors de la période surchargée des fêtes, d'octobre à décembre, il faut un petit plus. **Absolut** a choisi de consacrer cette nouvelle édition limitée à la culture florissante de la musique électronique de club. Inspiré par le minimalisme des rythmes répétitifs, le graphisme est sobre, et confiné au bas de la bouteille afin que la surface miroir puisse briller et refléter son environnement. Cet enrobage semi-transparent mis au point pour l'occasion souligne la silhouette de la bouteille mais permet également de voir le contenu à travers le verre, afin que la vodka, le verre et l'enveloppe accrochent et reflètent la lumière, pour créer un effet « Electrik » fait de subtiles nuances de bleu.

ABSOLUT
ABSOLUT ELECTRIK

Creative Direction: Mattias Lindstedt
Managing Direction, Strategy Direction:
Jonas Andersson
Planning: Johan Hesslefors
Client Direction: Carina Gustafson
Client Management: Sofia Törling, Jenny Ilola
Senior Design: Anna Yo Lee, Dag Forsberg
Client: The Absolut Company
Global Marketing Management, Absolut,
Limited Editions: Elin Furelid
Trade Marketing Direction, Absolut Vodka:
Dimitri Jansen
Absolut Global Brand Management, Design:
Caroline Mörnås
Packaging Development Direction: Erik Näf
Photography: Bohman + Sjöstrand
Case Movie: Milford
Company: Brand Union Stockholm
Country: Sweden
Category: Limited editions, limited series,
event creations

SILVER PENTAWARD 2016

BULLEIT BOURBON

Design: Jon Davies, Martyn Wallwork, Ben Cox
Company: Butterfly Cannon
Country: UK
Category: Limited editions, limited series,
event creations
GOLD PENTAWARD 2017

Bulleit Bourbon needed a pack that would
stand out on the shelf but still retain the brand's
straight-talking Kentucky style. The package
designers created a hessian cloth Lewis bag with
triple-stitched seams and industrial-sized magnetic rivets, which help to retain Bulleit's distinct
bottle shape. The Lewis bag can be removed
for consumers to crush ice inside, in order to
make the brand's signature cocktail, the Bulleit
Mint Julep.

Bulleit Bourbon brauchte eine Verpackung,
die im Regal herausticht, aber dennoch das
bodenständige Kentucky-Image der Marke beibe-
hält. Die Verpackungsdesigner entwarfen einen
Beutel aus Sackleinen mit Dreifachnaht und
extragroßen magnetischen Nieten, durch die
die typische Flaschenform von Bulleit sichtbar
bleibt. Der Leinenbeutel kann abgenommen und
zum Eiszerkleinern verwendet werden, um den
bekannten Cocktail der Marke, den Bulleit Mint
Julep, herzustellen.

Bulleit Bourbon avait besoin d'un packaging
qui se distinguerait dans les rayons, tout en conser-
vant son style direct et franc typique du Kentucky.
Les designers ont créé un sac en toile de jute Lewis
à triples coutures, avec des rivets magnétiques de
taille industrielle qui soulignent la forme caractéristique de la bouteille de Bulleit. Les consommateurs peuvent utiliser le sac Lewis pour y écraser
de la glace afin de préparer le cocktail vedette de la
marque, le Bulleit Mint Julep.

The brief was to create the design for **Johnnie Walker Black Label** of the future, to feature in the movie *Blade Runner 2049*. The hourglass-shaped bottle from the original *Blade Runner* was refined by introducing the classic 24-degree angle cut in at the top and base that is a trademark on Johnnie Walker bottles. The result is a bold, futuristic bottle shape balanced around the iconic label. A high-gloss black coating covers the top and base, framing the vibrant whiskey color and accentuating the sharp, straight edges of the glass. A short neck and oversized square stopper finish the unique design. Just 42,000 limited-edition bottles were created and they sold out globally across 23 markets within weeks—*Johnnie Walker, The Director's Cut.*

Die Vorgabe lautete, ein Zukunfts-Design für **Johnnie Walker Black Label** zu entwerfen, das in dem Film *Blade Runner 2049* verwendet werden sollte. Die wie eine Sanduhr geformte Flasche aus dem ersten *Blade-Runner*-Film wurde durch die oben und unten eingefügten klassischen Einschnitte im 24-Grad-Winkel, einem Markenzeichen der Johnnie-Walker-Flaschen, veredelt. Das Ergebnis ist eine kraftvolle, futuristische Flaschenform mit dem berühmten Etikett im Zentrum. Ober- und Unterteil der Flasche sind mit schwarzem Hochglanzlack überzogen, der die leuchtende Whisky-Farbe einrahmt und die schneidigen, geraden Glaskanten betont. Ein kurzer Hals und ein übergroßer, viereckiger Verschluss runden dieses herausragende Design ab. Nur 42 000 Flaschen dieser Sonderedition wurden hergestellt, und sie waren auf 23 Märkten weltweit innerhalb weniger Wochen ausverkauft – *Johnnie Walker, The Director's Cut.*

La mission était de créer une bouteille de **Johnnie Walker Black Label** futuriste, afin qu'elle apparaisse dans le film *Blade Runner 2049*. La bouteille en forme de sablier du premier *Blade Runner* a été redéfinie en utilisant la découpe à un angle de 24 degrés en haut et à la base, caractéristique des bouteilles de Johnnie Walker. Le résultat est une forme futuriste et pleine de personnalité, équilibrée autour de l'étiquette emblématique. Un revêtement haute brillance recouvre le haut et la base, encadrant la couleur profonde du whisky et accentuant les angles aigus et droits du verre. Ce design singulier est couronné par un col court et un bouchon carré surdimensionné. Seules 42 000 bouteilles en édition limitée ont été créées, et elles se sont vendues en quelques semaines sur 23 marchés du monde entier – *Johnnie Walker, The Director's Cut.*

JOHNNIE WALKER BLACK LABEL THE DIRECTOR'S CUT

Executive Creative Direction: David Palmer
Creative: Nick Johnson, Chris Jeffreys
Artwork: Simon Bradley
3D: Jodie Rudge
Senior Account Management: Gemma Boardman
Production: Dani Wedderburn
Company: Love
Country: UK
Category: Limited editions, limited series, event creations

GOLD PENTAWARD 2018

KARHU

Creative Direction: Matt Thompson
Senior Design: Ashleigh Lambert
Design: Samuel Harvey
Client Business Direction: Linda Rytterstig
Print Direction: David Clabon
Company: Design Bridge London
Country: UK
Category: Limited editions, limited series,
event creations
SILVER PENTAWARD 2018

CARLSBERG
THE KØBENHAVN COLLECTION

Design: Spencer Buck, Jonathan Turner-Rogers, Laura Lancaster, Claire Bassett, Steven Yendole, Lottie Pettinger, Matt Hitchcock, Sam Hadley
Company: Taxi Studio
Country: UK
Category: Limited editions, limited series, event creations

SILVER PENTAWARD 2017

PEPSI

Design: PepsiCo Design & Innovation, PepsiCo Global Beverage R&D
Company: PepsiCo Design & Innovation
Country: USA
Category: Limited editions, limited series, event creations

GOLD PENTAWARD 2019

The **Pepsi/NFL Laces Can and Influencer Kit** was created to celebrate 16 years of partnership between Pepsi and the NFL for Super Bowl LIII. The Influencer Kit was launched the week leading up to the big game in Atlanta and included a decorative Pepsi-blue can enthroned in a specially-designed custom carton. Inspired by the form and feel of a football, the Pepsi/NFL Laces can is heavily textured and formed to mimic the laces on an actual football, creating excitement and enhancing the recipient's sensory experience of the product.

Das **Pepsi/NFL Laces Can und Influencer Kit** wurde entworfen, um 16 Jahre Partnerschaft zwischen Pepsi und der NFL (US-amerikanische Football-Profiliga) zum 58. Superbowl zu feiern. Das Influencer Kit wurde in der Woche vor dem großen Spiel in Atlanta vorgestellt und beinhaltete eine dekorative Dose Pepsi Blue, die in einem eigens entworfenen Karton prominent präsentiert wurde. Inspiriert von der Form und der Haptik eines Footballs, ist die Pepsi/NFL Dose stark strukturiert und so geformt, dass sie die Schnüre eines echten Footballs nachahmt, Begeisterung erzeugen und die sensorische Produkterfahrung des Kunden verstärken soll.

Le **Pepsi/NFL Laces Can and Influencer Kit** a été créé pour fêter les 16 ans de partenariat entre Pepsi et la NFL pour le Super Bowl LIII. Lancé la semaine précédant le grand match à Atlanta, cet Influencer Kit incluait une cannette bleue Pepsi décorative et présentée dans une boîte spécialement conçue. La cannette Pepsi/NFL Laces, qui évoque la forme et le toucher d'un ballon de football américain, est texturée et imite le lacet d'un vrai ballon. Le produit résulte attrayant et améliore l'expérience sensorielle du consommateur.

BECK'S

CCO: Alexander Schill
Executive Creative Direction: Michael Wilk
Photography: Johann Cohrs
Motion Design: Dennis Fritz
Copywriting: Joy Chakravorty
Management Supervision: Lars Holling
Senior Account Management: Sabrina Schwarz
Marketing Management: Susanne Koop
(Anheuser Busch AB InBev)
Company: Serviceplan
Country: Germany
Category: Limited editions, limited series,
event creations

GOLD PENTAWARD 2020

ARCHIE ROSE

Creative Direction: Matthew Squadrito
Illustration: Kian 'Horisumi' Forreal
Design: Robbie North
Company: Squad Ink
Country: Australia
Category: Limited editions, limited series, event creations

BRONZE PENTAWARD 2018

RHUM CLÉMENT

Design and Illustration: Linea Team
Company: Linea – The Spirit Valley Designers
Country: France
Category: Limited editions, limited series,
event creations
SILVER PENTAWARD 2019

CHRISTMAS ABSINTHE 2010

Design: Kevin Shaw
Company: Stranger & Stranger
Country: UK
Category: Self-promotion

GOLD PENTAWARD 2011
AVERY DENNISON PRIZE

For its 12th Christmas gift *Stranger & Stranger* chose to resurrect the glory days of absinthe and created a bespoke single batch of only 250 bottles. To produce the desired labelling they dug up some old-school printers who worked their craft die-stamping the inks and embossing pure cotton-fibre paper. "Absinthe, mother of all happiness, O infinite liquor, you glint in my glass green and pale like the eyes of the mistress I once loved..." (Gustave Kahn).

Stranger & Stranger entschieden sich, für ihr 12. Weihnachtsgeschenk die glorreichen Tage des Absinths wiederaufersehen zu lassen, und gaben eine maßgeschneiderte Einzelcharge mit 250 Flaschen in Auftrag. Für die gewünschte Etikettierung wurden ein paar altmodische Drucker mit Stahlstich-Technik ausgegraben und so die reine Baumwollpapierfaser bedruckt. „Absinth, Mutter allen Glücks, oh endlose Spirituose, funkelst in meinem Glase grün und bleich wie die Augen jener, die ich einst liebte …" (Gustave Kahn).

Pour son 12ᵉ cadeau de Noël, *Stranger & Stranger* a choisi de ressusciter la grande époque de l'absinthe et a créé un lot unique et sur mesure de seulement 250 bouteilles. Pour l'étiquette, l'entreprise est allée chercher des imprimeurs à l'ancienne qui estampent l'encre et travaillent en relief le papier en pures fibres de coton. « Absinthe, mère des bonheurs, ô liqueur infinie, tu miroites en mon verre comme les yeux verts et pâles de la maîtresse que jadis j'aimais … » (Gustave Kahn).

FISH CLUB WINE

Brand Strategy Direction: Stepan Avanesyan
Creative Direction: Stepan Azaryan
Art Direction: Christina Khlushyan
Design: Eliza Malkhasyan
Company: Backbone Branding
Country: Armenia
Category: Distributors'/retailers' own brands, private labels

GOLD PENTAWARD 2018

ALBERT HEIJN
EXCELLENT COFFEE PERLA

Design Direction: Ditte Glebbeek
Brand and Account Direction: Evelyn Hille
Illustration: Patrick Seymour, Maarten Rijnen
Client Management: Anneloes Andringa, Maurits van Beek
Company: dBOD
Country: Netherlands
Category: Distributors'/retailers' own brands, private labels

GOLD PENTAWARD 2017

BANDIDO COFFEE CO.

Design: Ben Christie, David Azurdia, Mike Fischer,
Jessica Sutherland
Company: Magpie Studio
Country: UK
Category: Distributors'/retailers' own brands, private labels

SILVER PENTAWARD 2018

IKEA PÅTÅR

Creative Direction: Marie Wollbeck
Senior Art Direction: Stefan Sundström, Martin Gylje
Art Direction and Ilustration: Erik Dolk
Illustration: Henrik Naessén
Graphic Design: Linn Svensson
Junior Art Direction: Gustav Karlsson Thors
Senior Account Direction: Annika Rabe
Account Direction: Petra Blanking
Company: BAS ID
Country: Sweden
Category: Distributors'/retailers' own brands, private labels

SILVER PENTAWARD 2017

BIONIC BOTTLE & AQUA JELLY

Concept: Uwe Melichar
Structural Packaging, Design Factor Concept and Visualizations: Heiko Nietzky, Deluma
Company: Factor Design
Country: Germany
Category: Packaging concept

SILVER PENTAWARD 2017

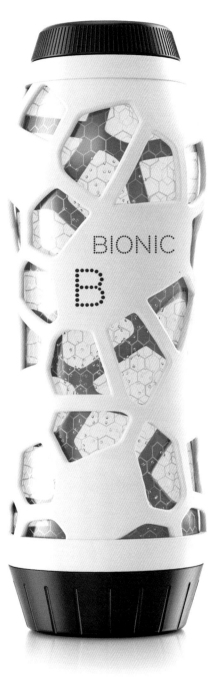

SHAOXING YELLOW WINE

Creative, Design and Illustration: Guanzi
Copywriting: Cherry Lu
Company: Beijing ChiZha Company
Country: China
Category: Distributors'/retailers' own brands,
private labels
SILVER PENTAWARD 2020

HIKAMI YONMARU – JUNMAI DAIGINJO

Creative Direction: Naomi Yamamoto
Package Art Direction: Maria Hirokawa
Graphic Art Direction: Ikki Kobayashi
Production: Sachiko Takamine
Bottle: Seieido Printing
Wrapping Paper: Tozan Washi
Client: Suisen Shuzo
Company: Shiseido
Country: Japan
Category: Distributors'/retailers' own brands, private labels

SILVER PENTAWARD 2019

OILOSOO

Brand Strategy: Lusie Grigoryan
Creative Direction, Design Idea and Graphic Design: Stepan Azaryan
Art Direction and Illustration: Mariam Stepanyan
Project Management: Marianna Atshemyan
Copywriting: Grace Jerejian
Company: Backbone Branding
Country: Armenia
Category: Distributors'/retailers' own brands, private labels

GOLD PENTAWARD 2020

OCTOPUS

Design: Pavla Chuykina
Company: Pavla Chuykina
Country: Russia
Category: Packaging concept

GOLD PENTAWARD 2019

The elegance of the **Octopus Rum** bottle shifts toward a playful dimension with this conceptual idea that transforms the traditional look of a wax seal flowing down a bottle to create the head and tentacles of an octopus. Looking every bit the sentry, the wax sea creature guards the contents of the bottle from errant oxygen or prying hands. With the simple addition of two embossed eyes, the designer brings Billy the octopus to life, creating an emotional connection between consumer and brand.

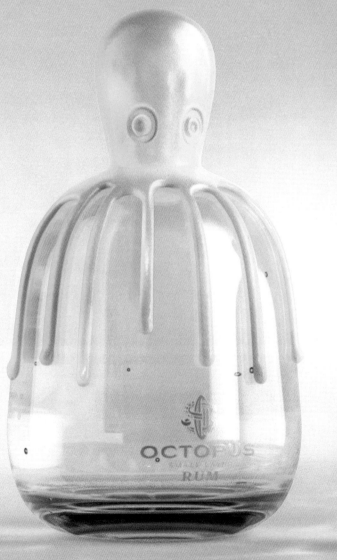

Die Eleganz der **Octopus Rum**-Flasche spielt mit der Idee, das Aussehen eines die Flasche herunterfließenden Wachssiegels so zu transformieren, dass es zu einem Oktopus wird. Wie ein Wachposten beschützt das Seeungeheuer den Inhalt der Flasche vor Sauerstoff oder spitzen Fingern. Durch die zwei eingeprägten Augen lässt der Designer Oktopus Billy lebendig wirken und schafft so eine emotionale Bindung zwischen Konsument und Marke.

L'originalité de la bouteille **Octopus Rum** tient à son aspect ludique, l'habituel cachet de cire dégoulinant sur les côtés pour créer la tête et les tentacules d'un poulpe. Telle une sentinelle, la créature marine en cire garde le contenu de la bouteille à l'abri de l'oxygène ambient ou de mains fureteuses. En ajoutant deux yeux en relief, le designer donne vie à Billy le poulpe et crée un lien émotionnel entre le consommateur et la marque.

XIAOHUTUXIAN

Creative Direction: Xiongbo Deng
Design: Xing Liu
Illustration: Xing Liu
Company: ShenZhen Lingyun Creative
Packaging Design
Country: China
Category: Packaging concept

SILVER PENTAWARD 2020

CORN WHISKY

Creative Direction: Yoshio Kato
Art Direction: Yoshio Kato, Eijiro Kuniyoshi
Design: Kenji Takahashi
Company: Kotobuki Seihan Printing
Country: Japan
Category: Packaging concept

BRONZE PENTAWARD 2019

The packaging for **Corn Whiskey** was designed to look like the product's main ingredient: corn. The "husks" that form the outer packaging are not just for aesthetics; they also help protect the bottle from damage. This conceptual piece is a great example of how package design can be straightforward, fun and effective.

Die Verpackung von **Corn Whiskey** wurde so entworfen, dass sie genau wie die Hauptzutat des Produkts aussieht: Mais. Die „Hülsen", die die äußere Verpackung bilden, sind nicht nur ästhetisch, sie helfen außerdem, die Flasche vor Bruch zu schützen. Dieses konzeptionelle Stück ist ein tolles Beispiel dafür, wie Verpackungs-design unkompliziert, lustig und effektiv sein kann.

Le packaging pour **Corn Whiskey** a été conçu pour simuler le principal ingrédient du produit, à savoir le maïs. Les « feuilles » qui forment le packaging externe ne sont pas simplement esthétiques, elles servent aussi à protéger la bouteille. Cette création conceptuelle illustre bien comment un emballage peut être à la fois simple, amusant et utile.

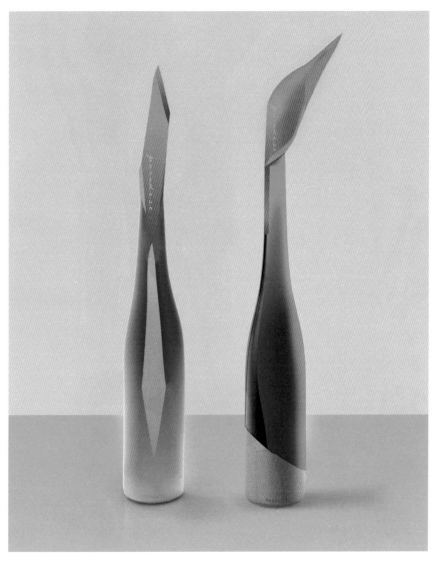

PARADISE
Design: Siyu Yu
Supervision: Hu Ji-Jun
School: Shanghai Institute of Visual Arts (SIVA)
Country: China
Category: Packaging concept (student)
BRONZE PENTAWARD 2020

PU 'ER TEA CUBE

Design: Yongzhou Ma, Boxuan Yu, Shilei Niu, Hao Zhu
School: Changsha University of Science and Technology
Country: China
Category: Packaging concept (student)

BRONZE PENTAWARD 2020

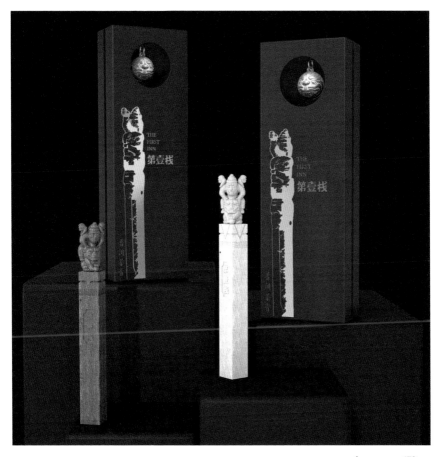

TWIST

Design: Huang Jiayin
Supervision: Hu Jijun
School: Shanghai Institute of Visual Arts (SIVA)
Country: China
Category: Packaging concept (student)

SILVER PENTAWARD 2019

SERÉ BREVE

Creative Direction and Design: Carlota Carrillo, Mercè Puig
School: Escuela Superior de Diseño de La Rioja (Esdir)
Country: Spain
Category: Packaging concept (student)

BRONZE PENTAWARD 2019

KWARTA

Design: Piotr Wiśniewski
Company: Opus B Brand Design
Country: Poland
Category: Packaging concept
GOLD PENTAWARD 2017

SAVAGE GARDEN

Design: Nikita Konkin
Country: Russia
Category: Packaging concept
GOLD PENTAWARD 2018

DAIWA
MINERAL WATER
Design: Yukiko Sakakura
3D Visualization: Kodai Kaneta
Company: Daiwa Can Company
Country: Japan
Category: Packaging concept
SILVER PENTAWARD 2017

HAKUSHU ELEMENTS

Creative Direction: Akiko Furusho
Art Direction and Design: Keisuke Kataoka
Photography: Hiroki Kubo
Company: Suntory
Country: Japan
Category: Packaging concept

SILVER PENTAWARD 2017

HANPPURI

Executive Direction: Kangkook Lee
Creative Direction: Yuljoong Kim
Design: Yeonmi An
Company: CJ Cheiljedang
Country: South Korea
Category: Packaging concept

BRONZE PENTAWARD 2018

THE BITE OF THE FRUITS

Design: Kodai Kaneta
Company: Daiwa Can Company
Country: Japan
Category: Packaging concept
SILVER PENTAWARD 2018

SLOW
Design: Piotr Wiśniewski, Aleksandra Wiśniewska
Company: Opus B Brand Design
Country: Poland
Category: Packaging concept
BRONZE PENTAWARD 2018

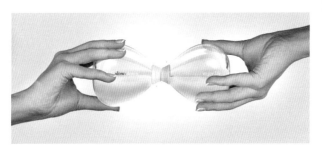

SODA WATER

Design: Yaquan Wei
School: Academy of Art University
Country: China
Category: Packaging concept

BRONZE PENTAWARD 2017

HAPPY GHOST

Design: Pavla Chuykina
Company: Pavla Chuykina
Country: Australia
Category: Packaging concept
PLATINUM PENTAWARD 2020

This conceptual piece for **Happy Ghost** is based on the iconic image of a ghost in a white shroud, which made its first appearance in 1916. Today this eerie spirit can be seen haunting the shelves of off-licences. To create this character, the design uses a deep indentation at the bottom of the bottle, along with a pair of spooky eyes, whilst the colouring of the glass creates a dark fog and mystical atmosphere.

Dieses konzeptionelle Stück für **Happy Ghost** basiert auf dem Bild eines Geists im weißen Laken, das 1916 das erste Mal auftauchte. Heute kann man dieses schaurige Gespenst in den Regalen von Wein- und Spirituosenhändlern spuken sehen. Das Design nutzt die Wölbung am Boden der Flasche. In Kombination mit einem Paar gespenstischer Augen bildet die Vertiefung den Charakter des Geists, während die Farbe des Glases dunklen Nebel und eine mystische Atmosphäre erzeugt.

Cette création pour le rhum **Happy Ghost** s'inspire de la typique image du fantôme sous un voile blanc, dont la première apparition remonte à 1916. Cet esprit surnaturel se retrouve aujourd'hui à hanter les rayons des débits de boissons. Le personnage prend vie grâce à la forme du profond renfoncement à la base de la bouteille et à une paire d'yeux lugubres, sans compter la teinte du verre qui crée une brume obscure et une atmosphère mystique.

PIPE
Design: Xiangxin Li
Supervision: Gu Chuan-Xi
School: Shanghai Institute of Visual Arts (SIVA)
Country: China
Category: Packaging concept (student)
SILVER PENTAWARD 2020

MAETI

Design: Mercè Puig
School: Escuela Superior de Diseño de
La Rioja (Esdir)
Country: Spain
Category: Packaging concept (student)

BRONZE PENTAWARD 2019

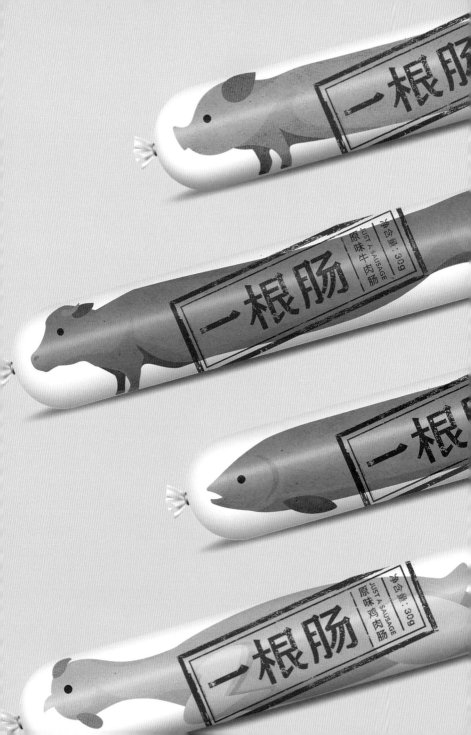

Best of the category
Bread, cereals and pasta
Dairy or soya-based products
Spices, oils and sauces
Fish, meat, poultry
Fruit and vegetables
Soups, ready-to-eat dishes, fast food

food

Fast-food restaurants and takeaway
Confectionery and sweet snacks
Savory snacks
Desserts, sweet foods and confection dishes
Food trends
Cross-category ranges
Limited editions, limited series, event creations
Distributors'/retailers' own brands, private labels
Packaging concept

The rice manufacturer **Shirokuma no Okome** adopted a polar bear as their brand image and needed a redesign to incorporate the charming illustrations. This design is not so much about the physical product (rice), but about elevating the brand into a new position in the market, distinguishing it from competitors by appealing to the emotions of the consumer.

Der Reishersteller **Shirokuma no Okome** eignete sich einen Eisbären als Markenzeichen an und brauchte ein neues Design, das die charmanten Illustrationen einbezog. Hier geht es nicht so sehr um das eigentliche Produkt (Reis), sondern mehr darum, die Marke auf dem Markt neu zu platzieren. Indem man auf die Emotionen der Kunden abzielt, gelingt eine Unterscheidung von der Konkurrenz.

La marque de riz **Shirokuma no Okome** a adopté un ours polaire comme mascotte, et avait besoin d'un nouveau design pour utiliser ces charmantes illustrations. Ce concept n'est pas tant centré sur le produit concret (du riz), mais sur la promotion de la marque à une nouvelle position sur le marché, en faisant appel aux émotions du consommateur pour la distinguer de ses concurrents.

SHIROKUMA NO OKOME

Art Direction: Ryuta Ishikawa
Design: Ryuta Ishikawa, Yukie Taka
Illustration: Masami Sakamoto
Company: Frame
Country: Japan
Category: Best of the category
PLATINUM PENTAWARD 2018

The brand ethos of Peruvian chocolate makers **Candela** is "Do it right, do what's right." We can see that this Platinum Pentaward-winning design by Infinito was definitely "done right." Candela pride themselves on an operation that is environmentally friendly and ethically responsible, so their packaging design had to embody this ethos. The hand-drawn illustrations show the physical hands of the producers hard at work, while the diverse ranges of bold colors represent the natural setting from which the chocolate originates.

Das Firmenethos des peruanischen Schokoladenherstellers **Candela** lautet „Mach's gut, tu Gutes". Man sieht auf den ersten Blick, dass dieses mit dem Platinum Pentaward ausgezeichnete Design von Infinito auf jeden Fall „gut gemacht" ist. Candela ist stolz darauf, ein umweltfreundlicher und ethisch verantwortungsvoller Betrieb zu sein, und das sollte sich natürlich im Package-Design widerspiegeln. Die handgemalten Illustrationen zeigen die hart arbeitenden Hände der Erzeuger, während die jeweils unterschiedliche Kombination aus klaren Farben die natürliche Umgebung repräsentiert, aus der die Schokolade stammt.

La philosophie de la marque de chocolat péruvienne **Candela** est « Faites-le bien, faites ce qui est juste ». On peut voir que ce packaging d'Infinito qui a remporté un Platinum Pentaward a sans aucun doute été « bien fait ». Candela s'enorgueillit d'être une entreprise éthique et respectueuse de l'environnement, et son packaging devait incarner cet esprit. Les illustrations dessinées à la main montrent les mains physiques des producteurs au travail, tandis que les différentes palettes de couleurs vives représentent l'environnement naturel d'où vient le chocolat.

CANDELA
Creative Direction: Alfredo Burga
Design: Amanda Hirakata, Pamela Espino
Illustrations: Pamela Espino
Project Management: Branko Bojovic, Joaquin Valdez, Talia Peschiera
General Management: Claudia Boggio
Company: Infinito
Country: Peru
Category: Best of the category
PLATINUM PENTAWARD 2017

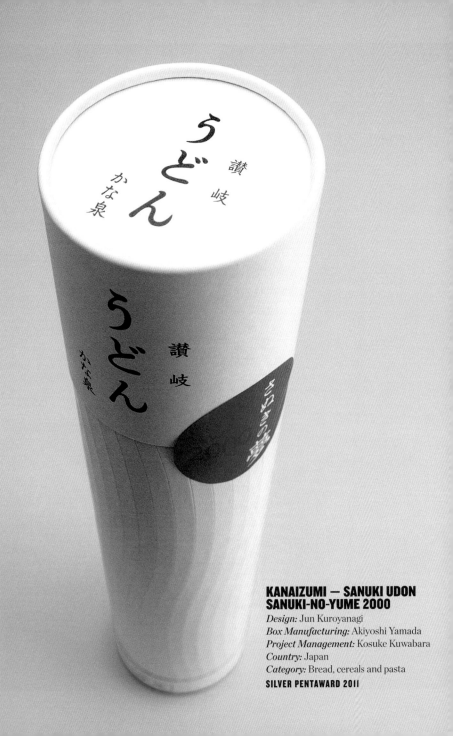

讃岐

うどん

かな泉

讃岐

うどん

かな泉

さぬきの夢

**KANAIZUMI — SANUKI UDON
SANUKI-NO-YUME 2000**
Design: Jun Kuroyanagi
Box Manufacturing: Akiyoshi Yamada
Project Management: Kosuke Kuwabara
Country: Japan
Category: Bread, cereals and pasta
SILVER PENTAWARD 2011

RACCONTI DEL CAMPO

Design: Barbara Cesura, Giacomo Stefanelli,
Annalisa Durante, Marina Durante
Company: Neom
Country: Italy
Category: Bread, cereals and pasta

SILVER PENTAWARD 2017

BAKEHUSET
NORWEGIAN BREAD

Design: Mathias Disen, Erling Norderud Hansen
Project Leader: Karianne Stenby
Client Direction: Caroline Von Hoiningen Huun
Creative Direction: Mathias Disen
Company: Scandinavian Design Group
Country: Norway
Category: Bread, cereals and pasta

GOLD PENTAWARD 2014

Norges BRØD

VESLEFRIKK

Kornbrød

"Jeg ønsker at ingen kan nekte
meg det første jeg ber om",
sa Veslefrikk.

Bakehuset

Norges BRØD

HULDRA

Speltloff

Brun stakk hadde a, og ho gikk
midt i myra. Kjær og myrgytter
vørte ho aldri det grann.

Bakehuset

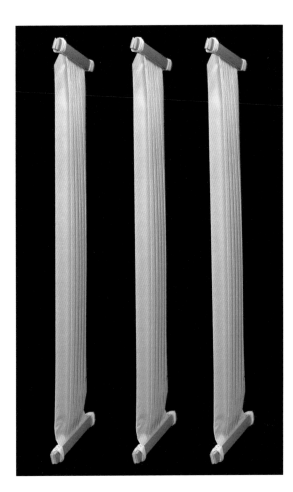
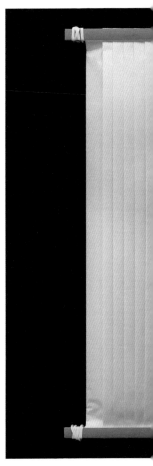

KISHIMEN

Art Direction and Graphic Design:
Hidekazu Hirai
Graphic Design: Maya Segawa
Company: Peace Graphics
Country: Japan
Category: Bread, cereals and pasta
GOLD PENTAWARD 2017

Kishimen noodles are made using the "hand-stretching" technique, a traditional Japanese noodle-making method. No knives are used but the noodles are stretched over and over again to make them thinner then hung from a bamboo rod for drying. The paper packaging containing the noodles is held together with pieces of bamboo at both ends and fastened with rubber bands. The paper is folded multiple times to duplicate the special method that is used to create the noodles. The materials of the packaging, namely, paper, bamboo and rubber, are inexpensive but the design gives a luxurious impression.

Kishimen-Nudeln werden auf traditionelle japanische Art „handgezogen". Dabei werden keine Messer benutzt; die Nudeln werden immer wieder zusammengelegt und auseinandergezogen, bis sie dünn genug sind, und anschließend zum Trocknen an einem Bambusstab aufgehängt. Die Papierverpackung der Nudeln ist an beiden Seiten mit Bambusstäben verschlossen, die mit Gummibändern fixiert sind. Das Papier ist mehrfach gefaltet, um die Herstellungsmethode der Nudeln abzubilden. Die für die Verpackung verwendeten Materialien Papier, Bambus und Gummi sind preisgünstig, aber das Design erweckt dennoch einen luxuriösen Eindruck.

Les nouilles **Kishimen** sont fabriquées à l'aide de la technique traditionnelle japonaise d'étirage à la main. Les artisans n'utilisent pas de couteaux. Les nouilles sont étirées sans relâche jusqu'à ce qu'elles soient très fines, puis elles sont pendues sur un bâton de bambou pour les faire sécher. Le packaging en papier contenant les nouilles est maintenu à chaque extrémité par des morceaux de bambou tenus par des élastiques. Le papier est plié plusieurs fois pour évoquer la méthode de fabrication des nouilles. Les matériaux du packaging, c'est-à-dire le papier, le bambou et le caoutchouc, sont bon marché. Mais le concept dégage une impression de luxe.

ΜΥΛΟΙ ΑΓ. ΓΕΩΡΓΙΟΥ

Αλεύρι Σίκαλης
για όλες τις χρήσεις

1 κιλό ℮

ΜΥΛΟΙ ΑΓ. ΓΕΩΡ

Αλεύρι για όλ
για γλυκιές και α.

ΧΩΡΙΣ ΓΛΟΥΤΕΝΗ

1 κιλό ℮

ST. GEORGE'S MILLS

Design: Mousegraphics team
Sculpture: Martha Foka
Company: Mousegraphics
Country: Greece
Category: Bread, cereals and pasta
GOLD PENTAWARD 2018

St. George's Mills flour is described as "suitable for all uses" and it is tested in an "experimental bakery." These phrases inspired a creative approach to the packaging design. Costume and stage designer Martha Foka was hired to bake a series of dough sculptures using the flour and these were photographed against a soft monochrome background. The implication is that flour is a versatile ingredient that can be used to create all kinds of delicious foods.

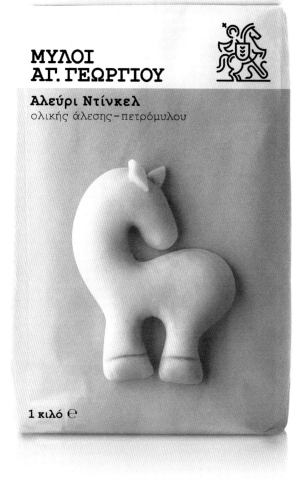

ΜΥΛΟΙ
ΑΓ. ΓΕΩΡΓΙΟΥ

Αλεύρι Ντίνκελ
ολικής άλεσης – πετρόμυλου

1 κιλό ℮

Das Mehl von **St. George's Mills** wird als „Allzweckmehl" beschrieben und in einer „experimentellen Backstube" getestet. Diese Begriffe gaben den Impuls zu einem kreativen Ansatz im Verpackungsdesign. Die Masken- und Bühnenbildnerin Martha Foka wurde beauftragt, eine Reihe von kleinen Teigskulpturen aus dem Mehl zu backen, die dann vor einem matten, monochromen Hintergrund fotografiert wurden. Die Implikation besteht darin, dass Mehl eine vielseitige Zutat ist, aus der sich alle möglichen Köstlichkeiten herstellen lassen.

La farine **St. George's Mills flour** « convient à toutes les utilisations » et est testée dans une « boulangerie expérimentale ». Ces mentions ont inspiré la démarche créative pour le packaging. La créatrice de costumes et de décors Martha Foka a été engagée pour cuire une série de sculptures en pâte réalisées à l'aide de la farine, qui ont ensuite été photographiées sur un fond monochrome aux couleurs douces. Le message est que cette farine est un ingrédient polyvalent pour dans toutes sortes de préparations délicieuses.

FENGFAN

Design: Li Sun, Rongrong Duan
Company: Rong Design
Country: China
Category: Bread, cereals and pasta
BRONZE PENTAWARD 2018

APOFCO

Design: Leodot design team
Company: Leodot
Country: China
Category: Bread, cereals and pasta

BRONZE PENTAWARD 2018

RICEMAN

Brand Strategy Direction: Stepan Avanesyan
Creative Direction: Stepan Azaryan
Project Management: Meri Sargsyan
Design: Stepan Azaryan, Eliza Malkhasyan
Modelling Design: Armenuhi Avagyan
Illustration: Marieta Arzumanyan,
Elina Barseghyan
Company: Backbone Branding
Country: Armenia
Category: Bread, cereals and pasta
PLATINUM PENTAWARD 2019

The brand idea for **Riceman** was based on humanising the rice-growing process, so the name and the packaging were developed to symbolise intensive human labour and the identity of the farmer. Illustrations of the farmers' diverse emotional expressions like self-confidence, satisfaction and empathy were used to reflect their daily lives, whilst the lid of the bag is in the form of the traditional Asian farmer's hat, marked inside with measurements. With tall and short size bags containing either the long grain or short grain rice, the overall design and packaging elements express the idea of human involvement, closeness to nature and the regional origin of the product.

Die Markenidee für **Riceman** basiert auf dem Anspruch auf einen fairen Reisanbau – der Name und die Verpackung wurden entwickelt, um die intensive menschliche Arbeit und die Identität der Bauern zu symbolisieren. Illustrationen von verschiedenen Gesichtsausdrücken der Bauern wie Selbstbewusstsein, Zufriedenheit und Empathie wurden benutzt, um das tägliche Leben abzubilden, während der Deckel die Form eines asiatischen Bauernhuts hat, der gleichzeitig als Messbecher für Reis genutzt werden kann. Die Beutel enthalten entweder Langkorn- oder Rundkornreis. Das Gesamtdesign und die Verpackungselemente drücken die Idee der menschlichen Beteiligung, die Nähe zur Natur und die regionale Herkunft des Produkts aus.

L'idée de la marque **Riceman** était d'humaniser la culture du riz : le nom et le packaging ont ainsi été pensés pour symboliser le travail humain intensif et l'identité du producteur. En représentant plusieurs sentiments des exploitants, comme la confiance en soi, la satisfaction et l'empathie, les illustrations reflètent leur quotidien, alors qu'un cache de la forme du traditionnel chapeau du paysan asiatique repose sur le haut avec les mesures de riz inscrites à l'intérieur. Les sacs de diverses tailles renferment du riz à grain court ou long, et tant le design global que les éléments du packaging transmettent l'intervention de l'homme, la proximité avec la nature et l'origine locale du produit.

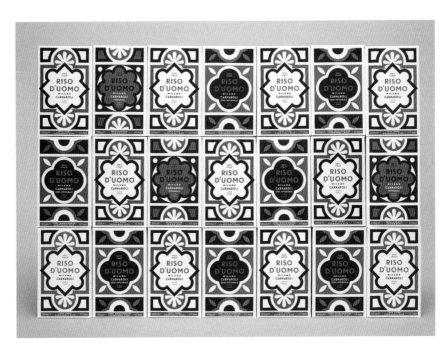

RISO D'UOMO

Managing Partner: Caz Hildebrand
Design Associate: Billy Bridgeworth
Company: Here Design
Country: UK
Category: Bread, cereals and pasta

SILVER PENTAWARD 2018

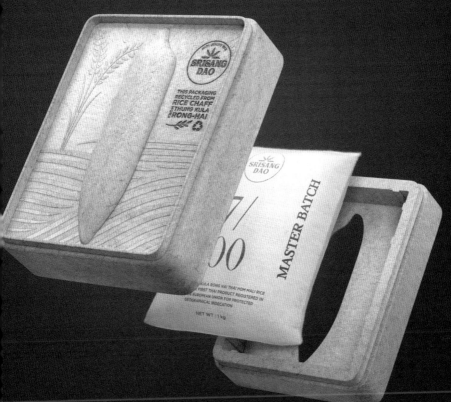

SRISANGDAO RICE

Executive Creative Direction: Somchana Kangwarnjit
Design: Rutthawitch Akkachairin, SKJ
Retouching: Pantipa Pummuang,
Thiyada Akarasinakul, Somporn Thimkhao
Company: Prompt Design
Country: Thailand
Category: Bread, cereals and pasta

GOLD PENTAWARD 2020

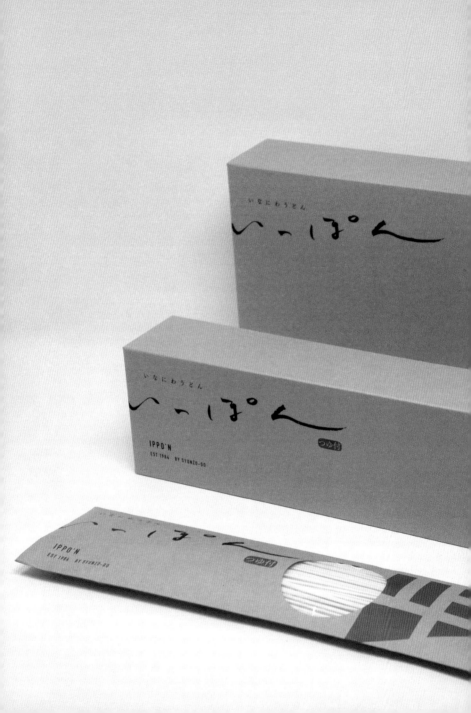

IPPO'N

Art Direction and Graphic Design:
Masahiro Miyazaki
Client: Inaniwa Udon Syunzodo
Company: Miyazaki Design Office
Country: Japan
Category: Bread, cereals and pasta
GOLD PENTAWARD 2019

IPPO'N was established as the new name in the rebranding of a Japanese noodle brand. Inaniwa udon are made in the Inaniwa area in Akita prefecture in Japan and are hand-stretched dried noodles that are slightly thinner than regular udon. The word ippon refers to a single line in Japanese, reflecting the character of the straight, beautiful udon, whilst *ippo* also means "the first step", perfect for launching a rebranded product.

IPPO'N ist der neue Name einer japanischen Nudelfirma. Inaniwa Udon werden in Inaniwa in der Akita Region Japans hergestellt und sind handgeformte getrocknete Nudeln, die etwas dünner als herkömmliche Udon sind. Das Wort *ippon* bezieht sich im Japanischen auf eine einzelne Linie, die den Charakter der geraden, hübschen Udon widerspiegelt, während *ippo* auch „der erste Schritt" bedeutet, der perfekt passt, um ein Produkt nach dem Rebranding wieder auf den Markt zu bringen.

IPPO'N est le nom qui a été adopté pour le rebranding d'une marque japonaise de nouilles. Élaborées dans la région d'Inaniwa de la préfecture d'Akita au Japon, les inaniwa udon sont des nouilles sèches étirées à la main, légèrement plus fines que les udon standard. En japonais, *ippon* désigne une ligne, à l'image des belles nouilles droites, alors que le terme *ippo* signifie « le premier pas », idéal pour le lancement d'un produit à l'image revisitée.

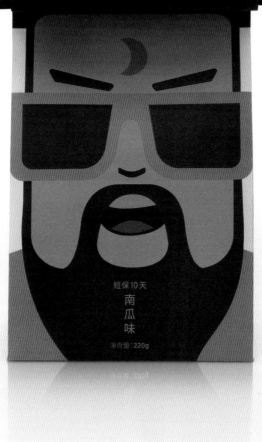

**QING YI NONG NONG
"LORD BAO" RYE BREAD**
Design: Jingfang Mei
Company: Hangzhou Dongyun Advertising Design
Country: China
Category: Bread, cereals and pasta
BRONZE PENTAWARD 2020

CHILIUXIAN

Design: The Mars Creative Team
Company: Shenzhen Baixinglong
Creative Packaging
Country: China
Category: Bread, cereals and pasta

SILVER PENTAWARD 2020

QUEENS of DAIRY

INTRODUCING

The
Grazeful

QUEEN
JERSEY

BARISTA
COFFEE MILK

4.3% eiwitten   4.8% vetten
NIET GEHOMOGENISEERD
1 LITER VERSE MELK

QUEENS OF DAIRY

Design: Vincent Limburg, Heidi Boersma, Leon Bosboom
Company: Guts & Glorious
Country: Netherlands
Category: Dairy or soya-based products
GOLD PENTAWARD 2017

Cows produce the fresh Jersey milk known as **Queens of Dairy** and the brand image acknowledges this, showing the cows as royalty. The design is not a typical milk design; dairy products for professional baristas is a new, up-and-coming category. The design is fresh and contemporary in color and appearance and is printed on a transparent label with metallic inks.

Von Jersey-Kühen stammt die frische Milch, die unter dem Namen **Queens of Dairy** bekannt ist. Das Erscheinungsbild der Marke trägt dem Rechnung, indem es eine Kuh als Königin zeigt. Das Design ist für Milch eher ungewöhnlich; Milchprodukte für professionelle Baristas sind eine neue Kategorie, die stark im Kommen ist. Dieser Entwurf, mit metallischen Druckfarben auf ein transparentes Etikett gedruckt, wirkt in seiner Farbgebung und seinem Erscheinungsbild frisch und zeitgemäß.

Les vaches produisent le lait frais de Jersey connu sous le nom de **Queens of Dairy** et l'image de marque leur rend hommage en les montrant comme des personnages royaux. Il ne s'agit pas d'une bouteille de lait classique. Les produits laitiers pour les baristas professionnels sont une nouvelle catégorie qui a le vent en poupe. Le graphisme est frais et contemporain par son style et ses couleurs, et est imprimé à l'encre métallisée sur une étiquette transparente.

AMADO CHARRA

Creative Direction and Graphic Design:
Daniel Morales, Javier Euba
Company: Moruba
Country: Spain
Category: Dairy or soya-based products

GOLD PENTAWARD 2018

Amado Charra artisanal cheese is named in honor of the maternal grandmother of the Salamanca family who make it, but the entire family pours their hearts and souls into the labor-intensive and very demanding work. This is reflected in the packaging, with a heart-covered wrapper, framed by hearts, and containing a variety of images from family life. Cheese packaging is traditionally conservative, without the use strong graphics, so this innovative concept sets Amado Charra apart.

Die Produzentenfamilie des handgemachten Käses **Amado Charra** stammt aus Salamanca. Sein Name ehrt die Großmutter mütterlicherseits, aber natürlich ist an dem arbeitsintensiven, mühsamen Herstellungsprozess die ganze Familie mit Leib und Seele beteiligt. Das spiegelt sich in der Verpackung: Das Einwickelpapier ist mit Herzen bedruckt, auf denen Szenen aus Alltag und Familienleben abgebildet sind. Käseverpackungen sind traditionell eher konservativ und verzichten auf ausdrucksstarke Grafiken, daher hebt dieses innovative Konzept den Amado-Charra-Käse von anderen ab.

Le fromage artisanal **Amado Charra** a été baptisé en l'honneur de la grand-mère maternelle de la famille originaire de Salamanque qui le fabrique, mais tous ses membres s'investissent corps et âme dans ce travail très exigeant. Le packaging reflète cela avec un emballage couvert de cœurs qui encadrent des images de la vie de famille. Les emballages de fromages sont conservateurs par tradition, et n'affichent pas de graphisme fort, c'est pourquoi ce concept innovant différencie Amado Charra de ses concurrents.

TOTEN EGG

Creative Direction and Design:
Morten Throndsen
Design: Eia Grodal, Jana Hestevold
Company: Strømme Throndsen Design
Country: Norway
Category: Dairy or soya-based products

BRONZE PENTAWARD 2018

MOO PREMIUM FOODS
Design: Mousegraphics team
Illustrations: Ryn Frank
Company: Mousegraphics
Country: Greece
Category: Dairy or soya-based products
SILVER PENTAWARD 2017

Балаам

КЕФ
ДОМ
КОРОТ
ГОДНО

2%

Балаам

МОЛОКО

ПАСТЕРИЗОВАННОЕ
ПИТЬЕВОЕ

2%

СЛИВОЧНОЕ

НАТУРАЛЬНЫЙ
ПРОДУКТ

82,5%

THE LU
PO

BRIE
ИЙ

ный

150 G

VALAAM

Creative Direction: Alexey Fadeev
Art Direction: Nikita Ivanov
Account Management: Anna Rozhnova
Company: Depot WPF
Country: Russia
Category: Dairy or soya-based products

SILVER PENTAWARD 2018

FRATELLI SPIRINI

Creative Direction: Igor Khramtsov
Company: Gordost
Country: Russia
Category: Dairy or soya-based products

BRONZE PENTAWARD 2017

The outside of **Fratelli Spirini**'s soft cheese packaging has an image of a cute cow, stressing the natural origin of the cheese: it's as if cows not only produce cheese, but also sell it with no middlemen involved. The holder case with the cut-out shapes of ears and horns makes the product stand out on the grocery store shelf and the color emphases differentiate it from other cheese brands. The presence of an Italian flag and a traditional food certification badge are an additional indication of the traditional Italian cheese-making process.

Die Käse-Packungen von **Fratelli Spirini** zeigen ein paar hübsche Kühe. So wird die natürliche Herkunft des Produkts betont, ganz so, als erzeugten die Kühe den Käse nicht nur, sondern verkauften ihn auch gleich selbst, ohne das Zutun irgendwelcher Händler. Durch den Pappumschlag mit den ausgeschnittenen Ohren und Hörnern fällt das Produkt im Laden auf, und die Farbvarianten unterscheiden es von anderen Marken. Die italienische Flagge und ein traditionelles Lebensmittelzertifikat sind weitere Hinweise auf die traditionelle Herstellung des italienischen Produkts.

Le packaging du fromage à pâte molle **Fratelli Spirini** est décoré d'une jolie vache pour souligner l'origine naturelle du produit : c'est comme si les vaches ne se contentaient pas de produire du fromage, mais le vendaient aussi sans intermédiaire. L'emballage avec les découpes en forme d'oreilles et de cornes fait ressortir le produit dans les rayons, et les accents de couleur le différencient des autres marques de fromage. La présence du drapeau italien et d'un label de certification alimentaire traditionnel indiquent un processus de production de fromage italien traditionnel.

YANGYANGLA

Design: Xiongbo Deng
Company: Shenzhen Lingyun Creative
Packaging Design
Country: China
Category: Dairy or soya-based products
SILVER PENTAWARD 2018

A-MOLOKO

Design: Vlad Ermolaev
Company: Ermolaev Bureau
Country: Russia
Category: Dairy or soya-based products

BRONZE PENTAWARD 2013

MENGNIU
MODERN FARMING

Creative Direction: Guanru Li
3D Design: Yujun Cai
Graphic Design: Guanru Li, Jiacheng Zhang,
Yujun Cai, Zhenxing Shi
Company: L3 Branding Experience
Country: China
Category: Dairy or soya-based products
BRONZE PENTAWARD 2018

AVGOULAKIA

Art Direction: Antonia Skarkari
Design and Illustration: Andreas Deskas
Company: A.S. Advertising
Country: Greece
Category: Dairy or soya-based products
GOLD PENTAWARD 2019

This design for **Avgoulakia's** organic egg packaging conveys the uniqueness of the brand in a modern and playful way, enriched with vivid, bright pops of colour. The chicken/egg dilemma may ask "which came first: the chicken or the egg?" but with these cartons the chickens definitely steal the show. Enchanted by the power of stories, a visual narrative was created about chickens with interesting and unusual qualities: with Captain Machi for free-range eggs, Madame Coco for organic eggs and Miss Nelly for barn-laid eggs.

Dieses Design mit lebhaften, leuchtenden Farbhighlights für die **Avgoulakia**-Bio-Ei-Verpackung übermittelt die Einzigartigkeit der Marke auf eine moderne und spielerische Art. Das Huhn/Ei-Dilemma stellt die Frage: „Wer war zuerst da: das Huhn oder das Ei?" Mit diesen Kartons stehlen definitiv die Hühner den Eiern die Show. Verzaubert von der Kraft einer Geschichte entstand eine visuelle Narrative über Hühner mit interessanten und eigenartigen Qualitäten: Captain Machi steht für Eier aus Freilandhaltung, Madame Coco für Bio-Eier und Miss Nelly für Eier aus Bodenhaltung.

Rehaussé de touches de couleurs vives, ce design moderne et amusant pour les boîtes d'œufs biologiques d'**Avgoulakia** transmet bien toute l'originalité de la marque. Le dilemme « Qui de l'œuf ou de la poule est apparu en premier ? » n'est pas résolu, mais ici c'est clairement l'animal qui vole la vedette. Le pouvoir reconnu des histoires a conduit à cette narration visuelle sur les poules, qui n'est pas sans intérêt et curiosités : on y trouve Captain Machi pour les œufs de poules élevées en libre parcours, Madame Coco pour les œufs biologiques, et Miss Nelly pour les œufs pondus en étable.

AV GOU LA KIA

we incubate the taste

ORGANIC
eggs

from royal hens

GR-BIO-15
Agriculture EU

 GREEK PRODUCT

MADAME
COCO
the royal

6

MEDIUM
fresh
eggs

AV GOU LA KIA

we incubate the taste

FREE-RANGE
eggs

from free-range &
rebellious hens

 GREEK PRODUCT

CAPTAIN
MACHI
the rebel

6

MEDIUM
fresh
eggs

AV GOU LA KIA

we incubate the taste

BARN
eggs

from carefree &
laid-back hens

 GREEK PRODUCT

MISS
NELLY
the carefree

6

MEDIUM
fresh
eggs

ANI DAIRY

Brand Strategy: Stepan Avanesyan
Creative Direction and Design: Stepan Azaryan
Project Management: Meri Sargsyan
Art Direction and Illustration: Mariam Stepanyan
Copywriting: Grace Jerejian
Company: Backbone Branding
Country: Armenia
Category: Dairy or soya-based products

GOLD PENTAWARD 2020

SMÖR BUTTER
Design: Mousegraphics team
Industrial Design: Nikos Kastanakis
Company: Mousegraphics
Country: Greece
Category: Dairy or soya-based products
SILVER PENTAWARD 2020

BON FROMAGE

Creative Direction: Paco Adín
Account Direction: Lourdes Morillas
Project Management: Susana Seijas
Company: Supperstudio
Country: Spain
Category: Dairy or soya-based products

SILVER PENTAWARD 2019

ZUIVELLEVEN

Founding Partners and Creative Direction:
Heidi Broersma, Vincent Limburg
Company: Guts&Glorious, Brand and
Packaging Designers
Country: Netherlands
Category: Dairy or soya-based products
BRONZE PENTAWARD 2019

JUMBO PLANTAARDIGE ZUIVEL
Design and Art Direction: Menno Mulder
Company: OD Designstudio
Country: Netherlands
Category: Dairy or soya-based products
SILVER PENTAWARD 2019

YILI

Brand Team: Bian Wu, Xi Wang,
Xu Jing, Hua Wang
Account Management: Crystal Cai,
Vera Ye, Benjamin Wei
Creative: Serean Tan, Vivina Li
Strategy: Minggo Li, Queenie Zhang,
Orchid Pan, Hu Meng
Color Management: Leo Lai, Fone Zhang
Bottle Design: Jingyu Guo
Company: Inner Mongolia Yili Group
Country: China
Category: Dairy or soya-based products
BRONZE PENTAWARD 2020

PIMENTON DE LA VERA
LAS HERMANAS

Design: Isabel Cabello
Company: Cabello x Mure
Country: Spain
Category: Spices, oils and sauces

GOLD PENTAWARD 2017

The paprika condiment **Las Hermanas** by Pimenton de la Vera comes in three varieties: spicy, sweet and sweet and sour. The new packaging design features original illustrations that show "Las Hermanas," a feminist Roman Catholic organization for Hispanic women, wearing traditional costumes from the region where the paprika is produced. The metallic colors of the cans differentiate between the three different flavors.

Das Paprikagewürz **Las Hermanas** von Pimenton de la Vera gibt es in drei Varianten: scharf, edelsüß sowie süßsauer. Das neue Verpackungsdesign zeigt Original-Illustrationen mit Bildern von „Las Hermanas", Mitgliedern einer feministischen katholischen Organisation für hispanische Frauen. Sie tragen die traditionelle Tracht der Region, in der das Paprikapulver hergestellt wird. Die Farben der metallischen Dosen dienen zur Unterscheidung der drei Geschmacksrichtungen.

Le paprika **Las Hermanas** de Pimenton de la Vera est un condiment qui est proposé en trois variantes : épicé, doux et aigre-doux. Le nouveau packaging porte des illustrations originales qui montrent « Las Hermanas », une organisation catholique féministe pour les femmes hispaniques, portant des costumes traditionnels de la région où est produit le paprika. Les couleurs métallisées des boites aident à différencier les trois variantes.

CUAC

Design: Isabel Cabello, Ana Mure
Company: Cabello x Mure
Country: Spain
Category: Spices, oils and sauces

GOLD PENTAWARD 2018

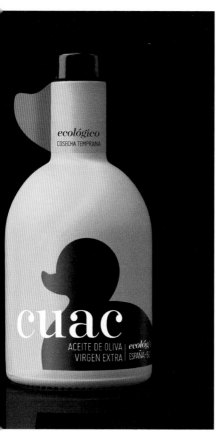

Cuac is a brand of organic extra-virgin olive oil from the province of Jaen in the south of Spain. The olive grove is located in a nature park known by local children as "Finca los Patos" (farm of the ducks) since the surrounding reservoirs are full of them. This is why the brand image is a rubber duck, a product with positive childhood associations, which also alludes to the name of the park. In the premium line, necklaces with a beak and tail shape are glued onto the bottle to reinforce the design. Its minimalist and clear aesthetic indicates that it is an ecological product.

Cuac ist ein natives Olivenöl extra in Bioqualität aus der Provinz Jaen im Süden Spaniens. Der Olivenhain befindet sich in einem Naturpark, den die dort wohnenden Kinder als „Finca los Patos" (Farm der Enten) kennen, denn die umliegenden Speicherseen sind voll von diesen Tieren. Deshalb ist das Markenzeichen der Firma eine Gummiente, ein Objekt, das positive Kindheitserinnerungen weckt und zugleich auf den Namen des Parks anspielt. Bei den Premium-Produkten wurden Manschetten in Schnabel- und Bürzelform an die Flaschen geklebt, um das Design zu verstärken. Seine klare, minimalistische Ästhetik verweist darauf, dass es sich um ein ökologisch erzeugtes Produkt handelt.

Cuac est une marque d'huile d'olive extra vierge écologique de la province de Jaén, dans le sud de l'Espagne. L'oliveraie se trouve dans un parc naturel que les enfants du coin connaissent sous le nom de « Finca los Patos » (ferme des canards), car les étangs environnants en sont pleins. C'est pourquoi l'image de la marque est un canard en caoutchouc, un produit qui possède des associations positives avec l'enfance. Pour la ligne haut de gamme, des formes de bec et de queue sont collées sur la bouteille pour renforcer le design. Cette esthétique minimaliste et épurée indique qu'il s'agit d'un produit écologique.

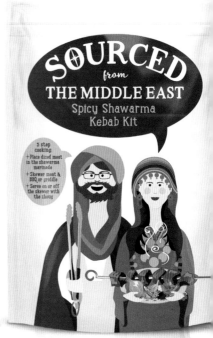

SOURCED

Design and Illustration: Hayley Bishop
Creative Direction: David Pearman
Account Management: Amy Strachey
Account Direction: Chris White
Company: This Way Up
Country: UK
Category: Spices, oils and sauces

BRONZE PENTAWARD 2017

AMOR É CEGO

Concept, Strategy and Naming: Rita Rivotti
Design: João R. Saúde
Company: Rita Rivotti Wine Branding & Design
Country: Portugal
Category: Spices, oils and sauces

SILVER PENTAWARD 2017

CORTIJO
SPIRITU SANTO

Design: Isabel Cabello
Company: Cabello x Mure
Country: Spain
Category: Spices, oils and sauces

SILVER PENTAWARD 2017

ARBEQUINA
ECOLÓGICO · ORGANIC

100%
auténtico
zumo
de aceituna
ECOLÓGICO COSECHA 2016/17

ORGANIC

CORTIJO
SPIRITU_SANTO
EXTRA VIRGIN OLIVE OIL

SABINO BASSO

Design: Mario Cavallaro, Stefano Marra,
Annamaria Varallo, Simonetta Pagliuca
Company: Nju Comunicazione
Country: Italy
Category: Spices, oils and sauces

SILVER PENTAWARD 2018

THE WILTSHIRE CHILLI FARM
SAUCES, PRESERVES, GRINDERS

Company: Buddy
Country: UK
Category: Spices, oils and sauces
SILVER PENTAWARD 2016

JOZO

Creative Strategy: Robert Kuiper,
Arthur van Hamersveld
Strategy: Robert Kuiper, Leontine de Groot
Creative Concept: Arthur van Hamersveld
Art Direction: Jantine Knijnenburg,
Arthur van Hamersveld
Design: Jantine Knijnenburg
Photography: TwentyTen, Amsterdam
Client Direction: Leontine de Groot
Company: Brandnew
Country: Netherlands
Category: Spices, oils and sauces
BRONZE PENTAWARD 2017

MIKE'S HOT HONEY

Art Direction: Clark Goolsby
Design: Mallory Parsons, Luke Woody
Company: Chase Design Group
Country: USA
Category: Spices, oils and sauces
BRONZE PENTAWARD 2018

OLIO MERICO
Art Direction: Baptiste Vallon
Strategy Direction: Gaîlle Vallon
Company: Un homme une femme
Country: France
Category: Spices, oils and sauces
BRONZE PENTAWARD 2018

AHAEAN LAND

Research, Design and Prototype Development:
KM Creative
Art Direction: Michalis Kanonis
Ceramic Manufacturing: Attikki Keramiki
Photography: Marios Theologis
Client: Ahaean Land
Company: KM Creative
Country: Greece
Category: Spices, oils and sauces

GOLD PENTAWARD 2019

The source of inspiration for the design of each ceramic container for the **Ahaean Land** products is the name and the history of each olive grove region, which reflect the unique culinary palette of each olive oil. In the olive groves, the crop is collected at two points in the season, with the early collection producing the fresh extra virgin green olive oil, and the later one the extra virgin olive oil. The ceramic containers distinguish between these by their colour, with white for the green olive oil and black for the mature olive oil. The Aheleon logo foil sticker on the containers highlights the sophisticated olive oil production process as well as the handmade ceramic containers.

Die Inspirationsquelle für das Design der Keramikbehälter der **Ahaean Land**-Produkte ist der Name und die Geschichte, die hinter jeder Olivenregion steckt, die die einzigartige kulinarische Palette des Olivenöls widerspiegeln. In den Olivenhainen wird die Frucht zu zwei Zeitpunkten in der Saison geerntet. Bei der frühen Ernte wird das frische grüne Olivenöl extra nativ hergestellt, bei der zweiten das reife Olivenöl extra nativ. Die Keramikbehälter unterscheiden durch ihre Farbe zwischen beiden Sorten — mit einem weißen Behälter für das grüne Olivenöl und einem schwarzen für das reife Olivenöl. Der folierte Aufkleber des Aheleon-Logos auf dem Behälter unterstreicht den anspruchsvollen Herstellungsprozess des Öls sowie der handgefertigten Keramikbehälter.

Le design de chaque récipient en céramique des produits de la marque **Ahaean Land** s'est inspiré du nom et de l'histoire de chaque région d'oliveraies, à l'image de la palette de saveurs unique de chaque huile d'olive. La récolte des olives se fait à deux moments au cours de la saison : la première collecte produit l'huile d'olive vierge extra fruité vert, la seconde l'huile d'olive vierge extra fruité mûr. Cette distinction est marquée par la couleur des récipients en céramique : le blanc pour l'huile aux accents de verdure, le noir pour l'huile maturée. L'adhésif métallisé du logo Aheleon dénote la sophistication du processus de fabrication et des récipients artisanaux en céramique.

PEDRO BERNARDO

Art Direction and Graphic Design: Ana Lobo
Digital Design: Cristian Ángel
Photography: Brandrid team
Company: Brandrid
Country: Spain
Category: Spices, oils and sauces
GOLD PENTAWARD 2020

MARINA PALUSCI
Design: Mario Di Paolo
Company: Spazio Di Paolo
Country: Italy
Category: Spices, oils and sauces
BRONZE PENTAWARD 2019

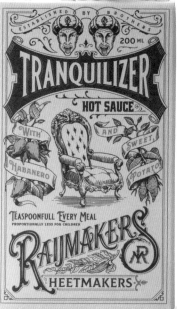

ESTABLISHED BY BROTHERS

200 ML

TRANQUILIZER

HOT SAUCE

WITH · AND

HABANERO · SWEET POTATO

TEASPOONFULL EVERY MEAL

PROPORTIONALLY LESS FOR CHILDREN

RAIJMAKERS

AR

HEETMAKERS

ESTABLISHED · USE WITH CAUTION · BY BROTHERS

BRAIN BUZZER

CAROLINA REAPER & GINGER

EXTREME · HOT SAUCE

200ML BOTTLED

RAIJMAKERS

AR

HEETMAKERS

RAIJMAKERS HEETMAKERS
Design: Jeroen de Kok
Art Direction: Niels Alkema
Design Management: Jan-Willem Glaubitz
DTP: Sofie Manuputty
Illustration: Michael Hinkle
Company: OD Designstudio
Country: Netherlands
Category: Spices, oils and sauces
SILVER PENTAWARD 2019

NONGFU WANGTIAN

Design: ShenZhen BOB Design team
Company: ShenZhen BOB Design
Country: China
Category: Spices, oils and sauces
PLATINUM PENTAWARD 2020

The philosophy of **Nongfu Wangtian** is that plants are cultivated naturally without any human intervention. They respect the rules of nature and reject any additives. The creative idea of this product packaging is that by transferring the shape of the chilli pepper to the container, it brings the experience of picking chillies directly to the customer. Its distinctive and fun design will make it the first to be noticed on the shelves, enticing consumers to buy it and try it out, and to share with friends and family.

Die Philosophie von **Nongfu Wangtian** ist, dass Pflanzen auf natürliche Weise und ohne menschliche Trickserei angebaut werden. Die Regeln der Natur werden respektiert und jegliche Zusatzstoffe abgelehnt. Durch das Übertragen der Chiliform auf die Verpackung wird die Erfahrung des Pflückens mit dem Kunden geteilt. Mit seinem unverwechselbaren und spielerischen Design fällt diese Soße in den Regalen auf und sorgt für Freude ein Produkt, das man gerne weiterempfiehlt.

Selon la philosophie de **Nongfu Wangtian**, les plantes sont cultivées naturellement sans intervention de l'homme, dans le respect des règles de la nature et sans aucun additif. Pour ce produit, l'idée créative consiste à donner à l'emballage la forme d'un piment afin d'offrir au consommateur une expérience de cueillette. Grâce à son design original et amusant, il est inratable dans les rayons et motive les consommateurs à l'essayer et à le partager en famille et entre amis.

LEVANTES FAMILY FARM

Creative Direction and Design:
Alexandros Gavrilakis
Illustration: Virginia Andronikou
Copywriting: Olympia Aivazi
Company: AG Design Agency
Country: Greece
Category: Spices, oils and sauces
SILVER PENTAWARD 2019

As a new player in the category, **Blue Goose** had to stand out from other organic meat products, and set about this by making its quality plain to see. To promote its health benefits a simple template was created to equate humane preparation with a product that was good for consumers. The stylized design, with hand-drawn cows, chickens and fish, emphasizes a premium, artisanal product, rather than showing the usual farm imagery, while the details inside the animal outlines refer to the natural environment and conditions in which each was raised. The overall visual focus succeeded in significantly increasing distribution in the Canadian market.

Als neuer Player seiner Kategorie wollte sich **Blue Goose** neben anderen Anbietern organischer Fleischprodukte sichtbar positionieren, am besten und einfachsten durch sichtbare Qualität. Zur Hervorhebung der gesundheitlichen Vorteile schuf man ein einfaches Grundmuster, das humane Tierhaltung und Konsumentennutzen gleichsetzt. Das stilisierte Design zeigt keine üblichen Bauernhofbilder, sondern betont dieses handwerkliche Premiumprodukt mit von Hand gezeichneten Kühen, Hühnern und Fischen. Die Details in den Zeichnungen beziehen sich auf die natürliche Umgebung und die Bedingungen, unter denen die Tiere aufwachsen. Dieser visuelle Fokus sorgte erfolgreich für eine wesentliche Verbreitung auf dem kanadischen Markt.

Nouveau venu dans la catégorie, **Blue Goose** devait s'imposer sur le marché et faire passer clairement un message de qualité. Pour vanter ses effets salutaires, cette création simple cherche à transmettre l'idée d'une préparation respectueuse et d'un produit sain. Le design stylisé, avec des vaches, des poules et des poissons dessinés à la main, souligne l'aspect artisanal et de qualité, alors que les détails dans le corps des animaux renvoient à l'environnement naturel et aux conditions dans lesquelles ils ont été élevés. L'approche visuelle a réussi à augmenter de façon notable sa distribution sur le marché canadien.

BLUE GOOSE

Executive Creative Direction: Dave Roberts
Creative Direction: Tom Koukodimos
Design: Flavio Carvalho (senior),
Anna Sera Garcia (senior), Oleg Portnoy
Copywriting: Pip Scowcroft, Laurent Abesdris
Illustration: Ben Kwok
Typography: Ian Brignell
Production: Karla Ramirez
Graphic Artist: Johnlee Raine
Company: Sid Lee
Country: Canada
Category: Fish, meat, poultry
GOLD PENTAWARD 2014

POACH PEAR
ARTISAN FOODS
180G

DUCK &
ORANGE
PATÉ

POACH PEAR
ARTISAN FOODS
180G

PORK
RILLETTE

POACH PEAR
ARTISAN FOODS
180G

PORK &
WALNUT
RILLETTE

POACH PEAR
ARTISAN FOODS
180G

CHICKEN &
PEPPERCORN
PATÉ

POACH PEAR
ARTISAN FOODS
180G

CHICKEN
PATÉ

POACH PEAR
ARTISAN FOODS
180G

PIG

POTTED

POACH PEAR
ARTISAN FOODS
180G

DUCK, CHICKEN
& PORCINI
RILLETTE

POACH PEAR
ARTISAN FOODS
180G

CHICKEN
& THYME
PATÉ

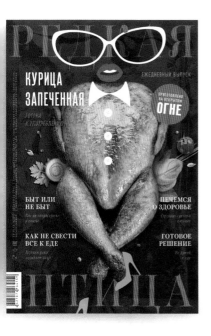

UNCOMMON BIRD

Creative Direction: Vladimir Fedoseev
Art Direction: Ksenia Ohotnikova
Direction of Strategy: Daria Sholomitskaya
Design: Suzanna Belkina
Account Management: Katerina Gurina
Company: Otvetdesign
Country: Russia
Category: Fish, meat, poultry
BRONZE PENTAWARD 2017

POACH PEAR

Design: Geoff Bickford
Company: Dessein
Country: Australia
Category: Fish, meat, poultry
SILVER PENTAWARD 2017

DESIDERIO RODRÍGUEZ

Design: Antonio Cornejo Lobato,
Jorge Augusto Pèrez, Antonio
Calleja Salado
Company: La Boîte
Country: Spain
Category: Fish, meat, poultry
BRONZE PENTAWARD 2018

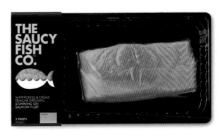

THE SAUCY FISH COMPANY

Design Director: Ben Greengrass
Account Director: Simon Preece
Designer: Stephen Woowat
Project Manager: Jan Hirst
Company: Elmwood
Country: UK
Category: Fish, meat, poultry

GOLD PENTAWARD 2010

The insight for **The Saucy Fish Company** was that the consumer was frightened by the thought of cooking fish, that they didn't know what to do with it, or how to serve it. Elmwood went on to create a brand that demystified and reduced risk, communicating to consumers that it's safe, easy to buy and cook fish. Building on a trend towards more flavoursome, dynamic food, the company designed a range of fish and sauce combinations.

Die **Saucy Fish Company** erkannte, wie verunsichert Verbraucher sind, wenn sie Fisch zubereiten sollen, weil sie nicht wissen, wie er zu verarbeiten oder zu servieren ist. Elmwood schuf daraufhin eine Marke, die das Problem entmystifizierte und das Risiko senkte. Dem Verbraucher wird vermittelt, wie einfach Fisch zu kaufen, sicher zu verarbeiten und zuzubereiten ist. Das Unternehmen greift den Trend zu wohlschmeckender und dynamischer Nahrung auf und schafft eine Produktpalette mit Fisch- und Saucenkombinationen.

L'idée de départ pour **The Saucy Fish Company** était que le consommateur est intimidé à l'idée de cuisiner du poisson, il ne sait pas quoi en faire, ni comment le servir. Elmwood a créé une marque qui démystifie et réduit les risques, en faisant comprendre au consommateur qu'il n'aura aucun mal à acheter et cuisiner du poisson. Tirant parti des tendances d'une alimentation savoureuse et dynamique, The Saucy Fish Company a conçu cette gamme de poissons et sauces combinés.

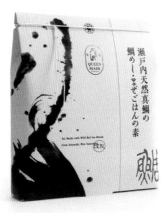

QUEEN MADE

Client: Ehime Kaisan
Art Direction and Graphic Design:
Koji Matsumoto
Illustration: Aya Matsumoto
Design Studio: Grand Deluxe
Company: Grand Deluxe
Country: Japan
Category: Fish, meat, poultry
GOLD PENTAWARD 2019

AYU KIMURA

Creative Direction, Art Direction and Design:
Masahiro Minami
Client: Kimura Suisan Corp
Company: Masahiro Minami Design
Country: Japan
Category: Fish, meat, poultry
GOLD PENTAWARD 2020

THE BEST

This is a packaging redesign for **AYU Kimura**, a dried sweet fish which is a very rare product in Japan. There it is common practice to cut fish in half, flay it and eat it dried – a type of processed fish called *himono*. Reducing the water content prevents the fish from spoiling and makes it more delicious. The gold paper packaging was designed to resemble the bamboo colander used in the traditional drying process. It's flat and simple, yet appears three-dimensional and woven, which adds to the high-quality feel of the product.

Das ist ein neues Verpackungsdesign für **AYU Kimura**-Trockenfisch, der in Japan eine Delikatesse ist. Dort ist es üblich, den Fisch, *Himono*, in zwei Hälften zu schneiden, zu enthäuten und getrocknet zu essen. Die Reduzierung des Wassergehalts verhindert, dass der Fisch verdirbt, und macht ihn schmackhafter. Die Verpackung aus Goldpapier wurde so gestaltet, dass sie dem Bambussieb ähnelt, das für den traditionellen Trocknungsvorgang verwendet wird. Die Dreidimensionalität des scheinbar gewobenen Siebs trägt zur hochwertigen Haptik des Produkts bei.

Le packaging pour la marque **AYU Kimura** a connu une refonte. Ce poisson séché sucré est un produit extrêmement rare au Japon et se prépare selon une méthode traditionnelle : l'animal est coupé en deux moitiés, ouvert et consommé séché (himono). Sa teneur en eau étant moindre, le poisson se conserve et acquiert une saveur délicieuse. Le papier doré de l'emballage a été pensé pour rappeler la passoire en bambou employée dans le procédé de séchage traditionnel. Il est plat et simple, mais semble pourtant en trois dimensions et tressé, ce qui contribue à transmettre la grande qualité du produit.

QIDELONGDONGQIANG

Design: Yifu Pan, Han Zhen
Creative Direction: Yifu Pan
Company: IFPD Studio
Country: China
Category: Fish, meat, poultry

SILVER PENTAWARD 2020

UNCLE PIG'S OLD BACON

Design: Zhou Jingkuan
Illustration: Hu Yunfeng
Company: Shenzhen Left and Right Packaging Design
Country: China
Category: Fish, meat, poultry
SILVER PENTAWARD 2019

KADONAGA SEAFOODS PICKLED FISH
Creative Direction and Art Direction:
Toshiki Osada (Bespoke)
Creative Direction and Copywriting:
Kenichi Yasuda (Sakura)
Design: Shogo Seki
Illustration: Tatsuya Kobayashi
Production: Mode
Company: Sakura, Bespoke
Country: Japan
Category: Fish, meat, poultry
SILVER PENTAWARD 2020

RICH GROUP

Design: Zhangyong Hou
Company: Zhongshihuanmei (Dalian) Advertising
Country: China
Category: Fish, meat, poultry
BRONZE PENTAWARD 2019

AYU KIMURA

Creative Direction, Art Direction and Design:
Masahiro Minami
Client: Kimura Suisan Corp
Company: Masahiro Minami Design
Country: Japan
Category: Fish, meat, poultry
BRONZE PENTAWARD 2020

HI LEMON

Creative Direction: Bo Shen
Design: Bo Shen
Illustration: Xiaoqin Pu
Photography: Bo Shen
Client: Peng Li Lemon
Company: Beyond Brand Company
Country: China
Category: Fruit and vegetables

GOLD PENTAWARD 2019

To break out of the conventional design of produce packaging, **Hi Lemon** features a fun and clever box that protects and transports the fruit. The simple folds of the packaging materials and amusing motif help emphasise the distinguishing characteristics of the brand. The key visual image on the packaging is that of a fashionable and "cool" gentleman, whilst the main colour is a bright lemon hue, matching the product inside and creating a brand image of style and energy.

Um aus dem konventionellen Verpackungsdesign für Obst auszubrechen, bringt **Hi Lemon** eine lustige und intelligente Box heraus, welche die Frucht sowohl transportiert als auch schützt. Die einfach gefaltete Verpackung und das amüsante Motiv tragen dazu bei, die herausragenden Merkmale der Marke zu betonen. Das visuelle Hauptmerkmal der Verpackung ist ein modebewusster, „cooler" Gentleman, während die Grundfarbe ein kräftiger Zitronenton ist, der zum Produkt in der Box passt und ein Markenimage voller Stil und Energie widerspiegelt.

Pour rompre avec le design habituel des emballages de produits frais, **Hi Lemon** présente une boîte drôle et astucieuse qui protège les fruits pendant leur transport. Le pliage du carton et le motif amusant viennent renforcer les caractéristiques distinguant la marque. L'image visuelle du packaging est celle d'un gentleman chic et avenant, et la couleur principale est un jaune citron vif en accord avec le produit, ce qui communique une image de marque stylisée et dynamique.

MOYO® YOUR NATURAL SWEETS

Design: Merel van Tellingen
Art Direction: Menno Mulder
Project Management: Fleur Gerritsen
DTP: Dvora Levy
Company: OD Designstudio, FLEX/design
Country: Netherlands
Category: Fruit and vegetables

SILVER PENTAWARD 2020

BOON BARIQ

Creative Direction: Stepan Azaryan
Project Management: Meri Sargsyan
Design: Stepan Azaryan, Eliza Malkhasyan
Illustration: Elina Barsegyan
Company: Backbone Branding
Country: Armenia
Category: Fruit and vegetables

SILVER PENTAWARD 2019

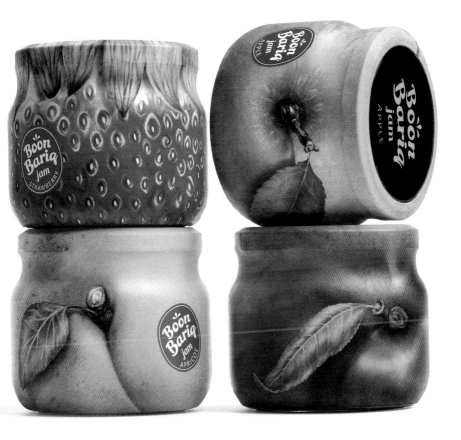

ORANGINAL

Design Lead: Yujie Chen
Design: Fengming Chen, Ching-Lang Chen,
Jiarong Zeng, Shuzhuan Huang, Haiyong Wang,
Guoxiang Zheng, Qing Yu, Mengxuan Cai
Company: inDare Design Strategy Limited
Country: China
Category: Fruit and vegetables
SILVER PENTAWARD 2020

The fresh navel oranges for **Oranginal** are picked in Zigui County, western Hubei. The cultivation of navel oranges by fruit farmers is depicted in the illustrations, whilst the packaging uses traditionally woven bamboo baskets to refer to the harvest process and the culture of traditional Chinese crafts. In addition, the label on the packaging, which is reminiscent of a pair of hands, is made of ecological materials, which are recyclable and easily decompose. Special attention and awareness to environmental protection characterise the inside and outside of the packaging.

Die frischen Navelorangen von **Oranginal** werden im Bezirk Zigui, im Westen von Hubei gepflückt. Der Anbau der Navelorangen durch Obstbauern wird in den Illustrationen dargestellt, während die Verpackung traditionell geflochtene Bambuskörbe nutzt, um auf den Ernteprozess und die Kultur des chinesischen Kunsthandwerks zu verweisen. Zusätzlich ist das Etikett, das an ein Paar Hände erinnert, aus recycelbarem Material hergestellt. Das Innere und Äußere der Verpackung charakterisieren ein besonderes Bewusstsein für den Umweltschutz.

Les oranges navel pour **Oranginal** sont cueillies dans le district de Zigui, dans le Hubei occidental. Des illustrations expliquent la culture de cette variété d'oranges par des producteurs fruitiers ; le packaging prend quant à lui la forme des traditionnels paniers en bambou tressé pour évoquer la récolte et la culture de l'artisanat chinois traditionnel. L'étiquette sur l'emballage rappelle une paire de mains et est faite de matériaux écologiques recyclables et compostables. Une attention et une conscience toutes particulières portées à la protection de l'environnement se retrouvent tant à l'intérieur qu'à l'extérieur du packaging.

JOHANNES

Design and Illustration: Irene Ibañez
Photography: Twentyten
Company: Guts&Glorious, Brand and
Packaging Designers
Country: Netherlands
Category: Fruit and vegetables

BRONZE PENTAWARD 2020

GAEA
WILD HORTA
Design: Mousegraphics team
Company: Mousegraphics
Country: Greece
Category: Fruit and vegetables

GOLD PENTAWARD 2017

PO HU CHENG HUI FARM

Design: Qi Yuan
Company: Leadshow
Country: China
Category: Fruit and vegetables

BRONZE PENTAWARD 2017

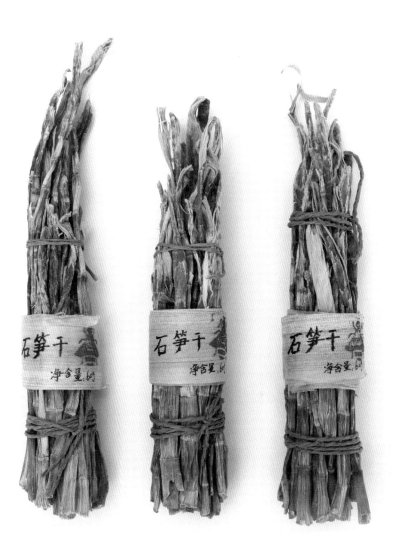

QING YI NONG NONG
DRIED VEGETABLES

Design: Jingfang Mei
Company: Hangzhou Dongyun Advertising Design
Country: China
Category: Fruit and vegetables
BRONZE PENTAWARD 2020

PRIME STAR

Creative Direction: Mikhail Gubergrits
Art Direction: Sergey Lavrinenko
Illustration: Eiko Ojala, Oleg Grinko
Design: Evgeniya Zelautdinova
Company: Linii Group
Country: Russia
Category: Soups, ready-to-eat dishes, fast food

SILVER PENTAWARD 2015

The Cube is a contemporary and sustainable in-air dining experience for **SAS Scandinavian Airlines**. Inspired by takeaway culture, the smart design saves up to 51 tons of plastic per year with FSC certified cardboard items and a PLA coating that delivers the same technical capabilities, strength and efficiency as plastic when used in a food processing environment. The cubical shape makes the content very easy to eat and leaves enough space on your table to continue to work, read or watch a movie, whilst the separately packed condiments give the passenger the freedom to customise their meal. With goals to lessen their carbon impact by 2030, this initiative towards more sustainable travel involves minimising waste and use of fossil fuel plastics through a sustainable food packaging solution.

Dieser Würfel ist das zeitgemäße und nachhaltige „Geschirr" auf den Flügen der **SAS Scandinavian Airlines**. Inspiriert von der Take-away-Kultur, spart das intelligente Design mit FSC-zertifizierten Produkten aus Karton mit PLA-Beschichtung 51 Tonnen Plastik pro Jahr ein. Es hat dieselben technischen Fähigkeiten, dieselbe Stärke und Effizienz wie Plastik, wenn es im lebensmittelver-arbeitenden Umfeld eingesetzt wird. Die Würfelform macht es einfach, zu essen und gleichzeitig genug Platz auf dem Tisch zu haben, um weiter zu arbeiten, zu lesen oder einen Film zu sehen, während die einzeln verpackten Gewürze dem Passagier die Möglichkeit geben, seine Mahlzeit selbst zu würzen. Mit dem Ziel, die CO2-Bilanz bis 2030 zu senken, beinhaltet diese Initiative für nachhaltigeres Reisen die Minimierung von Verpackungsmüll und Plastik durch eine Lösung mit ressourcenschonenden Essensverpackungen.

The Cube est une expérience de repas en vol moderne et écoresponsable offerte par **SAS Scandinavian Airlines**. S'inspirant de la vente à emporter, ce design intelligent fait économiser jusqu'à 51 tonnes de plastique par an grâce aux éléments en carton certifié FSC et au revêtement PLA qui possède un potentiel, une résistance et une efficacité identiques au plastique dans un environnement agroalimentaire. La forme cubique facilite l'accès aux plats et libère assez de place sur la tablette pour continuer à travailler, lire ou regarder un film, alors que les condiments emballés séparément offrent aux passagers la possibilité de personnaliser leur repas. L'objectif étant de réduire l'impact carbone d'ici à 2030, cette initiative en faveur de voyages plus respectueux de l'environnement passe par la réduction des déchets et de l'utilisation de plastiques d'origine fossile via une solution durable de conditionnement alimentaire.

SAS SCANDINAVIAN AIRLINES
Product Design and Manufacturing: deSter team
Branding: Bold
Company: deSter
Country: Belgium
Category: Soups, ready-to-eat dishes, fast food
GOLD PENTAWARD 2020

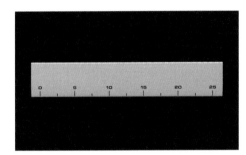

MANO PIZZA
Design: Goods team
Illustration: Samuel Nyholm
Company: Goods
Country: Norway
Category: Soups, ready-to-eat dishes, fast food
SILVER PENTAWARD 2019

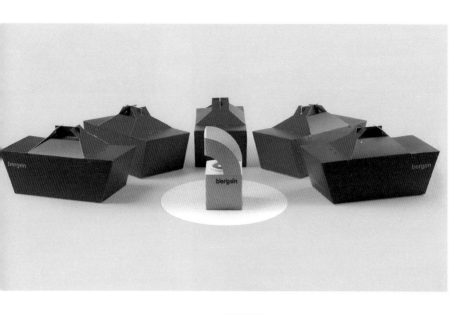

BERGEN

Creative Direction: Alexey Fadeev
Design Direction: Nikita Ivanov
Art Direction: Vera Zvereva
Design: Nikita Ivanov, Vera Zvereva
Project Management: Elena Melnik
Copywriting: Sasha Fedoseeva
Company: Depot Branding Agency
Country: Russia
Category: Soups, ready-to-eat dishes, fast food

BRONZE PENTAWARD 2019

Art Direction and Graphic Design:
Hidekazu Hirai
Graphic Design: Segawa Maya
Illustration: Fumiaki Muto
Company: Peace Graphics
Country: Japan
Category: Soups, ready-to-eat dishes,
fast food

SILVER PENTAWARD 2018

Nagoya Cochin -
natural taste of chicken
enjoyed in every chew.

The Nagoya Cochin is the first
variety of food chicken in Japan
produced in the 1880s by brothers
Sohei and Masaaki Kaito from
Saigoro Uruzi Clan, who considered
beef Nagoya chicken and Buff
Cochin from China. The Cochin
raising was discontinued in time,
but the customer voiced their
wishes to "enjoy the traditional
taste" again. In 1973, the Nagoya
prefectural government began
reproducing the Nagoya Cochin and
successfully revived its breed
through 16-year-long efforts. The
Nagoya Cochin is characterized by
its meaty texture and rich flavor
which deepens each time you chew
it, unlike any broiler stock.

◯ How to eat
Warm it up in boiling water
directly without opening the bag
or in a microwave oven after
moving the food out from the bag
to a plate and covering it with
plastic wrap. The food has been
pre-boiled to make it soft and
therefore keep in mind that the
meat can be easily separated from
the bones. Be careful with the
heated food to avoid burns.

BURGER KING
ANGRIEST WHOPPER

Head of Design: Bruce Duckworth
Creative Direction: Clem Halpin
Design: Jamie Nash
Artwork: James Chilvers
Senior Account Management: Nicola Eager
Company: Turner Duckworth
Country: UK
Category: Fast-food restaurants and takeaway

GOLD PENTAWARD 2017

For a 2016 limited-edition launch, Burger King adapted the original Angry Whopper into the ultimate **Angriest Whopper**, which had fiery jalapenos in a hot-sauce-infused angry-red bun. To accompany the launch, they created a media campaign around the idea of using fire from a volcano to flame-grill the Angriest Whoppers. The packaging made the graphic connection between the unique ingredient, the spicy jalapeno, and this special-edition Whopper's angry attitude. The shape of the jalapeno doubles up as angry, fiery, demonic eyes.

2016 machte Burger King aus dem Angry Whopper in einer Sonderaktion für kurze Zeit den ultimativ **Angriest Whopper**, der in einem mit scharfer Sauce zornesrot gefärbten Brötchen feurige Jalapeños enthielt. In der erweiterten Medienkampagne rund um das Produkt wird außerdem gezeigt, dass der Angriest Whopper auf Vulkanflammen gegrillt wird. Das Verpackungs-design schuf eine grafische Verbindung zwischen der Extrazutat, der scharfen Jalapeño, und der Grundstimmung dieses bösen Whoppers. Aus der verdoppelten Jalapeño werden zornige Augen mit feurigem, dämonischem Blick.

Pour un lancement en édition limitée de 2016, Burger King a repris l'Angry Whopper (le Whopper en colère) et en a fait l'**Angriest Whopper** (le Whopper le plus en colère), avec des piments jalapeño explosifs dans un petit pain rouge de courroux et imbibé de sauce piquante. Pour ac-compagner le lancement, Burger King a créé une campagne média autour de l'idée d'utiliser le feu d'un volcan pour griller à la flamme les Angriest Whoppers. Le packaging établit un lien visuel entre l'ingrédient caractéristique, le piment jala-peño, et l'humeur colérique de cette édition spé-ciale du Whopper. En forme de piment brillent des yeux démoniaques enflammés et furieux.

SAMURAI
JAPANESE CUISINE
Art Direction: Varduhi Antonyan
Illustration: Varduhi Antonyan
Graphic Design: Haykaz Khroyan
Company: Marog Creative Agency
Country: Armenia
Category: Fast-food restaurants and takeaway
SILVER PENTAWARD 2017

MENU

只々、手前は主君の為に、主君の願いを察知し、如何なる慈儀な事が在ろうとも、常に好鮮な物を供する所存でござる。

剣の達人 純

SAMURAI
JAPANESE CUISINE

BAGHRAMYAN AVE 2
+374 10 585670

TEa

Malmö Chokladfabrik produces high-quality chocolate and wanted to introduce cones to complement it, so a new design was needed. Using the brand's distinctive design elements, the cone design has strong flavor cues, graphic simplicity, and typographical detailing, strengthening visibility and accessibility. The design creates a friendly, happy vibe that invites trial and experimentation. The copy injects a humorous tone that perfectly fits the design itself.

MALMÖ CHOKLADFABRIK

Account Management: Johanna Agustin
Production Management: Johanna Larsson
Design: Mika Nilsson
Senior Design: Peeter Ots
Final Art: Anki Mac Pherson
Copywriting: Sara Boisen
Company: Pond Design
Country: Sweden
Category: Confectionery and sweet snacks

GOLD PENTAWARD 2018

Die **Malmö Chokladfabrik** produziert hoch-wertige Schokoladen und entschied passend dazu Waffeln anzubieten. Im Einklang mit den typi-schen Designelementen der Marke zeichnet sich das neue Waffeldesign durch eine klare Sorten-kennung, grafische Schlichtheit und typografische Details aus, die Sichtbarkeit und Zugänglichkeit erhöhen. Insgesamt erzeugt die Verpackung eine freundliche, fröhliche Stimmung, die zum Probie-ren und Experimentieren einlädt. Eine humorvolle Note in den Texten rundet das Design ab.

Malmö Chokladfabrik produit du chocolat de grande qualité et voulait lancer des cornets pour compléter sa gamme. Un nouveau design s'impo-sait donc. L'emballage reprend les éléments dis-tinctifs de la marque, avec des indices clairs sur le goût, une grande simplicité graphique et une typo-graphie détaillée, qui renforcent la visibilité et l'accessibilité. Le design crée un sentiment de convivialité et de bonne humeur qui invite à l'expé-rimentation. Le texte apporte une note d'humour qui correspond parfaitement au design.

CRUDE

Art Direction and Logo Design: Federico Galvani
Typography, Illustration and Graphic Design:
Anna Rodighiero
Photography: Federico Padovani
Printing: Grafiche Cosentino
Hot Foil: Kurz Luxoro
Company: Happycentro
Country: Italy
Category: Confectionery and sweet snacks
SILVER PENTAWARD 2017

The recipe for **Crude** is based on simple ingredients and this is reflected in the brand identity
of the chocolate, which is built around an intricate
structure of simple shapes, and typography that
shows the percentages of cocoa content – 70, 80,
90, 100 – in visual form. Two materials are used
in the packaging: a cheap recycled cardboard
commonly used for mass packaging, and luxurious
metallic foils, hot stamped in red, blue, copper and
rainbow colors.

Das Rezept für **Crude** basiert auf einfachen
Zutaten, und dieser Umstand spiegelt sich in
der Markenidentität der Schokolade wider. Das
Design besteht aus verschachtelten Arrangements
simpler Formen und Zahlen, die den Kakaogehalt
in Prozent – 70, 80, 90, 100 – visuell darstellen.
Zwei Materialien finden hier Verwendung: eine
preisgünstige, recycelte Pappe, wie man sie gewöhnlich zum Verpacken großer Warenmengen
benutzt, und luxuriöse, heißgeprägte Metallfolie
in Rot, Blau, Kupfer oder Regenbogenfarben.

La recette de **Crude** se base sur des ingrédients
simples, ce qui se reflète dans l'identité de marque
de ce chocolat : une structure complexe de formes
simples indique visuellement le pourcentage en
cacao (70, 80, 90, 100). L'emballage est fait de
deux matériaux : un carton recyclé bon marché
couramment utilisé pour le packaging de masse, et
des feuilles métallisées luxueuses, marquées à
chaud en rouge, bleu, cuivre et arc-en-ciel.

DELICATA

Design: ...,staat team
Company: ...,staat
Country: Netherlands
Category: Confectionery and sweet snacks
SILVER PENTAWARD 2018

MIA premium chocolate is part of a specialty food brand that is created and packaged entirely in Africa, from farm to factory. The name is an acronym standing for "Made in Africa" but it also represents the Latin word for "My" because everyone involved in the organization feels a sense of ownership for the products. The packaging was designed to reflect the brand's African origins, but not in a stereotypical way; instead, it reflects all that is great about the vibrance of modern Africa.

Die MIA-Premiumschokolade gehört zu einer Spezialitätenmarke, die ausschließlich in Afrika hergestellt und verpackt wird – von der Farm bis zur Fabrik. Der Name ist ein Akronym und steht für „Made in Africa", zugleich bedeutet es das lateinische Wort für „mein", denn alle an der Firma Beteiligten verstehen sich als Miteigentümer der Produkte. Die Verpackung sollte den afrikanischen Ursprung der Marke spiegeln, allerdings nicht auf stereotype Art und Weise; vielmehr evoziert sie all das, was an der Lebendigkeit des modernen Afrika so wunderbar ist.

Le chocolat haut de gamme MIA fait partie d'une marque de spécialités alimentaires entièrement produites et emballées en Afrique, de la ferme à l'usine. Ce nom est l'acronyme de « Made in Africa », mais représente aussi le mot latin pour « mienne » parce que toutes les personnes qui participent à cette organisation se sentent personnellement impliquées dans ces produits. Le packaging a été conçu pour refléter les origines africaines de la marque, mais en évitant les stéréotypes et en soulignant la vitalité de l'Afrique moderne.

MIA

Design: Jamie Helly, Aisling Walsh, Derek McGrath, Sheena Flynn, Emma Kate Horsfield, Katy Connell, Róisín Ní Ráighne, Alan Pollock
Company: Dynamo Branding
Country: Ireland
Category: Confectionery and sweet snacks
SILVER PENTAWARD 2018

CF 18 CHOCOLATIER
Photography: Lars Petter Pettersen (Coup)
Company: OlssønBarbieri
Country: Norway
Category: Confectionery and sweet snacks
GOLD PENTAWARD 2020

REAL HANDFUL

Design: Will Gladden, Claudio Vecchio
Illustration: Call Me George(s)
Company: Midday
Country: UK
Category: Confectionery and sweet snacks

GOLD PENTAWARD 2019

HONMIDO

Design: Bravis International team
Company: Bravis International
Country: Japan
Category: Confectionery and sweet snacks

SILVER PENTAWARD 2019

FORTNUM & MASON

Creative Direction: Chloe Templeman
Senior Design: Alice Douglas-Dean, Morgan Swain
Business Development: Alice Goss
Word Direction: Caroline Slade
Senior Production Project Management: Talitha Watson
Illustration: Paul Desmond
Company: Design Bridge London
Country: UK
Category: Confectionery and sweet snacks

SILVER PENTAWARD 2019

MACHIYENGA TREE TO BAR
Photography: Sumiko Miura
Company: Alejandro Gavancho
Country: Peru
Category: Confectionery and sweet snacks
BRONZE PENTAWARD 2020

POCKY THE GIFT

Creative Direction and Art Direction:
Yoshihiro Yagi
Planning and Copywriting: Haruko Tsutsui
Design: Taiji Kimura, Haruko Nakatani,
Satomi Okubo, Hirono Matsunaga
Planning: Takuya Fujita and Ryoya Sugano,
Mai Umegae and Kotaro Fujiwara
Construction Management: Masamitsu Usui
Company: Dentsu
Country: Japan
Category: Confectionery and sweet snacks
SILVER PENTAWARD 2020

ZOKOKO
Design: Edouard Ball, Jon Clark, Jodi Hooker,
Frederico Hernandez, Thomas Finn
Company: Webb Scarlett deVlam Sydney
Country: Australia
Category: Confectionery and sweet snacks
BRONZE PENTAWARD 2010

FRITO-LAY
TRUENORTH

Creative Director: Todd Simmons
Design: Bill Darling, Masha Zolotarsky, Jodie Gatlin
Production Director: Beth Kovalsky
Production Manager: Michele Miller
Strategists: Christina O'Neal, Tina Mehta
Account Director: Jessica Chalifoux
Company: Wolff Olins
Country: USA
Category: Savory snacks

BRONZE PENTAWARD 2009

PCHAK

Art Direction and Design: Stepan Azaryan
Illustration: Enok Sargsyan
Company: Backbone Branding
Country: Armenia
Category: Savory snacks

GOLD PENTAWARD 2017

Pumpkin seeds

XIANGKE SUNFLOWER SEEDS

Creative Direction: Zhou Jingkuan
Design Direction: Sun Linlin
Illustration: Yang Xue, Li Ziqiong
Company: Shenzhen Left and Right
Packaging Design
Country: China
Category: Savory snacks

GOLD PENTAWARD 2019

On the packaging for **Xiangke Sunflower Seeds** three animals that like to eat these seeds are featured: a monkey, a hamster and a parrot. The mouths of the animals are the same shape as the sunflower seeds, and their surprised and satisfied expressions suggest that the seeds are big and delicious. In order to make the brand's packaging all-embracing, the images of a man, a woman and an old man were also created, whose wide-open mouths reveal their appetite for the tasty seeds.

Auf der Verpackung von **Xiangke Sunflower Seeds** sind drei Tiere zu sehen, die sehr gerne Sonnenblumenkerne essen: ein Affe, ein Hamster und ein Papagei. Die Münder der drei Tiere haben dieselbe Form wie die Saat und ihre überraschten und zufriedenen Gesichtsausdrücke lassen vermuten, dass die Kerne groß und köstlich sind. Um die Verpackung der Marke allumfassend zu gestalten, wurden außerdem die Bilder zweier Männer und einer Frau entworfen, deren weitgeöffnete Münder zeigen, dass sie großen Appetit auf den schmackhaften Snack haben.

Sur le packaging des graines de tournesol de la marque **Xiangke**, trois animaux qui en sont amateurs, que sont le singe, le hamster et le perroquet, sont illustrés avec la bouche en forme de graine de tournesol. Leurs expressions de surprise et de satisfaction font comprendre que les graines sont aussi grandes que délicieuses. Et pour renvoyer une image plus complète, les visages d'un homme jeune, d'un autre âgé et d'une femme, tous avec la bouche grande ouverte, prouvent leur goût pour ces savoureuses graines.

BLACK EAT
Design: Peng Chong
Company: Pesign Design
Country: China
Category: Savory snacks
BRONZE PENTAWARD 2017

ένα
κουταλάκι
ζάχαρη

ένα
κουταλάκι
ζάχαρη

ένα
κουταλάκι
ζάχαρη

ένα
κουταλάκι
ζάχαρη

ένα
κουταλάκι
ζάχαρη

ένα
κουταλάκι
ζάχαρη

SUGARILLOS SUGAR STICKS

Design: Gregory Tsaknakis *Illustration:*
Ionna Papaioannou
Company: Mousegraphics
Country: Greece
Category: Desserts, sweet foods and
confection dishes

BRONZE PENTAWARD 2010

MATCHALL

Design Direction: Zhu Chao
Design: Zhu Chao, Wang Ruyi
Company: Mint Design
Country: China
Category: Desserts, sweet foods and
confection dishes

SILVER PENTAWARD 2018

森林抹茶曲奇
（烘烤糕点）
Forest Matcha Cookie

matchall

净含量:270g

ZHANGREN WORKSHOP

Design: Sichuan Guge Dynasty Brand Design team
Company: Sichuan Guge Dynasty Brand Design
Consultant
Country: China
Category: Desserts, sweet foods and
confection dishes

GOLD PENTAWARD 2015

The rice candy and crunchy candy made by
Zhangren Workshop are popular snacks
particular to the city of Dujiangyan in Sichuan
province. The packaging takes the form of a paper
bag sealed at the top with a length of hemp rope,
which in conjunction with the printed design
supplies the top-knot of the Taoist pictured.
This ingenious combination of tradition and
fashion achieves a strong visual impact, while the
clean design projects a sense of simplicity and
slight luxury.

Das von **Zhangren Workshop** hergestellte
Reiskonfekt und die Knusperbonbons sind in der
Stadt Dujiangyan in der Provinz Sichuan besonders beliebte Leckereien. Die Verpackung erscheint in Form einer Papiertüte, oben mit einer
Hanfschnur verschlossen, die zusammen mit dem
Printdesign dem Taoisten seinen Haarschopf
liefert. Diese raffinierte Kombination aus Tradition und Mode erzielt eine kraftvolle optische
Wirkung, während das klare Design Einfachheit
und leichten Luxus vermittelt.

Les bonbons de riz et les bonbons croquants
de **Zhangren Workshop** sont des en-cas popu-
laires de la ville de Dujiangyan, dans la province
du Sichuan. L'emballage est un sachet en papier
fermé par une cordelette de chanvre, qui avec le
dessin imprimé forme la houppe du taoïste repré-
senté. Ce design inspiré des traditions délivre un
impact visuel fort, et exprime simplicité et luxe
discret.

TK FOOD
ASSORTED FLAVOUR GIFT BOX

Design: Victor Branding creative team
Company: Victor Branding Design Corp.
Country: Taiwan
Category: Desserts, sweet foods and confection dishes

SILVER PENTAWARD 2011

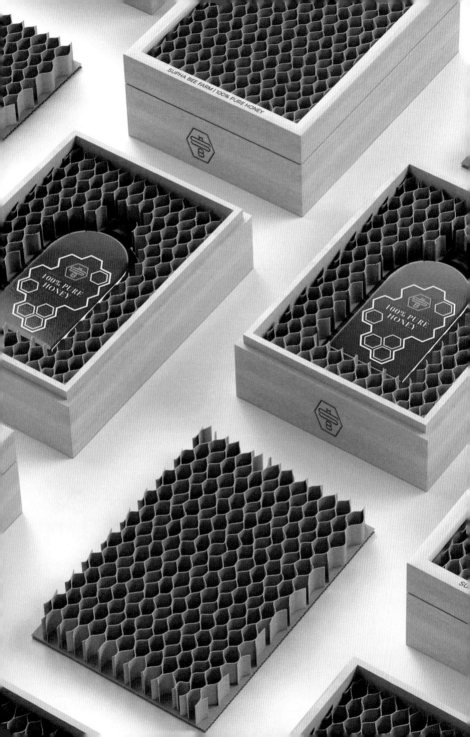

SUPHA BEE FARM HONEY

Executive Creative Direction:
Somchana Kangwarnjit
Design: Rutthawitch Akkachairin, SKJ,
Napapach Sunlee
Retouching: Pantipa Pummuang,
Thiyada Akarasinakul, Somporn Thimkhao
Company: Prompt Design
Country: Thailand
Category: Desserts, sweet foods and
confection dishes
GOLD PENTAWARD 2020

Supha Bee Farm is one of the two main honey producers in Thailand which has its own bee farms with bee rearing and breeding facilities. The outstanding product is 100% real pure honey with packaging that is specially designed and inspired by the structure of the beehive frame. The paper honeycomb is used together with the wooden box to emphasise the feeling that the honey bottle inside is directly from the beehive. The SB logo is designed simply to make it look similar to a bee.

Die **Supha Bee Farm** ist einer der beiden wichtigsten Honigproduzenten in Thailand, der eigene Bienenfarmen mit Bienenaufzucht und Brutanlagen besitzt. Das herausragende Produkt ist zu 100 % reiner Honig mit einer Verpackung, die speziell entworfen und von der Struktur des Bienenstockrahmens inspiriert wurde. Die Honigwabe aus Papier wird gemeinsam mit einer Box aus Holz verkauft, um das Gefühl zu unterstreichen, dass die darin enthaltene Honigflasche direkt aus dem Bienenstock kommt. Das SB-Logo ist so gestaltet, dass es einer Biene ähnlich sieht.

Supha Bee Farm est l'un des deux principaux producteurs de miel de Thaïlande possédant ses propres exploitations apicoles et installations d'élevage et de reproduction d'abeilles. Ce produit exceptionnel est un miel pur à 100 %, logé dans un emballage spécialement conçu et inspiré de la structure d'une ruche. Combiné à une boîte en bois, le papier alvéolé accentue l'impression que la bouteille de miel sort directement de la ruche. Le logo SB a été conçu pour ressembler à une abeille.

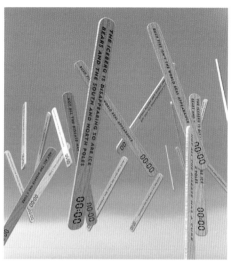
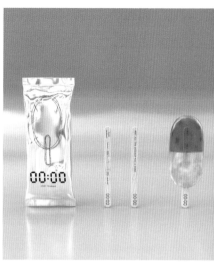
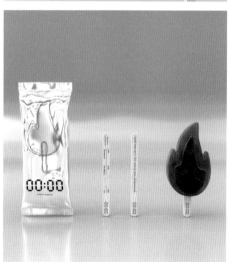
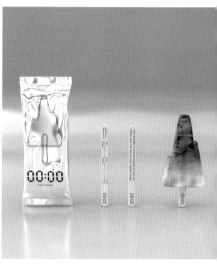

00:00

Design Lead: Yujie Chen
Design: Fengming Chen, Chinglang Chen, Jiarong Zeng, Yichao Fan, Qingwei Li, Haiyong Wang, Qing Yu
Company: inDare Design Strategy Limited
Country: China
Category: Desserts, sweet foods and confection dishes

SILVER PENTAWARD 2020

JEJU PREMIUM TART

Art Direction: Seoyoon Yang
Design: Seongmin Jeon, Hyeyoung Choi
Company: SPC Samlip
Country: South Korea
Category: Desserts, sweet foods and confection dishes

SILVER PENTAWARD 2019

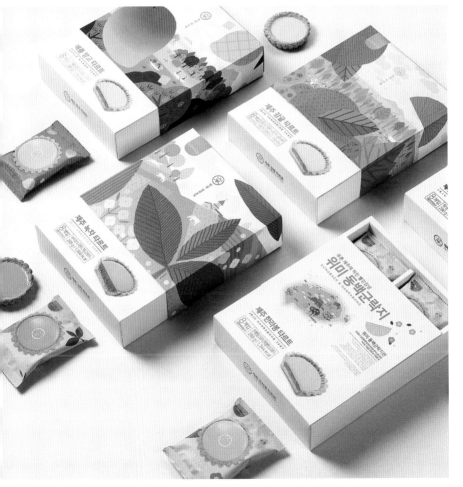

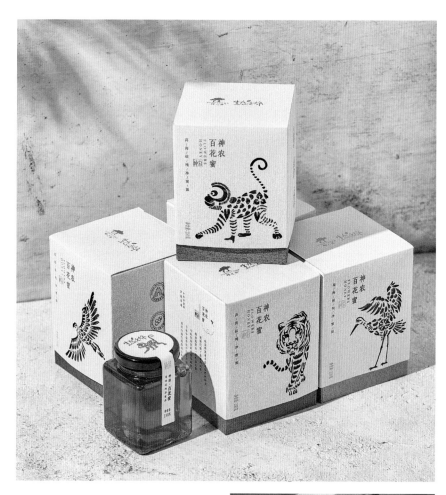

HONEY OF VARIOUS FLOWERS IN SHENGNONGJIA

Design: Xiang Shasha
Creative Direction: Zhang Yanhui
Customer Service Direction: Zhou Xiaoli
Illustration: Tong Meng
Company: Wuhan Pufan Advertising
Country: China
Category: Desserts, sweet foods and confection dishes

SILVER PENTAWARD 2020

THREE TREASURES OF CHAOZHOU

Design Guidance: Yang Zhen
Design: Xu Yi Fei, Yang Jia Lu, Hu Yu Bin, Lin Qing Yi
Company: Firewolf Design
Country: China
Category: Food trends

SILVER PENTAWARD 2019

LOGOTHETIS ORGANIC FARM

Creative Direction: Antonia Skaraki
Design: Andreas Deskas, Valia Alousi,
Evri Makridis
Copywriting: Sotiria Theodorou
Company: A.S. Advertising
Country: Greece
Category: Food trends

SILVER PENTAWARD 2020

MR. FANG'S STORE

Design: Sozo Design, Mr. Fang's Store
Company: Hangzhou SOZO Industrial Design
Country: China
Category: Food trends
SILVER PENTAWARD 2019

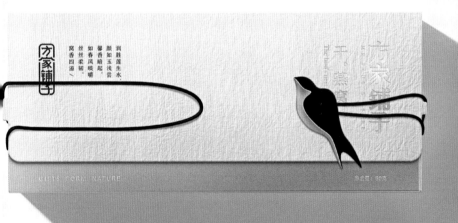

GAEA SNACKS

Design: Mousegraphics team
Company: Mousegraphics
Country: Greece
Category: Food trends
GOLD PENTAWARD 2018

The packaging of **Gaea** vegan snacks was initially designed for the Greek market then launched on the international market thereafter. Most vegan products use images of fresh food on their packaging design to suggest the idea of naturalness, but this takes a diametrically different solution. Each vegetable (carrot, gherkin, cauliflower) has been designed as an emblem printed across two color zones, borrowing principles from flag design. All product information is clearly stated on the front.

Die Verpackung der veganen Snacks von **Gaea** wurde ursprünglich für den griechischen Markt entworfen und erst danach auch international herausgebracht. Die meisten veganen Produkte werden in Verpackungen mit Bildern von frischen Lebensmitteln angeboten, um den Eindruck von Natürlichkeit zu erwecken, doch hier wird eine diametral entgegengesetzte Lösung gesucht. Jedes Gemüse (Karotte, Gurke, Blumenkohl) wird als Emblem auf zwei Farbzonen dargestellt, in Anlehnung an Prinzipien des Flaggendesigns. Alle Produktinformationen stehen deutlich sichtbar auf der Vorderseite.

Le packaging des snacks végans **Gaea** a initialement été conçu pour le marché grec, et a été lancé sur le marché international par la suite. La plupart des produits végans utilisent des images d'aliments frais sur leur packaging pour suggérer leur naturel, mais ici la démarche adoptée est diamétralement opposée. Chaque légume (carotte, cornichon, chou-fleur) devient un emblème stylisé imprimé sur deux zones colorées, selon un principe inspiré des drapeaux. Toutes les informations relatives au produit sont clairement indiquées sur le devant.

SWEET FREEDOM

Design: Moyra Casey, Kelly Bennett, Chris McDonald
Company: Afterhours
Country: UK
Category: Food trends

SILVER PENTAWARD 2017

SHINY WOODS

Design: Jingfang Mei
Company: Dong Yun
Country: China
Category: Food trends
GOLD PENTAWARD 2017

WOOLWORTHS
GOLD

Design: Claire Stenvert, Jessica Parisi
Creative Direction: Gavin Greenhalf
Styling: Gemma Lush
Photography: Andrew Dougal Stavert
Account Management: Jane Eaton
Head of Own Brand Packaging Design: Suzy Lake
Design Specialist: Sandra Dagher
Company: Marque Brand Consultants
Country: Australia
Category: Cross-category ranges

BRONZE PENTAWARD 2014

VAN DER BURGH CHOCOLAAD
HANDGEMAAKTE CHOCOLADE

PURE CHOCOLADE
72% CACAO
100 GRAM

VAN DER BURGH CHOCOLAAD
HANDGEMAAKTE CHOCOLADE

PURE CHOCOLADE
54% CACAO
100 GRAM

VAN DER BURGH CHOCOLAAD
HANDGEMAAKTE CHOCOLADE

MELK CHOCOLADE
MET HELE HAZELNOOT
40% CACAO
100 GRAM

VAN DER BURGH CHOCOLAAD
HANDGEMAAKTE CHOCOLADE

MELK CHOCOLADE
MET AMANDEL
40% CACAO
100 GRAM

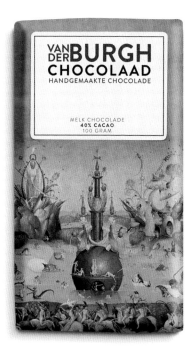

In 2016 the city of 's-Hertogenbosch commemorates the 500th anniversary of the death of the painter Hieronymus Bosch, its most famous son. His utterly distinctive style and fantastic imagery are the basis for the **jHEROnimus** brand, which markets contemporary products inspired by the artist's works. Amongst a variety of different items to be sold in museum-shops around the world, the jHEROnimus chocolate has been handmade by the Van der Burgh Chocolaad company. A limited edition, its wrapper incorporates details from Bosch's works alongside simple graphic wallpaper motifs.

2016 gedenkt die holländische Stadt 's-Hertogenbosch des 500. Todestags von Hieronymus Bosch, dem berühmtesten Sohn der Stadt. Sein außerordentlich charakteristischer Stil und die fantastischen Gemälde bilden die Basis der Marke **jHEROnimus**, unter der moderne, vom Werk des Künstlers inspirierte Produkte vermarktet werden. Neben vielfältigen verschiedenen Artikeln, die in Museumsshops in aller Welt verkauft werden, stellt die Firma Van der Burgh Chocolaad die Schokolade jHEROnimus per Hand her. Die limitierte Edition zeigt Details der Werke von Bosch neben einfachen Tapetenmustern.

En 2016, la ville de Bois-le-Duc a commémoré le 500ᵉ anniversaire de la mort du peintre Jérôme Bosch, son enfant le plus célèbre. Son style tout à fait distinctif et ses images fantastiques sont la base de la marque **jHEROnimus**, qui vend des produits contemporains inspirés par les œuvres de cet artiste. Les différents articles vendus dans les musées du monde entier comprennent aussi le chocolat jHEROnimus, fabriqué à la main par l'entreprise Van der Burgh Chocolaad. En édition limitée, son emballage associe des détails des œuvres de Bosch à des motifs de papier peint graphique.

VAN DER BURGH CHOCOLAAD JHERONIMUS BOSCH

Design: Jeroen Hoedjes, Paul Roeters
Company: Studio Kluif
Country: Netherlands
Category: Limited editions, limited series, event creations

GOLD PENTAWARD 2015

MAROU, FAISEURS DE CHOCOLAT
MAROU CHOCOLATE FOR NATIONAL
GALLERY SINGAPORE

Design: Chi-An De Leo, Joshua Breidenbach,
William Sörqvist, Anna Tran
Company: Rice Creative
Country: Vietnam
Category: Limited editions, limited series,
event creations

GOLD PENTAWARD 2016

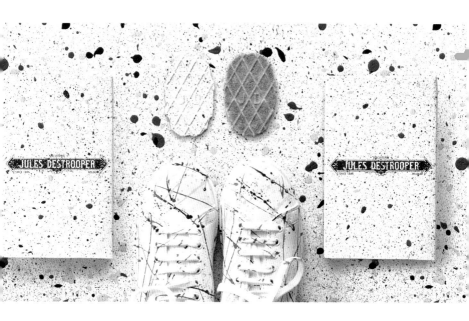

JULES DESTROOPER
130TH ANNIVERSARY

Creative Direction: Patrick De Grande
Design: Kobe De Keyzer, Vicky Acke
Stylist: Els Goethals
Company: Quatre Mains
Country: Belgium
Category: Limited editions, limited series,
event creations

GOLD PENTAWARD 2017

Jules Destrooper, master biscuitiers, decided to create a limited-edition gift to celebrate their 130th anniversary. They collaborated with Belgian chocolatier Dominique Persoone to hand-decorate a limited selection of 1,000 packs in the style of the Action painters. Dominique Persoone created a biscuit in the Belgian national colors: white-chocolate covered with yellow, black and red paint sprinkles. Each one was unique and came with its own identification number.

Meister-Biscuitier **Jules Destrooper** hat zur Feier des 130-jährigen Bestehens eine Geschenk-Edition in limitierter Auflage herausgebracht. Dafür wurde mit dem belgischen Chocolatier Dominique Persoone zusammengearbeitet, der eine Selektion von 1000 Kekspackungen im Stil des Action Painting von Hand dekorierte. Dominique Persoone kreierte Waffelkekse in den belgischen Nationalfarben: gelbe, schwarze und rote Sprenkel auf einem weißen Schokoladenüberzug. Jede Verpackung war einzigartig und trug eine eigene Seriennummer.

Jules Destrooper, maîtres biscuitiers, a décidé de créer un cadeau en édition limitée pour célébrer son 130ᵉ anniversaire. La marque a travaillé en collaboration avec le chocolatier belge Dominique Persoone pour décorer à la main une sélection de 1000 paquets dans le style de l'action painting. Dominique Persoone a créé un biscuit dans les couleurs nationales de la Belgique : chocolat blanc couvert de confettis jaunes, noirs et rouges. Chaque paquet est unique et possède son propre numéro d'identification.

Burger King's 2017 festive season packaging was designed as an invitation to their customers to join in the fun and celebrations. They are best known for their flame-grilling so the design combined festive icons with flames, viewed as in a photographic negative. The Whopper wrap became Santa's beard, over a fiery background, while takeaway bags allowed customers to become the bearded Mr Claus himself, as the bag could be held to your mouth, creating shareable, Insta-worthy packaging.

Burger Kings Jubiläumsverpackungen von 2017 sollten die Kunden zum Mitfeiern einladen. Die Marke ist besonders bekannt für ihre flame-grilled Burger, deshalb verband das Design festli-che Motive mit Bildern von Flammen, dargestellt wie auf einem Foto-Negativ. Das Whopper-Papier wurde zum Nikolausbart mit feurigem Hinter-grund, und bei den Tüten zum Mitnehmen konn-ten sich die Kunden selbst in den bärtigen Niko-laus verwandeln, indem sie sich die Tüte vor den Mund hielten – so entstanden instagramwürdige Verpackungsbilder, die sich gut mit Freunden teilen ließen.

Le packaging des fêtes de fin d'année de Burger King pour 2017 invitait les clients à se joindre aux célébrations et au divertissement. Burger King est connu pour sa viande grillée à flamme nue, c'est pourquoi le design combinait des images emblématiques de Noël et des flammes, traitées comme un négatif photographique. L'emballage du Whopper est devenu la barbe du Père Noël sur un fond ardent, tandis que les sacs à emporter permettaient aux clients de se transfor-mer en Père Noël en le plaçant devant leur bouche, ce qui offrait l'occasion de prendre une photo et de la partager sur Instagram.

BURGER KING
CHRISTMAS PACKAGING 2017

Executive Creative Direction: David Turner, Bruce Duckworth
Creative Direction: Clem Halpin, Christian Eager
Design: Jessie Froggett, Chris Simpson
Account Direction: Nicola Eager
Account Executive: Viviana Gardener
Company: Turner Duckworth
Country: UK
Category: Limited editions, limited series, event creations
GOLD PENTAWARD 2018

MONDELEZ
CADBURY

Creative Direction: Asa Cook
Design: Kirsty Struthers
Associate Creative Direction and Art Direction:
Rob Ellis (VCCP)
Associate Creative Direction and Copywriting:
Peter Reid (VCCP)
Company: Design Bridge London in collaboration
with VCCP London
Country: UK
Category: Limited editions, limited series,
event creations

GOLD PENTAWARD 2020

To help Age UK fight the loneliness epidemic, **Cadbury** were asked to donate their words and create the "wordless bar". Keeping things simple, the milk pour motif was left exactly where it normally appears on the standard bar, and a stripped back graphic style was used for maximum "quietness". The bar occupies an almost empty space on the shelf, which boldly stood out precisely because the design is so minimal. It's not until someone picks up the bar that they see the message in a milk splash speech bubble on the back of the pack, telling them that 30p per bar sold is donated to Age UK. The Cadbury purple and the milk pour are so distinctive that the bar is immediately recognisable.

Um der Organisation Age UK zu helfen, die Epidemie der Einsamkeit zu bekämpfen, wurde **Cadbury** gebeten, ihre Worte zu spenden und die „wortlose Tafel" zu kreieren. Das Motiv der Milchgläser ist genau dort platziert, wo es auch sonst auf den Schokoladentafeln zu finden ist, für maximale „Ruhe" wurde ein zurückgenommener grafischer Stil verwendet. Die Tafel belegt damit eine fast leere Stelle im Regal, die vor allem deswegen heraussticht, weil das Design so reduziert ist. Erst wenn jemand die Tafel in die Hand nimmt, sieht er die Botschaft auf der Rückseite der Packung mit dem Hinweis, dass 30 Pence pro verkaufter Tafel an Age UK gespendet werden. Das Cadbury-Lila und die fließende Milch sind so markant, dass die Tafel sofort wiedererkannt wird.

Pour combattre le fléau de la solitude, Age UK a demandé à **Cadbury** de proposer une « tablette sans mots ». Pour faire simple, l'image du lait versé a été conservée à sa place habituelle, et un style graphique dépouillé a été choisi pour une « tranquillité » absolue. La tablette occupe un espace quasiment vide en rayon et se fait clairement remarquer grâce à ce design si minimal. C'est seulement quand on prend la tablette que l'on peut voir au dos le message dans une bulle de texte en forme d'éclaboussure de lait, expliquant que pour chaque tablette vendue, 30 pence sont reversés à Age UK. Le violet Cadbury et le lait versé sont tellement caractéristiques que la tablette est immédiatement identifiable.

CARNERO

Creative Direction and Graphic Design:
Emanuele Basso
Creative Direction: Elena Carella
Graphic Design and Illustration: Federico Epis
Company: The 6th
Country: Italy
Category: Limited editions, limited series,
event creations

GOLD PENTAWARD 2019

Carnero is the first biltong, a type of dried
meat, produced in Italy. Inspired by the style of the
Golden Age of Italian graphic design, the front of
the packaging shows illustrations of Mr Carnero
playing with his cows: the classic cow and the spicy
cow. To help make the product stand out, the backs
of the packets show 25 different visuals of the
Carnero family and storyline, turning the pouches
into a mural when displayed all together.

INGREDIENTI

Carne di manzo, Pepe nero, Coriandolo,
Aceto, Noce moscata, Zucchero di canna,
Aromi naturali, Sale, Sale a basso
contenuto di sodio, Salsa
worchestershire, Bicarbonato
di sodio, Conservanti
Naturali, Antiossidante.

Carnero ist das erste Biltong, eine Art Trockenfleisch, das in Italien hergestellt wird. Inspiriert vom Stil des Goldenen Zeitalters des italienischen Grafikdesigns, zeigt die Vorderseite der Verpackung Illustrationen von Mr. Carnero, die mit dem Bild der Kuh spielen: die klassische Kuh und die scharfe Kuh. Damit das Produkt heraussticht, sind die Verpackungen mit 25 Bildern der Carnero-Familie und ihrer Geschichte gestaltet und verwandeln die Tüten, wenn sie alle nebeneinandergelegt werden, in ein Wandgemälde,

Carnero est le premier biltong, un type de viande séchée, produit en Italie. S'inspirant du style de l'âge d'or du design graphique italien, l'avant du packaging affiche des illustrations de M. Carnero jouant avec ses vaches, la classique et l'épicée. Pour singulariser le produit, l'arrière du paquet compte 25 illustrations de la famille Carnero et son histoire. Mis côte à côte, les emballages forment alors une véritable fresque.

FIGLIA

Creative Direction: Andy Reynolds
Design Direction: Gianluca Crudele
Design: Louisa Luk
Ceramic Artwork: Salvatore Caraglia
Client Management: Euginia Chui
Photography: Scott Kimble
Company: Superunion
Country: UK
Category: Limited editions, limited series,
event creations
SILVER PENTAWARD 2020

Figlia (meaning daughter in Italian) is a limited-edition batch of hand-crafted olive oil from Agricola Dargenio. The edition was inspired by the concept "Feminine by Nature", which relates to both the product and how it's made, whilst showing support for Agricola's first female CEO. Three hundred handmade ceramic bottles from the same region were created, and aside from a subtle stamp in the base, the bottles are purposefully left unlabelled so they may be repurposed. A series of illustrations were developed to form the foundations of their visual language, inspired by the bottle design and use of soft organic shapes to form delicate and minimal depictions of female faces. Like the bottles, the illustrations aim to celebrate the uniqueness of all things natural and come in a multitude of variations set around the same style and colour palette.

Figlia (bedeutet Tochter auf Italienisch) ist eine limitierte Charge handgemachten Olivenöls von Agricola Dargenio. Die Edition wurde von dem Konzept „von Natur aus weiblich" inspiriert, das sich sowohl auf das Produkt als auch auf die Herstellungsweise bezieht und gleichzeitig Unterstützung für Agricolas erste weibliche CEO zeigt. Es wurden dreihundert Keramikflaschen regional gefertigt und abgesehen von einem einfachen Stempel auf dem Boden, haben die Flaschen selbst absichtlich keine aufgeklebten Labels, damit sie wiederverwendet werden können. Für die Etiketten auf der Verpackung und die losen Schildchen an der Flasche wurde eine Reihe von Illustrationen angefertigt, die subtile Abbildungen von weiblichen Gesichtern zeigen. Wie die Flaschen zielen auch sie darauf ab, Natürlichkeit und Einzigartigkeit zu zelebrieren und wurden als Unikate angelegt, die sich in Form und Farbe voneinander unterscheiden.

Figlia (fille, en italien) est une collection en édition limitée d'huile d'olive artisanale d'Agricola Dargenio. Le concept derrière cette gamme est celui de « féminine par nature » associé au produit et à sa fabrication, et preuve du soutien à la première femme PDG d'Agricola. Trois-cents bouteilles en céramique ont été fabriquées à la main dans cette région et à part un discret tampon à leur base, elles sont délibérément dépourvues d'étiquette pour en faciliter le recyclage. Les illustrations réalisées posent les bases du langage visuel, qui s'aligne sur le design des bouteilles et joue avec des formes organiques pour représenter des visages féminins de façon délicate et minimale. Comme les bouteilles, ces illustrations visent à célébrer la singularité de toutes les choses naturelles et se déclinent en une foule de variantes autour du même style et de la même palette de couleurs.

LADY M MOONCAKE GIFT SET PACKAGE

Design: BXL Creative Design, Lady M Confections
Client: Lady M Confections
Company: Shenzhen Baixinglong Creative Packaging
Country: China
Category: Limited editions, limited series,
event creations

SILVER PENTAWARD 2020

BAKERY FACTORY

Art Direction: Seoyoon Yang
Design and Illustration: Hyeyoung Choi
Company: SPC Samlip
Country: South Korea
Category: Limited editions, limited series,
event creations

BRONZE PENTAWARD 2020

SHANGRI-LA INTERNATIONAL
HOTEL MANAGEMENT LTD

Creative Direction: Tim Siro
Senior Design: Christie Widjaja
Visualisation: Dea Jovita
3D Design Direction: Aaron Lim
Design: Elysa Tan, Pamela Ng
Illustration: Jason Liw
Senior Visualisation: Ong Jian'An
Visualisation Direction: Charles Galland
3D Technical Design Direction: Toh Meng Lee
Print and Production Team Lead: Calvin Low
Production Management: Fenson Cheng
Artwork: Vivian Vindu Dinata
Senior Client Management: Andie Ngoh
Client Executive: Nur Farzana
Company: Design Bridge Singapore
Country: UK
Category: Limited editions, limited series,
event creations
BRONZE PENTAWARD 2020

NOBLEZA DEL SUR

Creative Direction: Isabel Cabello
Design: Isabel Cabello
Design and Illustration: Ester Moreno
Company: Cabello x Mure
Country: Spain
Category: Limited editions, limited series,
event creations

BRONZE PENTAWARD 2019

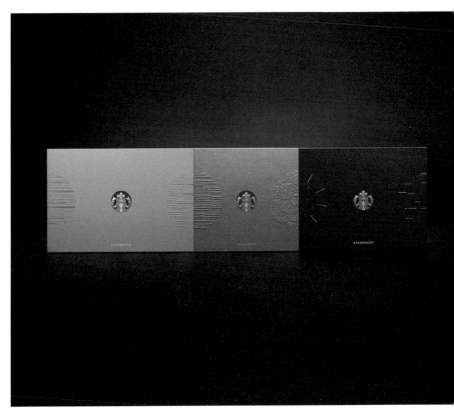

STARBUCKS

Senior Design: Carmen Lee
Design: WanFeng Wang
Senior Client Management: Ivy Wang
3D Technical Design Direction: Meng Lee Toh
Client Business Direction: Greenly Lu
Production Management: Fenson Cheng
Creative Direction: Tom Gilbert
Company: Design Bridge London
Country: UK
Category: Limited editions, limited series, event creations

SILVER PENTAWARD 2019

ARMATORE

Design: Lettera 7
Company: Armatore
Country: Italy
Category: Limited editions, limited series,
event creations

BRONZE PENTAWARD 2019

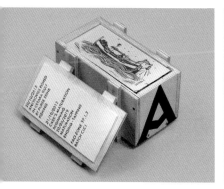

XING SHI SHAN BRAND DESIGN

Client: Nanlian Agricultural
Design: One More Design
Creative Direction: Xia Jiangnan, Zhang Haiqiang,
Meng Shenhui, Huang Fupeng, Mao Jian,
Qiu Yang
Company: One More Idea
Country: China
Category: Distributors'/retailers' own brands,
private labels

GOLD PENTAWARD 2020

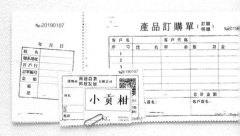

WAITROSE & PARTNERS

Creative Direction: Garrick Hamm
Client Services Direction: Wybe Magermans
Account Management: Bella Thompson
Design Direction: Mark Nichols
Design: Christopher Ribét, Becki Sewell,
Holly Mattacott-Cousins, Jane Harwood
Photography: Jonathan Gregson
Production Management: Mark Tosey
Artwork: Mark Tickner, Nursel Arslan
Retouching: Chris Fennel
Client and Head of Design
Waitrose & Partners: Ashley Vinall
Company: Williams Murray Hamm
Country: UK
Category: Distributors'/retailers' own brands,
private labels

BRONZE PENTAWARD 2019

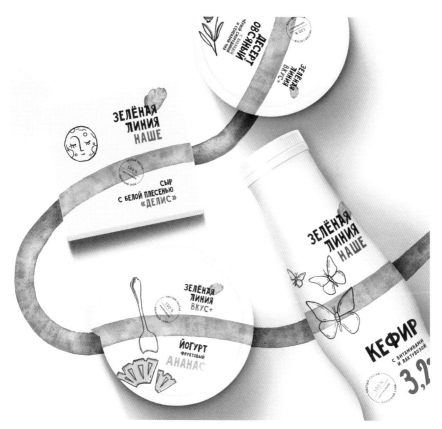

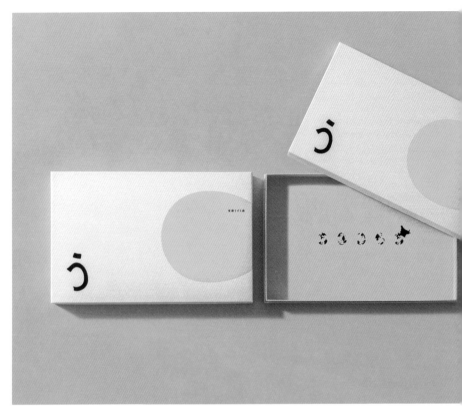

MURORAN UZURAEN

Art Direction: Nobuya Hayasaka
Creative Direction: Hitoshi Kobayashi
Design: Nobuya Hayasaka
Production: arica design
Client: Muroran Uzuraen
Company: arica design
Country: Japan
Category: Distributors'/retailers' own brands,
private labels
BRONZE PENTAWARD 2020

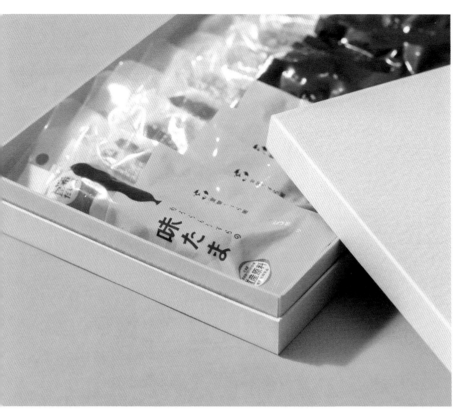

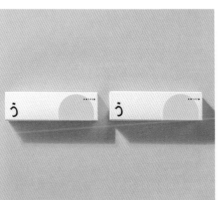

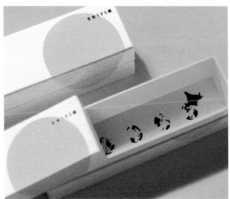

GREEN LINE PRIVATE LABEL

Creative Direction: Nadie Parshina
Art Direction: Ann Burlakina
Junior Design: Nikita Gavrilov
Account Management: Kate Dorokhina
Company: Ohmybrand
Country: Russia
Category: Distributors'/retailers' own brands,
private labels

BRONZE PENTAWARD 2020

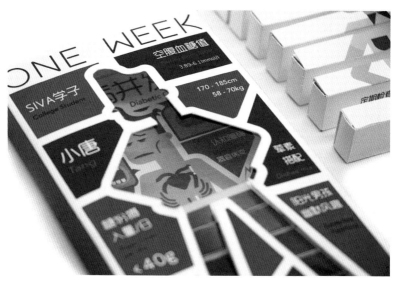

E&B

Design: Chen Xiaotong, Xiao Han
Design Direction: Michail Semoglou
School: Shanghai Institute of Visual Arts (SIVA)
Country: China
Category: Packaging concept (student)

BRONZE PENTAWARD 2019

Nord Stream is a range of tins within cardboard packets that contain preserved fish and seafood in five different varieties: sardines, smoked mussels, crab, octopus, and squid. Each variety has its own distinct graphic and its own colour. There is a hidden animation too: the picture on the top starts to move when you open the package. This interactivity involves the customer in a unique process of communication with the product.

Nord Stream bietet ein Sortiment von Fisch und Meeresfrüchten in Konserven mit Kartonumschlägen an. Die fünf Sorten sind Sardinen, geräucherte Muscheln, Krebsfleisch, Tintenfisch und Oktopus. Jede Sorte hat ihre eigene Grafik und Farbe. Dazu birgt die Verpackung eine Animation: Das Bild auf der Vorderseite gerät in Bewegung, wenn man die Verpackung öffnet. Durch dieses interaktive Element tritt der Kunde in einen ganz besonderen Kommunikationsprozess mit dem Produkt ein.

Nord Stream est une gamme de boîtes de conserve présentées dans des emballages en carton. Elles contiennent des conserves de poisson et de fruits de mer de cinq variétés : sardines, moules fumées, crabe, poulpe et calamar. Chaque variété possède un graphisme et une couleur différents. Il y a aussi une animation cachée : l'image sur le dessus de la boîte bouge lorsque vous ouvrez. Cette interactivité crée un processus de communication unique entre le client et le produit.

NORD STREAM

Art Direction: Artem Petrovsky
Senior Design: Jenya Petrovskaya
Photography: Vladimir Zotov
Technology: Andrey Shkola
Management: Olya Goryacheva
Company: Loco Studio
Country: Russia
Category: Packaging concept

GOLD PENTAWARD 2018

SWEET SKY COTTON CANDY
no artificial flavours or colours / for children +3
Blackberry cloud 60g
4387636801094

OPEN HERE

SWEET SKY
Blueberry cloud

TAKEOUT
Design: Wei-Chi Lin, Yi-Wen Hsu, Yu-San Weng
School: Ming Chi University of Technology
Country: Taiwan
Category: Packaging concept (student)
BRONZE PENTAWARD 2018

YINONG

Creative Direction: Jintao He
Design: Fanggui Chen
Illustration: Xiaofan Chen
Company: Shantou Datianchao Brand Planning
Country: China
Category: Packaging concept

GOLD PENTAWARD 2020

RAINY SEASONS

Design: Pavla Chuykina
Country: Russia
Category: Packaging concept
SILVER PENTAWARD 2017

BIBIGO
STEAM MANDU

Executive Direction: Kangkook Lee
Creative Direction: Yuljoong Kim
Design: Seongpyo Lee
Product Design: Kinam Hwang
Company: CJ Cheiljedang
Country: South Korea
Category: Packaging concept

BRONZE PENTAWARD 2018

JONAH'S

Associate Creative Direction: Chantal Roberti
Company: SGK Anthem – Amsterdam
Country: Netherlands
Category: Packaging concept
SILVER PENTAWARD 2020

TUNA FISH CAN
LIKENED TO A FISHING BOAT

Design: Sayaka Kawagoe
Company: Toyo Seikan Group Holdings
Country: Japan
Category: Packaging concept

GOLD PENTAWARD 2019

This conceptual piece for a tuna fish can tells the story of how fresh tuna from the sea ends up on our plates. With delightful details decorating the fishing-boat-shaped can, the package created for **Toyo Seikan Group Holdings** was designed to bring happiness to the family dinner table and create instant brand recognition around a popular everyday food.

Diese konzeptionelle Thunfischdose erzählt, wie frischer Thunfisch aus dem Meer auf unsere Teller gelangt. In Form eines Fischerboots, mit wundervollen Details verziert, wurde die Verpackung für **Toyo Seikan Group Holdings** entworfen, um Fröhlichkeit auf den Essenstisch zu bringen und um einen Wiedererkennungswert der Marke rund um ein beliebtes Alltagsessen zu schaffen.

Cette œuvre conceptuelle pour une boîte de conserve de thon explique comment le thon frais du grand large finit dans notre assiette. Parfaitement décorée, la boîte en forme de bateau de pêche a été conçue pour **Toyo Seikan Group Holdings,** afin de donner une touche joyeuse aux repas en famille et d'assurer la reconnaissance immédiate d'un aliment populaire de tous les jours.

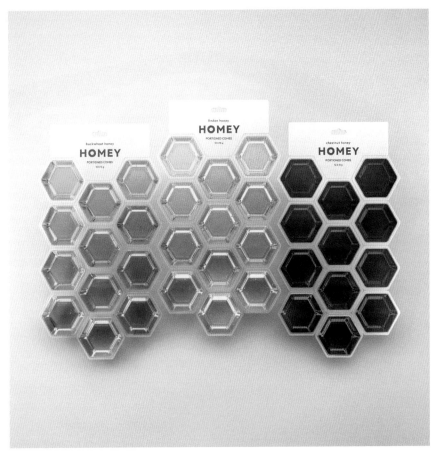

HOMEY

Art Direction: Katya Mushkina
CG Artwork: Bulgakov Nikita, Aleksey Shelukho
Copywriting: Aleksey Kalyan
Company: Katya Mushkina
Country: Russia
Category: Packaging concept

BRONZE PENTAWARD 2019

BEE-FEE

Design: Zuzanna Sadlik, Beata Faron
Company: Opus B Brand Design
Country: Poland
Category: Packaging concept
SILVER PENTAWARD 2019

JIANGGUO WAWA

Creative Direction: Haozhen Luo
Company: Beijing Heziguai Creative Design
Country: China
Category: Packaging concept
BRONZE PENTAWARD 2020

HOT WAVE

Design, Creative Direction and Photography:
Lin Wang
Supervision: Gu Chuan-Xi
School: Shanghai Institute of Visual Arts (SIVA)
Country: China
Category: Packaging concept (student)

GOLD PENTAWARD 2020

CLÓCLO

Creative Direction, Design and 3D Rendering
Design: África Álvarez Bueriberi
Instruction: Mónica Yoldi, Gracia de Prado, Marcos Gallo
School: Escuela Superior de Diseño de La Rioja (Esdir)
Country: Spain
Category: Packaging concept (student)
GOLD PENTAWARD 2020

Clóclo is reusable organic egg packaging, intended to reduce the number of single-use containers. The set of different shapes and the graphic aesthetics emulate the appearance of the egg when it comes out of the shell, creating fluid forms that allow retailers to set up attractive combinations at the point of sale. Made of bent poplar wood, there are three styles which differentiate between M, L and XL eggs. Initially created with four egg slots, the structure can be easily scaled up to 6, 12 or more based on the consumer's needs.

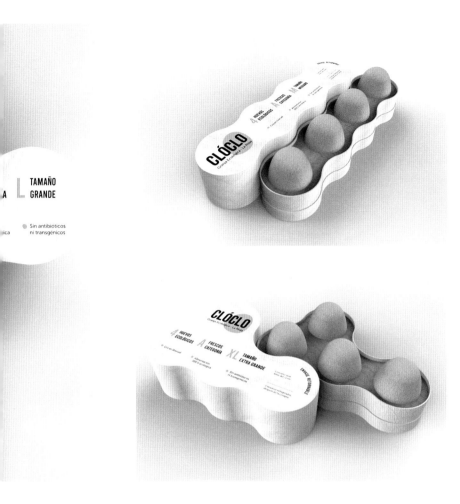

TAMAÑO
A L GRANDE

Sin antibioticos
ni transgénicos

Clóclo ist eine wiederverwendbare biologische Eierverpackung, die darauf abzielt, die Anzahl von Einmal-Verpackungen zu reduzieren. Das Set aus verschiedenen Formen und die grafische Ästhetik ahmen das Ei nach, wenn es aus der Schale kommt. Die fließenden Formen ermöglichen es dem Einzelhändler, attraktive Kombinationen im Laden zu bilden. Aus biegsamem Pappelholz hergestellt, gibt es drei verschiedene Stile für die Größen M, L und XL. Vorerst mit Platz für vier Eier hergestellt, kann die Struktur einfach auf sechs, zwölf oder noch mehr Eier, je nach Bedürfnissen des Konsumenten, erweitert werden.

Clóclo est un emballage réutilisable pour œufs bio servant l'objectif de réduire le nombre de boîtes d'un seul usage. Les formes variées et l'esthétique graphique imitent l'aspect d'un œuf quand on en casse la coquille, ce qui donne des figures fluides idéales pour composer des combinaisons attrayantes dans les points de vente. Fabriquées en bois de peuplier courbé, les boîtes sont disponibles dans trois styles selon la taille M, L et XL des œufs. D'abord pensé pour quatre compartiments, cet emballage peut facilement passer à 6, 12 ou plus selon les besoins des consommateurs.

BOUDIN SAN FRANCISCO

Design and Art Direction: Yi Mao
Photography: Jack Strutz
Hand Modelling: Lemon Zhai
Instruction: Andrew Gibbs, Jessica Deseo
Advisor: Gerardo Herrera
School: ArtCenter College of Design
Country: USA
Category: Packaging concept (student)

GOLD PENTAWARD 2019

Boudin SF is a bakery and restaurant chain originally from San Franciscom known for its sourdough bread. It was established in 1849 by Isidore Boudin, the son of a family of master bakers from Burgundy, France, by blending the sourdough prevalent among miners in the Gold Rush with French techniques. Today, it is famous for its sourdough boule with clam chowder inside of it. This rebranding and packaging design recognises sustainability as longevity and delivers Boudin SF's same spirit but with a 21st-century vibe. This conceptual piece is part of a project from ArtCenter College of Design's first 100% plastic-free packaging course.

Boudin SF ist eine Bäckerei- und Restaurant-kette, die ursprünglich aus San Francisco stammt und für ihr Sauerteigbrot bekannt ist. Sie wurde 1849 von Isidore Boudin, dem Sohn einer Familie von Meisterbäckern aus Burgund, gegründet. Er kombinierte die Sauerteigkomponente, die bei den Minenarbeitern zur Zeit des Goldrauschs besonders beliebt war, mit französischen Back-techniken. Heute ist die Kette bekannt für Muschelsuppe im Sauerteigbrötchen. Das Design erkennt Nachhaltigkeit als Langlebigkeit an und verknüpft Boudin SFs Erbe mit dem Schwung des 21. Jahrhunderts. Dieses konzeptionelle Stück ist Teil eines Projekts des ersten 100 % plastik-freien Verpackungskurses des ArtCenter College of Design.

Boudin SF est une chaîne de boulangeries et de restaurants originaire de San Francisco et qui est réputée pour son pain au levain. Fondée en 1849 par Isidore Boudin, fils d'une famille bourgui-gnonne de maîtres boulangers, elle doit son succès au mariage du savoir-faire français de la boulange-rie et du levain que les chercheurs d'or cultivaient à cette époque. Aujourd'hui, Boudin est célèbre pour sa chaudrée de palourdes servie dans une boule de pain au levain. Ce design de rebranding et de packaging fait rimer durabilité et longévité et transmet la même philosophie de Boudin SF, mais avec une approche du 21ᵉ siècle. Cette œuvre conceptuelle fait partie d'un projet pour le premier cours de création de packagings 100 % sans plas-tique à l'ArtCenter College of Design.

STANDARD

Design: Olga Prokhorova
Tutoring: Leonid Slavin, Alexander Nazarenko
School: British Higher School of Art and Design
Country: Russia
Category: Packaging concept (student)
BRONZE PENTAWARD 2020

SEE'S CANDIES

Design: Donna Kang
Photography: James chou
School: ArtCenter College of Design
Country: USA
Category: Packaging concept (student)

SILVER PENTAWARD 2019

Best of the category
Beauty
Perfumes and cosmetics
Garments

body

Health care
Body care
Distributors'/retailers' own brands, private labels
Packaging concept

MATSUKIYO

Design: William Woduschegg, Hideto Matsuo,
Yoshihiko Miyagi, Sayaka Ichiki, Yusuke Arai,
Koici Fujimura, Kanako Yaginuma
Company: Interbrand
Country: Japan
Category: Best of the category

PLATINUM PENTAWARD 2017

This packaging design for **Matsukiyo** toilet
paper tackles the age-old Japanese embarrass-
ment about purchasing personal hygiene products.
Interbrand Japan, the designers behind this
Platinum Pentaward-winning design, claim to have
made toilet paper cool by giving it attitude! The
exterior of the packaging is illustrated with full-
size images of everyday objects of similar shapes.
This humorous idea creates the illusion that something other than a pack of toilet rolls is being car-
ried—perhaps a baby, or a boom box.

Dieses Verpackungsdesign für **Matsukiyo**-
Toilettenpapier setzt bei der uralten Verlegenheit
der Japaner beim Kauf von Körperhygiene-Arti-
keln an. Die Designer von Interbrand Japan, die
hinter diesem mit dem Pentaward in Platin ge-
krönten Entwurf stehen, behaupten, durch sie
wäre Toilettenpapier cool geworden, indem sie
dem Produkt Unbefangenheit und Pep verliehen
haben! Die Außenseite ihrer Verpackung zeigt
ganzflächige Bilder von alltäglichen Dingen ähnli-
cher Größe. Diese witzige Idee erzeugt die Illusion, man trage etwas ganz anderes mit sich herum
als ein Paket Toilettenpapier – zum Beispiel ein
Baby oder einen Ghettoblaster.

Ce concept de packaging pour le papier toilette
Matsukiyo trouve une solution à la gêne que
beaucoup de Japonais ressentent lorsqu'ils
achètent des produits d'hygiène personnelle. Les
designers d'Interbrand Japan derrière ce concept,
qui a remporté un Platinum Pentaward, affirment
avoir rendu cool le papier toilette en le dotant
d'une personnalité ! L'extérieur du packaging est
illustré d'images grandeur nature d'objets quoti-
diens de formes similaires. Cette idée pleine d'humour donne l'impression que le consommateur
porte autre chose qu'un paquet de papier toilette,
comme un bébé ou un gros radiocassette.

O BOTICÁRIO
EUDORA SOUL

Design: Luis Gustavo Bartolomei, Rodrigo Costabeber,
Alex Diniz, Hudson Abreu, Nathalia Zupo, Nancy Stegal,
Gabriela Simões
Company: B+G Designers
Country: Brazil
Category: Beauty

BRONZE PENTAWARD 2011

POLA
BA GRANDLUXE 2
Creative Direction: Takashi Matsui, Chiharu Suzuki
Art Direction: Haruyo Eto
Design: Kentaro Ito, Rumie Ito
Company: Pola
Country: Japan
Category: Beauty
BRONZE PENTAWARD 2014

**ORIENTAL PRINCESS
BENEFICIAL**
Design: Somchana Kangwarnjit, Thiyada Akarasinakul,
Ratikorn Kesornjarung, Chirut Maneengam,
Sirin Poopiamsakdi, SKJ, Pongpipat Jetsadalak
Company: Prompt Design
Country: Thailand
Category: Beauty
BRONZE PENTAWARD 2016

The brief was to create packaging that would differentiate this new line of cosmetics in a highly competitive market. There are two basic design elements: a bright and unusual shade of yellow and a bold typeface, which combine to form a strong brand identity. The name of the brand, **Asarai**, dominates the all-yellow surface of each product in straight, imposing linearity but is introduced on the outer tubular box as a quirky play on the design lexicon: every time the tube's upper part closes on the lower part it fits differently. The brand name letters are thus fragmented, rearranged, visually cut, and conceptually completed by chance.

ASARAI

Design: Mousegraphics team
Company: Mousegraphics
Country: Greece
Category: Beauty
GOLD PENTAWARD 2018

Der Auftrag lautete, eine Verpackung zu entwerfen, um diese neue Kosmetiklinie auf einem wettbewerbsintensiven Markt auffallen zu lassen. Das Design besteht aus zwei Grundelementen: einem ungewohnt kräftigen Gelb und einer individuellen Schrift, die gemeinsam für eine starke Markenidentität sorgen. Der Name **Asarai** dominiert die einfarbig gelbe Oberfläche jedes Artikels in direkten, imposanten Buchstaben, wird auf der Umverpackungsröhre jedoch zum spitzfindigen Spiel: Jedes Mal, wenn der obere Teil der Röhre zum Schließen auf den unteren gesetzt wird, entsteht ein neues Bild. Die Buchstaben des Markennamens werden fragmentiert, zerschnitten, und ganz zufällig neu zusammengesetzt.

La mission était de créer un packaging qui différencierait cette nouvelle ligne de cosmétiques sur un marché extrêmement concurrentiel. Le design se base sur deux éléments qui se combinent pour donner une puissante identité de marque : une couleur jaune vif inhabituelle et une police de caractères gras. Le nom de la marque, **Asarai**, monopolise la surface entièrement jaune de chaque produit avec une linéarité imposante. Sur la boîte extérieure tubulaire en revanche, il prend une dimension ludique inattendue : chaque fois que la partie supérieure du tube se referme sur celle du bas, sa position est différente. Les lettres du nom de la marque sont alors fragmentées, réarrangées, visuellement coupées et conceptuellement formées au hasard.

DEREK L|DEREK L|DEREK L|DEREK L|DEREK L|DEREK L|DEREK L|DEREK L|DEREK L|DEREK L|DEREK L
IO CROS|IO CROS|IO CROS|IO CROS|IO CROS|IO CROS|IO CROS|IO CROS|IO CROS|IO CROS|IO CROS
SILENT ST|LOOKING GL|HI-FI|DRUNK ON|AFLOAT|RAIN DAY|SOMETHING|ELLIPSIS|BLACKOUT|2AM KISS
EAU DE PAR|EAU DE PAR|EAU DE PAR|EAU DE PAR|EAU DE PAR|EAU DE PAR|EAU DE PAR|EAU DE PAR|EAU DE PAR|EAU DE PAR
175ML-5.9 FL|175ML-5.9 FL|175ML-5.9 FL|175ML-5.9 FL|175ML-5.9 FL|175ML-5.9 FL|175ML-5.9 FL|175ML-5.9 FL|175ML-5.9 FL|175ML-5.9 FL

DEREK LAM
IO CROSBY

Design: Sayuri Shoji
Company: Sayuri Studio
Country: Japan
Category: Beauty

SILVER PENTAWARD 2017

body **375**

POLA
BA SERIES SERUM REVUP
Creative Direction: Takashi Matsui
Art Direction: Haruyo Eto
Design: Mai Karin Kamiyama, Rieko Nakamura,
Shingo Isobe
Company: Pola
Country: Japan
Category: Beauty
BRONZE PENTAWARD 2017

1937

Creative Direction and Design: Muggie Ramadani
Company: Bold Scandinavia
Country: Denmark
Category: Beauty
SILVER PENTAWARD 2018

CHIOTURE

Creative Direction: Guozheng Jiang, Dan Chen
Strategy Consulting Direction: Yang Shu
Product Design: Xinnan Zhang, Zilei Jiao
Account Executive: Jin Li
Company: Shanghai Nianxiang Brand Design
& Consulting
Country: China
Category: Beauty

PLATINUM PENTAWARD 2020

This basic make-up kit for **Chioture**, a vibrant and youthful make-up brand, focuses on the ritual surrounding the use of the product. Chioture stands for chic + capture and refers to the brand's idea of a "young fashion hunter" seeking "the simple life". With its adorable camera-like look, the innovative design of this loose powder case and brush effectively communicates the fun characteristics of the brand. The user unscrews the "lens" to access the powder and pulls out the brush, which is securely stored in the "grip". The "viewfinder" shows the logo and also doubles as a dock for the brush.

Dieses Make-up-Set von **Chioture**, eine lebhafte und jugendliche Make-up-Marke, fokussiert sich auf das Ritual, das die Verwendung des Produkts umgibt. Chioture steht für chic + capture (dt. „einfangen") und bezieht sich auf die Idee der Marke eines „jungen Modejägers", der das „arglose Leben" sucht. Das innovative Design dieser Puderdose und des Pinsels mit seinem bezaubernden kameraähnlichen Look vermittelt die humorvolle Charakteristik der Marke wirkungsvoll. Der Nutzer schraubt die „Linse" ab, um an das Puder zu gelangen, und zieht den Pinsel hervor, der sicher im „Griff" verstaut ist. Der „Sucher" zeigt das Logo der Marke und kann gleichzeitig als Halterung für den Pinsel genutzt werden.

Ce kit de maquillage pour la marque juvénile et colorée **Chioture** est adapté à l'environnement habituel dans lequel il est utilisé. Chioture est la contraction de chic + capture et renvoie à l'idée d'une « jeune chasseuse de mode » en quête d'une « vie simple ». Avec un adorable look d'appareil photo, le design innovant de ce boîtier de poudre libre et son pinceau transmet parfaitement les amusantes particularités de la marque. L'utilisateur dévisse la « lentille » pour ouvrir le poudrier et extrait le pinceau logé dans la « poignée ». Le logo se trouve sur le « viseur », qui sert également de support au pinceau.

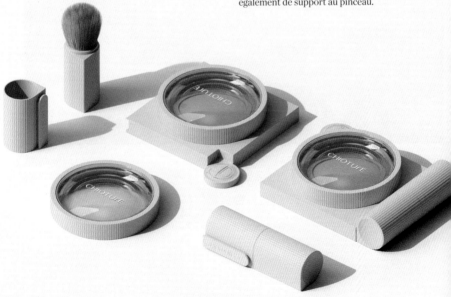

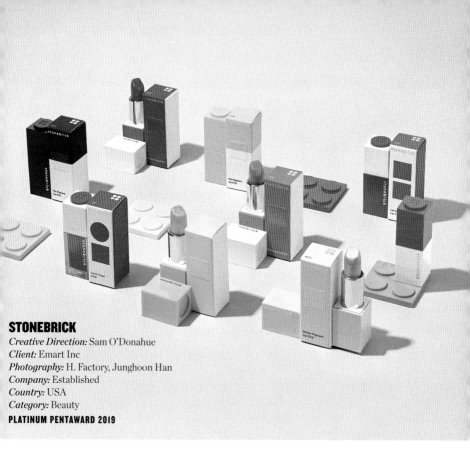

STONEBRICK

Creative Direction: Sam O'Donahue
Client: Emart Inc
Photography: H. Factory, Junghoon Han
Company: Established
Country: USA
Category: Beauty

PLATINUM PENTAWARD 2019

As a new line of makeup created for South Korea's largest retailer Emart, **Stonebrick** is the first fully customisable makeup range with individual magnetised components that snap together to create custom collections. The idea behind the line is to allow the customer to buy a tailor-made set of cosmetics in a playful, fun and joyful way. Lipsticks and face products also click together in different and exciting combinations for endless possibilities.

Als neue Make-up-Linie, die für Südkoreas größten Emart-Händler entworfen wurde, ist **Stonebrick** die erste komplett individualisierbare Make-up-Reihe mit einzelnen magnetischen Komponenten, die sich zu benutzerdefinierten Kollektionen zusammenfügen lassen. Die Idee ist es, dem

Kunden die Möglichkeit zu geben, ein auf spielerische Art maßgeschneidertes Kosmetikset zu erwerben. Auch Lippenstifte und Gesichtspflegeprodukte lassen sich in verschiedenen Kombinationen zusammenklicken.

Stonebrick est la nouvelle ligne de maquillage proposée par Emart, le plus grand détaillant de Corée du Sud. Il s'agit de la première gamme de produits de maquillage entièrement personnalisables, avec des éléments individuels aimantés qui s'assemblent pour former des collections uniques. L'idée est de permettre au consommateur d'acheter des produits cosmétiques personnalisés d'une manière amusante et originale. Les rouges à lèvres et les soins pour le visage se clipsent ensemble pour créer des combinaisons attrayantes infinies.

COLOUR ZONE

Creative Direction: Guozheng Jiang, Dan Chen
Graphic Design: Sijie Pei, Ke Zheng
Industrial Design: Zilei Jiao, Xinnan Zhang,
Lei Tang
Company: Shanghai Nianxiang Brand Design
& Consulting
Country: China
Category: Beauty
GOLD PENTAWARD 2019

The design for the make-up brand **Colour Zone** is built around the keywords contained in the brand's name. Using "zones of colour", the designer creates an exciting out-of-this-world look across the range of products. Shaped like a UFO, the products possess a futuristic colour gradient to highlight the wide range of unique colours available. Colour Zone reveals a parallel universe of make-up, offering endless possibilities for consumers to express themselves.

Das Design der Make-up-Marke **Colour Zone** basiert auf den im Markennamen enthaltenen Schlüsselwörtern. Mithilfe von „Farbzonen" hat der Designer eine aufregende Produktlinie geschaffen, die nicht von dieser Welt scheint. In Form von Ufos, zeigen die Produkte einen futuristischen Farbverlauf, um die einzigartige Vielfalt der erhältlichen Nuancen des Produkts hervorzuheben. Colour Zone offenbart damit ein Paralleluniversum des Make-ups, das den Konsumenten unendlichen Möglichkeiten bietet, sich selbst auszudrücken.

Le design pour la marque de cosmétiques **Colour Zone** se base sur les mots clés formant son nom. À l'aide de « zones de couleur », le designer a créé un intéressant look hors du commun pour toute la gamme de produits. Rappelant un OVNI, le produit affiche un dégradé futuriste pour souligner le large éventail de couleurs uniques disponibles. Colour Zone dévoile ainsi un univers parallèle de maquillage aux possibilités infinies pour que les consommateurs y trouvent un mode d'expression.

CHIOTURE

Creative Direction: Guozheng Jiang, Dan Chen
Strategy Consulting Direction: Yang Shu
Product Design: Xinnan Zhang, Zilei Jiao
Account Executive: Jin Li
Company: Shanghai Nianxiang Brand
Design & Consulting
Country: China
Category: Beauty

SILVER PENTAWARD 2020

SK:LK

Client: Beijing Youji Technology Development
Creative Direction: Tengxian Zou
Design: Tengxian Zou, Qi Tong, Yunfan Chen,
Yi Song
Render Division: Wenfang Ye
Company: Shanghai Version Design Group
Country: China
Category: Beauty

BRONZE PENTAWARD 2019

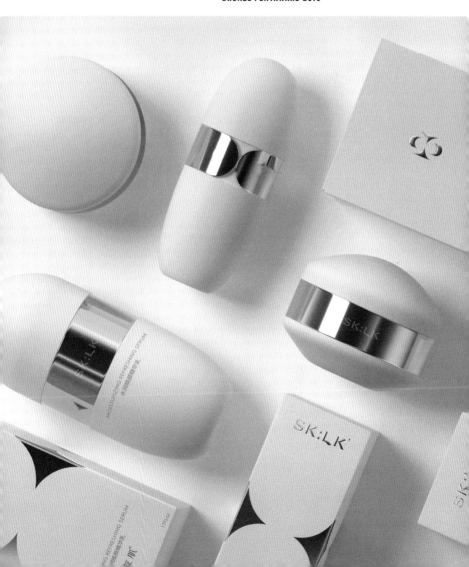

PHFORMULA
VITA

Design: Albert Puigdemont, Marta Montagut
Company: Puigdemont Roca
Country: Spain
Category: Perfumes and cosmetics

SILVER PENTAWARD 2015

FC KLUIF

Art Direction: Paul Roeters
Art Direction and Design: Jeroen Hoedjes
Company: Studio Kluif
Country: Netherlands
Category: Garments

SILVER PENTAWARD 2018

FJÄLLRÄVEN
BERGTAGEN

Packaging Design Direction: Linus Jiremark
Art Direction: Fredrik Lewander (Fjallraven)
Final Art: Annika Wikberg (Fjallraven)
Copywriting: Erik Hagelin (Fjallraven)
Research and Development: Thomas Hakansson
and Johanna Mollberg (Fjallraven)
Computer Generated Imagery: Nils Carlen and
Gabriel Von Gertten (Zenit Design Group)
Company: Packground
Country: Sweden
Category: Garments

SILVER PENTAWARD 2017

Rollor Express patented technology allows clothing to be rolled rather than folded for transport, and a raised edge prevents external pressure, so when the package is unrolled, the item of clothing is crease-free and ready to wear. The package's base is made of rollable corrugated cardboard with a foam rim. The roll is held together with a customizable handle with the logo or imprint of the fashion brand. This packaging is a typical "form follows function" design and it does what in the end is the purpose of packaging: gives the customer a pleasant experience and makes sure the product inside is presented at its best.

Mit **Rollor Express**, einer patentierten Technik, können Kleidungsstücke aufgerollt statt zusammengefaltet transportiert werden. Ein erhöhter Rand verhindert äußere Druckeinwirkung, sodass die Kleidung beim Auspacken faltenfrei und bereit zum Tagen ist. Das Grundelement der Verpackung besteht aus rollbarer Wellpappe mit einem Schaumstoffrand. Zusammengehalten wird die Rolle von einem individualisierbaren Griff, der das Logo oder einen Aufdruck der Modemarke enthält. Diese Verpackung ist ein typisches Beispiel für „form follows function" und erfüllt genau das, was letztendlich der Zweck jeder Verpackung ist: Sie gibt dem Kunden ein gutes Gefühl und sorgt dafür, dass das Produkt, das sich darin befindet, bestmöglich zur Geltung kommt.

ROLLOR EXPRESS

Design: Teun van der Laan, Robert Hoes,
Peter Hoogland
Company: Rollor
Country: Netherlands
Category: Garments
GOLD PENTAWARD 2017

La technologie brevetée de **Rollor Express**
permet d'enrouler les vêtements plutôt que de les
plier pour les transporter, et son bord relevé em-
pêche toute pression externe. Ainsi, lorsqu'on
déroule le vêtement, il est prêt à être porté, sans
plis. La base est en carton ondulé enroulable, avec
un bord en mousse. Le rouleau est maintenu par
une poignée qui peut être personnalisée avec le
logo ou l'identité de la marque. Ce packaging est
un concept typique du principe « la forme obéit à
la fonction », et remplit à merveille son rôle : offrir
au client une expérience agréable et conserver dans
des conditions optimales le produit qu'il contient.

CONVERSE
ALL WAH
Creative Direction: Dane Whitehurst
Design Cornerstone Converse: Gaby Granier
Company: Burgopak
Country: UK
Category: Garments
BRONZE PENTAWARD 2017

ADDA
Executive Creative Direction:
Somchana Kangwarnjit
Design: Ratthakorn Disjaiyen, Phanupong Maud,
SKJ, Pongpipat Jetsadalak
Retouchers: Thiyada Akarasinakul,
Pantipa Pummuang, Chalida Assawamongkholsiri
Company: Prompt Design
Country: Thailand
Category: Garments
SILVER PENTAWARD 2017

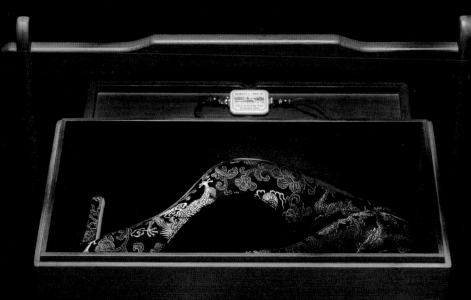

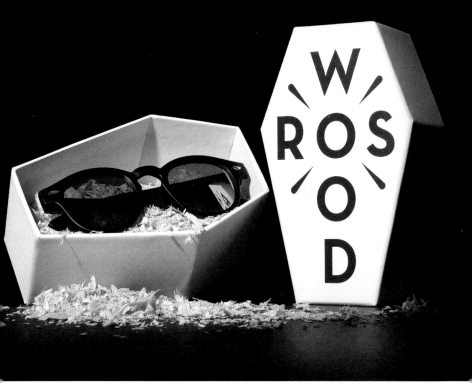

ROSWOOD

Concept Packaging and Design: F33
design team
Company: F33
Country: Spain
Category: Garments
BRONZE PENTAWARD 2018

THIMBLE PAN

Design: Patrick Pan
Company: Guangzhou Brand Vision Power AD
Country: China
Category: Garments
BRONZE PENTAWARD 2017

This re-invigorated packaging for **Petit Bateau**'s baby, kid and adult clothing and underwear uses the brand's history as the focus for its redesign. In 1918, Étienne Valton, the son of the brand's founder, had the idea to cut off the legs of long underwear, inventing the world's first baby pants. Inspired by the brand's transformative heritage, the design utilises a "cut out" as the packaging signature, which highlights the brand's iconic clothes in a simple and fun way. The pack's new structure also enables the brand to communicate its story and legendary attributes on the back of the pack while better protecting what is inside.

Für diese neu belebte Verpackung für **Petit Bateaus** Baby-, Kinder- und Erwachsenenbekleidung und Unterwäsche wurde die Geschichte der Marke als Schwerpunkt für das neue Design genutzt. 1918 hatte Étienne Valton, der Sohn des Markengründers, die Idee, die Beine der langen Unterhosen abzuschneiden, und entwarf so die erste Babyunterhose der Welt. Inspiriert durch das transformative Erbe der Marke, verwendet das Design einen „Ausschnitt" als Verpackungscharakteristik, die die Erfindung auf einfache und lustige Art hervorhebt. Die neue Struktur der Packung ermöglicht es der Marke auch, ihre Geschichte und legendären Eigenschaften auf der Rückseite der Verpackung zu kommunizieren und gleichzeitig den Inhalt besser zu schützen.

Ce packaging redynamisé des vêtements et sous-vêtements pour bébés, enfants et adultes **Petit Bateau** base sa refonte sur l'histoire de la marque. Étienne Valton, fils du fondateur de la marque, eut l'idée en 1918 de couper les jambes des sous-vêtements longs, ce qui donna naissance aux premiers pantalons bébé au monde. S'inspirant de cet héritage transformateur, le design choisit comme signe distinctif une découpe qui dévoile les vêtements emblématiques d'une façon simple et amusante. Ce nouvel agencement de l'emballage permet aussi à la marque de communiquer au dos son histoire et ses attributs légendaires, tout en protégeant davantage le produit qu'il renferme.

PETIT BATEAU

Managing Direction: Patrice Civanyan
Senior Design: Sarah Roberts
Design: Lysa Corporandy
Client: Petit Bateau
Company: Mutation
Country: France
Category: Garments
GOLD PENTAWARD 2020

SOUTHBANK WATSON OUTFITTER UK

Creative Direction: Paul Roeters
Design: Jeroen Hoedjes
Company: Studio Kluif
Country: Netherlands
Category: Garments

GOLD PENTAWARD 2019

Southbank Watson Outfitter UK's **Button Eye Shirt** is part of a collection of limited-edition handmade shirts. What makes the packaging of their products unique is their clever button-eye concept in combination with the striking illustrations on the gift boxes. The shirt's black button with its red thread plays an unexpected yet important role in the packaging, resulting in an "eye-conic" and playful design.

Das **Button Eye Shirt** von Southbank Watson Outfitter UK ist Teil einer Kollektion handgefertigter Hemden in limitierter Auflage. Was die Verpackung ihres Produkts einzigartig macht, ist ihr geniales Knopfaugen-Konzept in Kombination mit ihren markanten Illustrationen auf den Geschenkboxen. Der schwarze Knopf des Hemds mit seinem roten Zwirn spielt eine unerwartete und doch wichtige Rolle in der Verpackung, die sich in einem „Augen-scheinlichen" und spielerischen Design niederschlägt.

Le modèle **Button Eye Shirt** de Southbank Watson Outfitter UK appartient à une collection de chemises faites main en édition limitée. Le packaging de leurs produits est unique grâce à l'astucieux concept d'œil-bouton et aux illustrations éclatantes sur les coffrets-cadeaux. Le bouton noir cousu avec du fil rouge crée la surprise et devient le protagoniste du packaging, donnant un design amusant au premier coup d'œil.

FOUR SCHOLARS IN JIANGNAN

Creative Direction: Jingfang Mei
Company: Hangzhou Dongyun Advertising Design
Country: China
Category: Garments

SILVER PENTAWARD 2019

ROLLOR PACKAGING
Head of Design and Implementation:
Peter Hoogland
Packaging Design and Implementation Specialist:
Maarten Ornée
CEO and Founder: Teun van der Laan
CFO and Founder: Robert Hoes
Manufacturing: Smurfit Kappa MNL
Client: Loewe
Company: Rollor
Country: Netherlands
Category: Garments
BRONZE PENTAWARD 2019

GAMBOL
Creative Direction: Somchana Kanwarnjit
Creative Direction and Design:
Chalayoot Komalanimi
Art Direction: Nonpakorn Thiapairat
3D Rendering: Pichit Klungwijit
Illustration: Thanakim Thanomton
Company: Strong Design
Country: Thailand
Category: Garments
BRONZE PENTAWARD 2020

ALICE'S ADVENTURES IN WONDERLAND
Creative Direction, Art Direction
and Graphic Design: Koji Matsumoto
Company: Grand Deluxe
Country: Japan
Category: Garments
SILVER PENTAWARD 2020

HIDARIUCHIWA

Art Direction and Design: Ryuta Ishikawa
Company: Frame
Country: Japan
Category: Garments

BRONZE PENTAWARD 2019

Composition with Large Red Plane, Yellow, Black, Gray and Blue
Piet Mondrian, 1921

art
SOCKS

ARTSOCKS

Creative Direction: Stepan Azaryan
Project Management: Meri Sargsyan
Design: Christina Khlushyan, Eliza Malkhasyan
Company: Backbone Branding
Country: Armenia
Category: Garments

SILVER PENTAWARD 2019

GOLDEN ERA NUTRITION

Design: Zhanqiang Yang
Illustration: Wenwei Dai
3D: Zhihong Liang
Company: Going Design
Country: China
Category: Health care

SILVER PENTAWARD 2020

STARSHARING

Design: Wei Peng
Company: LionPeng Packaging Design Studio
Country: China
Category: Health care
BRONZE PENTAWARD 2019

CALLALY

Creative Direction: Chloe Templeman
Design: Faye Thomas
Sustainability Direction: Helen Hughes
Senior Production Management: Tal Watson
Senior Design: Cristina Tang
3D Branding Direction: Phil Bordet Stead
Design Direction: Natasha Dowdall,
Monique Bissell, Julian Waterson
Client Executive: Ellie Hammond-Hunt
Group Brand Experience Direction: Ed Mitchell
Company: Design Bridge London
Country: UK
Category: Health care
BRONZE PENTAWARD 2020

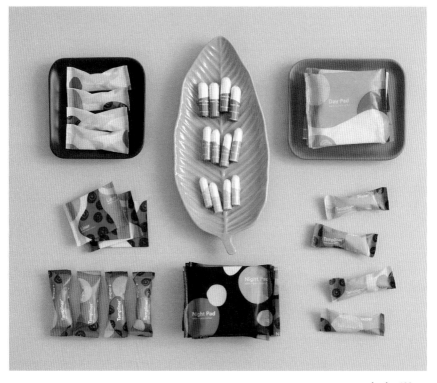

I'M PROBABLY
PMSING.
PERIOD.

OVARIES.
PERIOD.

IT'S JUST
BLOOD.

SAY IT LOUD.
PERIOD.
DONTHIDEITPERIOD.COM

DON'T HIDE IT. PERIOD.

Creative Direction: Neha Tulsian
Design: Sukriti Sahni
Photography: Raghav Kumar
Animation and Film-making: Nitin Shekhar
Social Media Management: Sukriti Sahni
Company: NH1 Design
Country: India
Category: Health care

SILVER PENTAWARD 2019

In India, myths and taboos around monthly periods often characterise menstruating women as unclean and impure. Even in urban areas, women still hesitate to ask for sanitary pads, and shopkeepers wrap menstrual products in newspapers and black plastic bags. As a way to help normalise the conversation around periods, **Don't Hide It. Period.** was launched. The limited-edition product uses this message as the main design concept. The phrase "don't hide it" was inspired by the sometimes embarrassing conversations around periods and seeks to remove the stigma around menstruation with its bold visuals and cheery wordplays.

In Indien charakterisieren Mythen und Tabus rund um die Monatsblutung menstruierende Frauen oft als unrein. Selbst in städtischen Gegenden trauen sich manche Frauen nicht, nach Damenbinden zu fragen, und Verkäufer verpacken Menstruationsprodukte in Zeitungen und schwarzen Plastiktüten. Um Gespräche über die Periode zu normalisieren, wurde **Don't Hide It. Period.** (dt. „Versteck es nicht") ins Leben gerufen. Das Produkt in limitierter Auflage nutzt seine Botschaft als Hauptdesignkonzept. Inspiriert von den manchmal peinlichen Dialogen über die Periode, brechen die starke Bildsprache und die selbstbewussten Sprüche das Stigma rund um die Menstruation auf. Die Doppeldeutigkeit des englischen Wortes "period" für „Periode" und „Punkt" am Satzende, macht die jeweilige Aussage zu einem echten Statement.

En Inde, les mythes et les tabous autour de la menstruation représentent souvent les femmes comme impures. Même dans les zones urbaines, les femmes hésitent encore à demander des serviettes hygiéniques, et les commerçants enveloppent les protections périodiques dans des feuilles de journaux et des sacs plastique noirs. **Don't Hide It. Period.** a été lancé pour essayer de normaliser la communication sur les règles. Le concept clé du design de ce produit en édition limitée est le propre message. La phrase « Don't hide it » (ne le cache pas) renvoient aux conversations parfois embarrassantes sur la menstruation et cherche à éliminer sa stigmatisation grâce à un visuel audacieux et des jeux de mots amusants, « period » ayant en anglais le double sens de règles et de point.

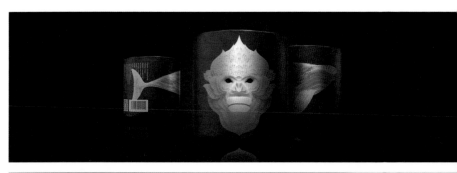

HILL SIDE

Creative Direction: Zhihua He
Design: Zhihua He
Client: Fengsheng Group
Company: Shanghai Version Design Group
Country: China
Category: Health care
SILVER PENTAWARD 2019

Hill Side is a new high-end brand of toilet paper which sees environmental protection and ecological balance as its core concepts. It uses special bamboo in the papermaking process, which is harvested by local farmers in Sichuan, supporting their incomes and respecting the ecological balance of the region. The black background gives a new look to traditional toilet roll packaging, featuring paper sculptures of endangered animals. The result is something that is both stylish and meaningful, aimed at young consumers who value the environment as well as the finer things in life.

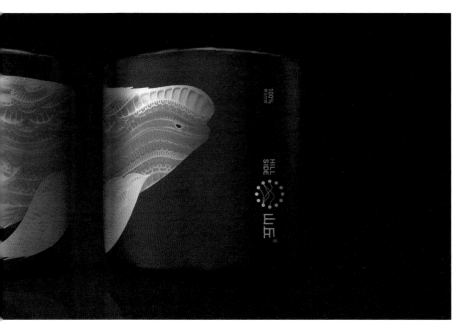

Hill Side ist eine neue luxuriöse Toilettenpapiermarke, die den Schutz der Umwelt und die ökologische Balance als das Kernkonzept ihrer Marke sieht. Bei der Papierherstellung benutzen sie Bambus, der von Bauern in Sichuan geerntet wird, um somit deren Einkommen zu unterstützen und das ökologische Gleichgewicht der Region zu respektieren. Der schwarze Hintergrund gibt der Toilettenpapierrolle einen modernen Look und zeigt Papierskulpturen bedrohter Tierarten. Das Resultat ist etwas, das sowohl stil- als auch bedeutungsvoll ist und sich damit an junge Verbraucher richtet, die die Umwelt aber auch die schönen Dinge des Lebens schätzen.

Hill Side est une nouvelle marque haut de gamme de papier toilette dont les concepts clés sont la protection de l'environnement et l'équilibre écologique. La fabrication du papier se fait à partir d'un bambou spécial récolté par des producteurs locaux à Sichuan : la marque assure ainsi leur revenus et respecte l'équilibre écologique de la région. Le fond noir tranche avec l'emballage traditionnel des rouleaux de papier toilette, présentant des photos de sculptures en papier d'animaux menacés d'extinction. Le produit obtenu est aussi sophistiqué que plein de sens et s'adresse aux jeunes consommateurs attachés à la défense de l'environnement et aux choses raffinées du quotidien.

CEIZO
Design: Qi Yuan
Company: Leadshow
Country: China
Category: Health care
SILVER PENTAWARD 2018

BAMBUPA

Design: Yuan Wang, Xi Li
Company: KDC brand
Country: China
Category: Health care
BRONZE PENTAWARD 2018

SOINS DE BEAUTÉ
MOERIE

Creative Agency: Moon Troops
Creative Direction and Graphic Design:
Motiejus Gaigalas
Photography: Marius Zicius
Company: Moon Troops
Country: Lithuania
Category: Health care

SILVER PENTAWARD 2017

MANUKA BEE
LIP CARE

Creative Direction: Guozheng Jiang
3D Design: Houcai Wang
Graphic Design: Dandan Chen
Business Direction: Lin Ling Wei
Company: OIB-Nianxiang
Country: China
Category: Body care

GOLD PENTAWARD 2017

CHUNJI
Design: Servaire & Co
Company: Marubi
Country: China
Category: Body care
GOLD PENTAWARD 2018

GREAT GRAPE
HYDRATING & MOISTURIZING
Cleanser

春纪
CHUNJI

GREAT GRAPE
HYDRATING & MOISTURIZING
Toner

GREAT GRA
HYDRATING & MOISTUR
Emulsion

Chunji is a care-conscious brand of cosmetics, made using high-quality natural ingredients that are ethically sourced. The simplicity and purity of the products led the designers to use color as the main ingredient of the visual identity of the package design. The overall effect is modern and youthful, with bold colors and fluent lines, making the products feel young and trendy.

Die Kosmetikmarke **Chunji** verwendet hochwertige, nach ethischen Grundsätzen erzeugte natürliche Inhaltsstoffe. Die Einfachheit und Reinheit der Produkte inspirierte die Designer, die visuelle Identität des Verpackungsdesigns vorrangig durch Farbe zu vermitteln. Der Gesamteindruck ist modern und jugendlich, klare Farben und fließende Linien lassen die Produkte jung und trendig wirken.

Chunji est une marque de cosmétiques consciente qui emploie des ingrédients naturels de grande qualité provenant de sources éthiques. La simplicité et la pureté des produits ont donné aux designers l'idée de baser l'identité visuelle du packaging sur la couleur comme composante principale. L'effet d'ensemble est moderne et jeune, avec des couleurs vives et des lignes fluides qui donnent au produit un style juvénile et tendance.

KANS
COSMETEA

Creative Direction: Guozheng Jiang
3D Design: Xinnan Zhang
Graphic Design: Dandan Chen
Business Direction: Lin Ling Wei
Company: OIB-Nianxiang
Country: China
Category: Body care

SILVER PENTAWARD 2017

Cosmetea is a skin-care brand in the East that uses tea as a key ingredient. The packaging is inspired by tea-sets, which have a long history in the East, going back thousands of years. The upper half of the bottle is the same as the top part of a traditional Gongdao mug for serving tea. The message is that skin care is just like drinking tea and perfect skin will be repaired every day, just as the soul is repaired when tea is drunk.

Der Hauptwirkstoff der **Cosmetea** Haut-pflegeserie aus Asien ist Tee. Inspiriert wurde die Verpackung von Teeservices, die in Asien eine jahrtausendealte Geschichte haben. Die obere Hälfte der Flasche hat die gleiche Form wie der obere Teil einer traditionellen Gongdao-Kanne. Die Botschaft lautet, dass es sich mit der Hautpfle-ge ebenso verhält wie mit dem Teetrinken: Eine perfekte Haut kann sich Tag für Tag regenerieren, genau wie die Seele sich beim Teetrinken erholt.

Cosmetea est une marque orientale de soins pour le visage dont l'ingrédient principal est le thé vert. Le packaging est inspiré des services à thé, dont la tradition est millénaire en Orient. La moi-tié supérieure du flacon est identique à celle d'une tasse à thé Gong Dao traditionnelle. Le message est que les soins du visage sont comme boire du thé : la peau est réparée chaque jour, tout comme le thé répare l'âme chaque jour.

FÉMME

Founder and CEO: Jonathan Ford
Creative Direction: Natalie Chung
Strategy Direction: Yael Alaton
Design: Jess Philips
Account Direction: Stuart McClelland
Company: Pearlfisher
Country: UK
Category: Body care
BRONZE PENTAWARD 2017

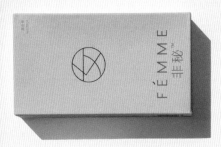

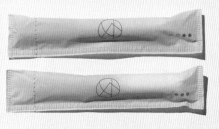

NATURELAB. TOKYO

Brand Direction: Hideaki Hosono
Art Direction & Design: Sayuri Shoji
Design: Manako Tagawa
Company: Sayuri Studio
Country: Japan
Category: Body care

SILVER PENTAWARD 2018

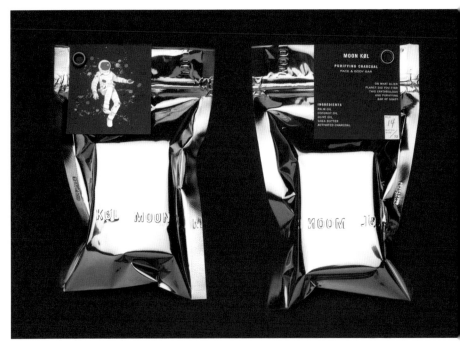

MOON KØL

Design: Sean Carter
Illustration: Rosie Gopaul
Production Design: Miles Linklater
Production: Joanne Henderson
Company: Carter Hales Design Lab
Country: Canada
Category: Body care

BRONZE PENTAWARD 2018

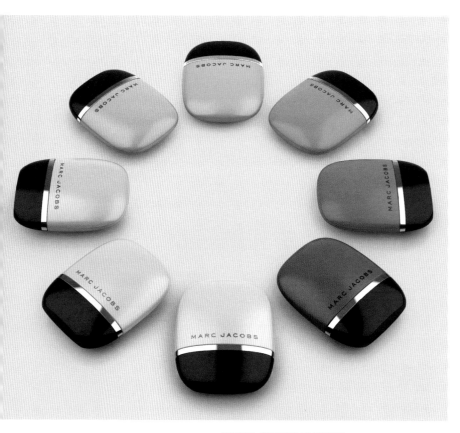

**MARC JACOBS BEAUTY
SHAMELESS FOUNDATION**

Creative Direction: Sam O'Donahue
Company: Established
Country: USA
Category: Beauty
BRONZE PENTAWARD 2018

SK:LK-BODY CARE

Client: Beijing Youji Technology Development
Creative Direction: Tengxian Zou, Zhihua He
Design: Tengxian Zou, Haoting Zhang, Wenfang Ye
Render Division: Wenfang Ye
Company: Shanghai Version Design Group
Country: China
Category: Body care

GOLD PENTAWARD 2020

SK:LK-BODY CARE is a set of body care products, from hair care and shampoo to shower gel. To highlight the purity and gentleness of the products, the design for this range was completely stripped back. All it consists of is a simple ripple pattern, which outlines the numbers 0, 1 and 2, on a fine, soft matte material to communicate the sequence in which it should be used.

SK:LK-BODY CARE ist ein Set von Körperpflegeprodukten, von Haarpflege und Shampoo bis hin zu Duschgel. Um die Reinheit und Sanftheit der Produkte zu unterstreichen, ist das Design für diese Reihe sehr minimalistisch. Es besteht aus nur einem Wellenmuster, das die Ziffern 0, 1 und 2 auf einem feinen, weichen und matten Material umreißt, und so die Reihenfolge vermittelt, in der die Produkte benutzt werden sollen.

SK:LK-BODY CARE est une gamme de produits de soin pour le corps incluant gel douche, shampooing et traitement capillaire. Pour transmettre la pureté et la douceur des produits, le design a été totalement épuré et se limite à un simple dessin ondulé qui trace les chiffres 0, 1 et 2 sur une surface matte et raffinée, indiquant ainsi l'ordre dans lequel utiliser les soins.

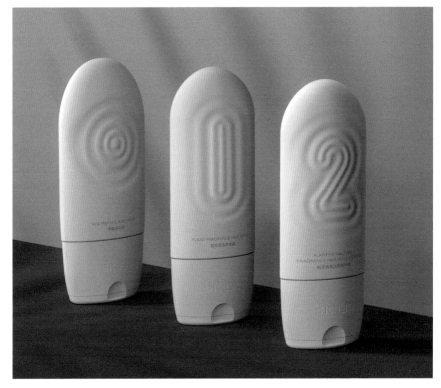

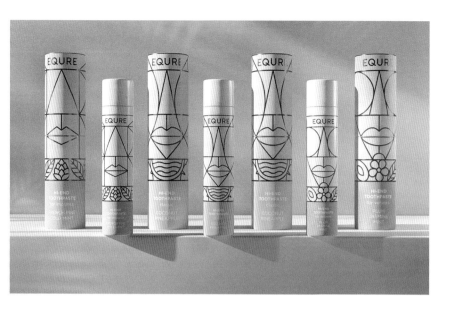

EQURE

Creative Direction: Valeria Repina
Art Direction: Alexandra Loginevskaya
Brand Strategy: Roman Pustovoit
Design: Polina Zagumenova
Company: Repina Branding
Country: Russia
Category: Body care

BRONZE PENTAWARD 2019

MARIONNAUD
SKIN CARE RANGE

Creative Direction: Sylvie Augendre,
Marie-Laurence Aubin
Company: Desdoigts
Country: France
Category: Distributors'/ retailers'
own brands, private labels

SILVER PENTAWARD 2016

BLOOMDALE EYEWEAR

Art Direction: Paul Roeters, Jeroen Hoedjes
Company: Studio Kluif
Country: Netherlands
Category: Best of the category
PLATINUM PENTAWARD 2018

Bloomdale is an eyewear brand that doesn't follow the typical brand codes. Instead of using photographs of models wearing their new products, they have a series of iconic portraits that were developed to underline the brand's tagline, "A Bloomdale for every face." These portraits play an important role in all their communications. Each box in the packaging range can be fitted with a different portrait depending on whether the client is a man, a woman, or a child. This way the optician makes a more personal statement to the client.

Boomdale ist eine Brillen- und Kontaktlinsenmarke, die sich den typischen Marken-Codes widersetzt. Anstelle der üblichen Fotos von Modellen, die neue Produkte tragen, arbeitet die Firma mit einer Reihe symbolhafter Porträts, die dem Slogan der Firma entsprechen: „Eine Bloomdale für jedes Gesicht." Diese Porträts stehen im Mittelpunkt der gesamten Markenkommunikation. Jede Schachtel aus dem Verpackungssortiment kann mit einem beliebigen Porträt versehen werden, je nachdem, ob der Kunde ein Mann, eine Frau oder ein Kind ist. Auf diese Weise kann der Optiker ganz persönlich auf seine Kunden eingehen.

Bloomdale est une marque de lunettes qui ne suit pas les codes typiques des marques. Au lieu d'utiliser des photographies de mannequins portant ses nouveaux produits, elle a recours à une série de portraits stylisés conçus pour rappeler le slogan de la marque : « Une paire de Bloomdale pour chaque visage ». Ces portraits jouent un rôle important dans toute sa stratégie de communication. Chaque boîte de la gamme peut être dotée d'un portrait différent, selon si le client est un homme, une femme ou un enfant. L'opticien peut ainsi offrir une approche plus personnalisée.

Outrageous volume
Dramatic volume mascara

MADE IN SEPHORA
Design: Solenne Joubert
Product Management: Pauline Prebois
Company: Sephora
Country: France
Category: Distributors' / retailers' own brands, private labels
SILVER PENTAWARD 2013

CRABTREE & EVELYN
EAU DE PARFUM

Creative Direction: Mary Lewis
Company: Lewis Moberly
Country: UK
Category: Distributors'/retailers'
own brands, private labels

BRONZE PENTAWARD 2014

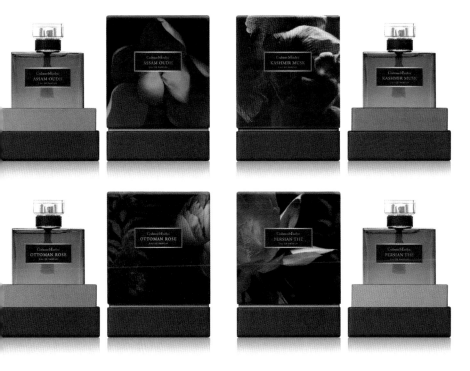

EMART
PURE

Chief Design: Hong Hyeon-ki
Direction: Lim Jun-soo
Company: Emart
Country: South Korea
Category: Distributors'/retailers' own brands,
private labels

GOLD PENTAWARD 2017

TUTU CHOUCHOU

Creative Direction: Yoshio Kato
Art Direction: Yoshio Kato, Mitsuharu Takehiro,
Eijiro Kuniyoshi
Design and Illustration: Kyo Sato
Company: Kotobuki Seihan Printing
Country: Japan
Category: Packaging concept
SILVER PENTAWARD 2017

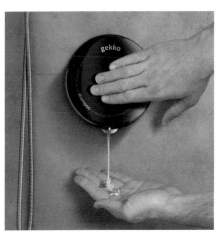

GEKKO

Design: Paweł Frej, Karolina Starowicz, Paweł Organ
Company: Opus B Brand Design
Country: Poland
Category: Packaging concept

SILVER PENTAWARD 2017

428

MINTED

Design: Sara Jones
Company: Anthem Benelux
Country: Netherlands
Category: Packaging concept

SILVER PENTAWARD 2018

TOTEM ROLLS

Creative Direction: Yoshio Kato
Art Direction: Yoshio Kato, Mitsuharu Takehiro,
Eijiro Kuniyoshi
Design and Illustration: Takaaki Hashimoto
Company: Kotobuki Seihan Printing
Country: Japan
Category: Packaging concept
GOLD PENTAWARD 2017

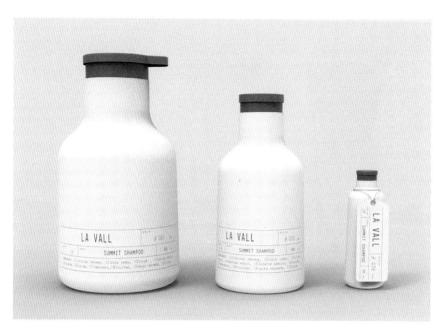

LA VALL

Design: Endika Gomez de Balugera, Sofía Cuba, Pablo Berges
Tutor: Alberto Cienfuegos, Guillem Virgili
School: Elisava School of Design & Engineering
Country: Spain
Category: Packaging concept (student)
BRONZE PENTAWARD 2018

LISTERINE

Design: Irina Altuna, Alejandra Amusquívar, Camila Robayo
School: Elisava School of Design & Engineering
Country: Spain
Category: Packaging concept (student)
BRONZE PENTAWARD 2018

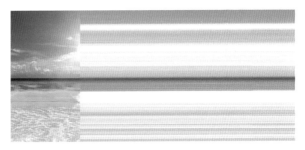

SEA FOAM

Design: Tanya Farba, Alexander Kirzhbaum,
Alexander Belyaev
School: British Higher School of Art and Design
Country: Russia
Category: Packaging concept (student)

GOLD PENTAWARD 2018

ALUMINUM POUCH
Design: Takashi Nomura
Company: Toyo Seikan Group Holdings
Country: Japan
Category: Packaging concept
BRONZE PENTAWARD 2017

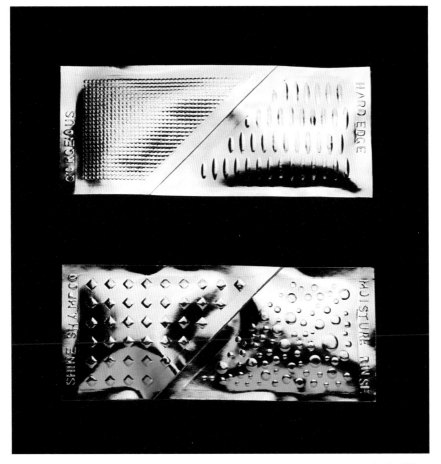

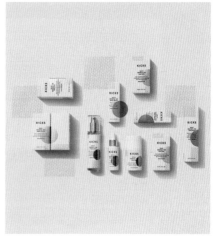

KICKS BEAUTY
SELF TAN

Creative Direction: Marie Wollbeck
Design Direction: Katrin Gullström
Design: Lovisa Ljungquist
Client Direction: Monika Varvne Uebel
Account Direction: Christine Schönborg
Company: BAS ID
Country: Sweden
Category: Distributors'/ retailers' own brands,
private labels

SILVER PENTAWARD 2019

THE BLACK MARKET

Creative Direction and Design: Marina Orvañanos
School: Elisava, Barcelona School of Design
& Engineering
Country: Spain
Category: Packaging concept (student)

SILVER PENTAWARD 2019

THE TROUPE

Design: Lavernia & Cienfuegos team
Company: Lavernia & Cienfuegos
Country: Spain
Category: Packaging concept

GOLD PENTAWARD 2020

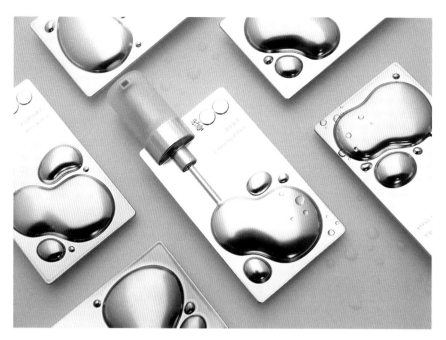

CODE 00-DESIGNED FOR POST-00S

Client: Symrise
Design: Yang Ming Jie
Company: Yang Design
Country: China
Category: Packaging concept

GOLD PENTAWARD 2019

Code 00 believes that the post-2000 generation has a unique and more independent knowledge of skincare products. To attract this target group, their product design concept uses science fiction films as its inspiration. The solid metal of the packaging turns into the liquid metal droplets of the product, whilst the logo highlights the "00", like a pair of curious eyes or the infinity symbol. The ingenious container perfectly suits this dual-purpose moisturising lip and cheek ointment, which is an innovation in itself.

Code 00 glaubt, dass die Post-2000-Generation ein einzigartiges und unabhängigeres Wissen über Hautpflegeprodukte hat. Um diese Zielgruppe anzusprechen, nutzt ihr Verpackungsdesignkonzept Science-Fiction-Filme als Inspirationsquelle. Die Verpackung verwandelt sich in flüssige Metalltropfen, während das Logo die „00" wie ein Paar Augen oder als das Unendlichkeitssymbol in Szene setzt. Dieser Behälter passt perfekt zu der zweifach verwendbaren feuchtigkeitsspendenden Lippen- und Wangenpflege, die an sich schon eine Innovation darstellt.

Code 00 croit que la génération Z possède des connaissances plus personnelles et indépendantes des produits cosmétiques. Pour attirer cette cible, le design des produits s'inspire des films de science-fiction. Avec une surface métallisée, le packaging figure des gouttes de métal liquide du produit, alors que le logo « 00 » s'affiche tel une paire d'yeux curieux ou le symbole de l'infini. L'ingénieux emballage va comme un gant à cette crème hydratante pour lèvres et pommettes, déjà toute une innovation en soi.

SIMPLY COSMETIC
Design: Vishal Vora
3D Visualisation: Rmadhun
Company: Sol Benito
Country: India
Category: Packaging concept
BRONZE PENTAWARD 2019

SO MUSH SUPPLEMENT

Executive Creative Direction: Somchana Kangwarnjit
Design: Rutthawitch Akkachairin, SKJ
Photography: Thiyada Akarasinakul, Pantipa Pummuang,
Somporn Thimkhao
Company: Prompt Design
Country: Thailand
Category: Packaging concept
SILVER PENTAWARD 2020

GOODBABY®

Supervision: Cao Xue (Guangzhou Academy of Fine Arts), Wang Liang (China Resources Sanjiu)
Art Direction: Duan Hongli (China Resources Sanjiu), Chen Jiayi (JiaYi (Guangzhou) Design)
Project Management: Xu Mengzhen (China Resources Sanjiu)
Graphic Design: He Ge (JiaYi (Guangzhou) Design)
Consumer Analysis: Man Lan (China Resources Sanjiu)
Market Analysis: Lin Huangtao (Guangzhou Academy of Fine Arts)
Company: China Resources Sanjiu Medical & Pharmaceutical
Country: China
Category: Packaging concept

BRONZE PENTAWARD 2020

CUBESSENCE

Creative Direction: Haozhen Luo
Company: Beijing Heziguai Creative Design
Country: China
Category: Packaging concept

SILVER PENTAWARD 2019

AKIO

Design: Robert Dadashev
3D Visualisation: Pavel Gubin, Aleksey Koler
Copywriting: Alex Kalyan
Art Direction: Katya Mushkina, Robert Dadashev
Tutoring: Leonid Slavin, Yevgeny Razumov
School: British Higher School of Art and Design
Country: Russia
Category: Packaging concept (student)
NXT-GEN PENTAWARDS 2020

More than anything, children love to play. **Akio** is a range of Japanese-style soap packaging that turns bathing into an amusing and interactive game. Thanks to the fun and graphic look of the containers, parents can distract a fussy child and keep them busy while they are getting clean. The removable kimono will surprise a toddler, grab their attention and help make bath time more fun and enjoyable.

Mehr als alles andere lieben Kinder das Spielen. **Akio** ist eine Reihe von Seifenverpackungen in Form von japanischen Figuren, die das Baden zu einem amüsanten und interaktiven Spiel machen. Dank des lustigen und grafischen Aussehens der Behälter können die Eltern ihr wählerisches Kind ablenken und beschäftigen, während sie es waschen. Der abnehmbare Kimono überrascht Kleinkinder, erregt ihre Aufmerksamkeit und hilft, die Badezeit lustiger und angenehmer zu gestalten.

Les enfants aiment jouer plus que tout autre chose. **Akio** est une marque de savons dont le packaging aux allures japonaises transforme la toilette en un divertissement interactif. Grâce à son look graphique amusant, les flacons permettent aux parents de distraire un enfant agité et de l'occuper pendant sa toilette. Le kimono amovible crée la surprise chez le bambin, retient son attention et fait de l'heure du bain un moment plus plaisant.

ART&FICT

Design: Evgeniia Zhuravleva
Tutoring: Leonid Slavin
Teaching: Yevgeny Razumov
3D Rendering: Dmitriy Saveliev
School: British Higher School of Art and Design
Country: Russia
Category: Packaging concept (student)

GOLD PENTAWARD 2019

There are two approaches that form the basis for the **Art & Fict** cotton bud creative. Many people clean their ears with cotton buds but don't realise that you can very easily damage your eardrums. The first approach is to illustrate this, using the colourful cotton swabs to create an image of Van Gogh's self-portrait with a bandaged ear. The second idea revolves around cotton swabs being used to apply makeup. In this case, the coloured swabs combine to form the image of Marilyn Monroe in the style of pop art.

Zwei Ideen stecken hinter der Wattestäbchen-Kreation von **Art & Fict**. Die Erste basiert auf dem Fakt, dass viele Menschen ihre Ohren mit Watte-stäbchen reinigen, aber nicht wissen, dass sie ihr Trommelfell dabei leicht beschädigen können. Van Goghs Selbstporträt mit verbundenem Ohr, zusammengestellt aus den gefärbten Spitzen der Stäbchen, steht dafür symbolisch ein. Die zweite Idee dreht sich um das Wattestäbchen, das zum Schminken zweckentfremdet wird. In diesem Fall bilden die Stäbchen ein Bild von Marilyn Monroe im Pop-Art-Stil.

Le design pour les cotons-tiges **Art & Fict** obéit à deux approches. Nombre de personnes se nettoient les oreilles à l'aide de bâtonnets ouatés sans être conscientes des risques pour leurs tympans. La première approche consiste à faire passer ce message en reproduisant à l'aide de cotons-tiges de couleur l'autoportrait de Van Gogh à l'oreille pansée. La seconde idée porte sur l'utilisation des bâtonnets pour le maquillage. Dans ce cas, la composition des cotons-tiges colorés forme l'image Pop art de Marilyn Monroe.

WHIRLPOOL HIGH-END NOURISHING MILK SET
Design: Tian-yi Zhang
Tutoring: Fang Jun
School: Shanghai Institute of Visual Arts (SIVA)
Country: China
Category: Packaging concept (student)
BRONZE PENTAWARD 2020

Best of the category
Perfumes
Make-up, body care, beauty products
Spirits
Fine wines, champagne

luxury

Gourmet food
Limited editions, limited series, event creations
Distributors'/retailers' own brands, private labels
Casks, cases, gift boxes, etc.
Packaging concept

BARDOT
LUXURY ICE CREAM BARS

Creative Direction: Tosh Hall
Design: Tosh Hall, Lia Gordon
Illustration: Jessica Minn, Michael Goodman
Lettering: Jessica Minn
Naming: Jen Jordan, Jason Bice
Production: Dan Ross
Account Direction: J.P. Sabarots
Client Management: Allison Hung
Company: Landor Associates, San Francisco
Country: USA
Category: Best of the category

PLATINUM PENTAWARD 2012
LUXEPACK PRIZE

The prestige Mexican ice-cream purveyor, Advanced Ice Cream Technologies, wanted to offer its carefully crafted, luxury products on the US market. With a name that sounded more like an innovator in cold storage than a producer of artisan iced confectionery, a new name and identity was required to convey the unparalleled decadence of the product, creating a sense of luxury, sensuality and desire. Meet the world's sexiest confection. The most decadent gelato is enrobed in graphic fantasy. Consumers may pick from the line-up or design their own. To eat now — or take away in its precious box, which, with a bit of magic, keeps it at the perfect temperature. Hold it. Lick it. Love it. **Bardot**.

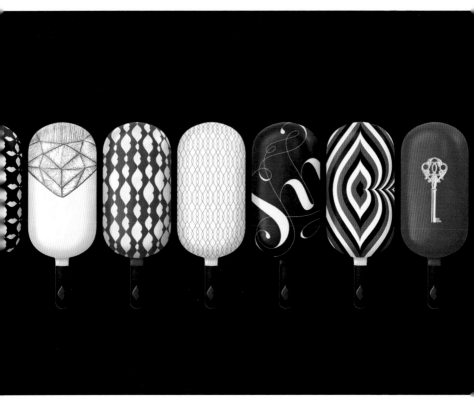

Der angesehene Eiscremelieferant Advanced Ice Cream Technologies aus Mexiko wollte seine sorgfältig hergestellten Luxusprodukte auch auf dem amerikanischen Markt feilbieten. Doch sein Name klingt eher nach Kühlschrankproduzent als nach dem Hersteller von kunstvollen Eisspezialitäten. So waren auch ein neuer Name und eine neue Identität fällig, um die beispiellose Dekadenz dieses Produkts und Luxus, Sinnlichkeit und Begehren zu vermitteln. Hier ist sie nun: die absolut heißeste „kalte Konfektion" der Welt. Dieses dekadenteste Gelato aller Zeiten kleidet sich in fantasievolle Zeichen und Muster. Die Kunden wählen zum Genießen ein Eis aus dem Angebot oder gestalten ihr eigenes. Zum sofortigen Verzehr oder zum Mitnehmen in der kostbaren Schachtel, in der das Eis mit nur ein bisschen Zauberei perfekt temperiert bleibt. Nimm es. Leck es. Liebe es. **Bardot**.

Le prestigieux glacier mexicain, Advanced Ice Cream Technologies, voulait proposer ses produits sophistiqués et luxueux sur le marché américain. Avec un nom qui évoque plus un fabricant de chambres froides qu'un glacier artisanal, il fallait trouver un nouveau nom et une nouvelle identité pour communiquer sur la décadence sans pareille du produit et créer une idée de luxe, de sensualité et de désir. La glace la plus sexy du monde est enrobée d'une débauche de graphisme. Les consommateurs peuvent choisir parmi les options proposées ou concevoir leur propre motif, à manger sur place ou à emporter dans sa boîte précieuse et magique, qui conserve la température parfaite. Prenez. Léchez. Adorez. **Bardot**.

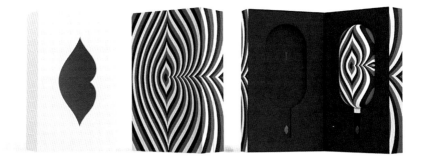

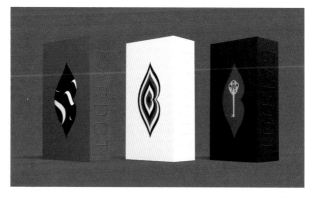

DIPTYQUE HOURGLASS 2.0

Design: Sebastien Servaire, Justine Dauchez,
Candido Debarros, Thomas Chouvaeff
Company: Servaire & Co
Country: France
Category: Best of the category

PLATINUM PENTAWARD 2018

Diptyque's Hourglass is an iconic home fragrance diffuser that was initially patented and designed in 2012. Its new design is in an hourglass shape to underline poetically the link between fragrance, time, and the home. It uses different colors of glass to differentiate the six fragrances. The cold-diffusing technology delivers perfume notes through ingenious wicks, which have been designed to extend the area the fragrance reaches through a new patent developed by Tecniplast. The Hourglass remains a sustainable, refillable product.

Das **Diptyque Hourglass** ist ein Raumduftverteiler mit Kultstatus, der ursprünglich 2012 entwickelt und patentiert wurde. Sein neues Design hat die Form einer Sanduhr, um die Verbindung von Duft, Zeit und Zuhause poetisch zu unterstreichen. Die sechs Duftnoten werden durch die Verwendung von sechs verschiedenen Glasfarbtönen unterschieden. Für die Kaltdiffusion der Düfte werden raffinierte Dochte benutzt, die nach einem neuen Patent von Tecniplast entworfen wurden, durch das der Bereich, in dem der Duft sich ausbreitet, erweitert werden konnte. Das Hourglass bleibt dabei ein nachhaltiges, wieder auffüllbares Produkt.

Le **sablier de dyptique** est un diffuseur de parfum pour la maison qui a été conçu et breveté en 2012. Son nouveau design en forme de sablier souligne avec poésie la relation entre le parfum, le temps et la maison. Il existe dans différentes couleurs de verre pour différencier les six parfums. La technologie de diffusion à froid délivre les notes parfumées à l'aide de bâtonnets ingénieux conçus pour augmenter la portée de la fragrance grâce à un nouveau brevet mis au point par Tecniplast. Le sablier est un produit durable et rechargeable.

ITAL SPIRITS
ITALICUS
Design: Stranger & Stranger team
Company: Stranger & Stranger
Country: UK
Category: Best of the category
PLATINUM PENTAWARD 2017

Italicus is a drink made from Italian bergamot and a carefully crafted selection of botanicals. Everything about the design of this bottle is quintessentially Italian. The typography evokes notions of traditional *Italia* while the tones of blue hint at its Mediterranean origins. There is a luxurious feel to the product that is translated through its gold-plated cap, which is inspired by Leonardo da Vinci. In a crowded market, this design immediately draws attention and is considered unique in the industry.

Italicus ist ein Getränk aus italienischer Bergamotte und einer erlesenen Mischung von Kräuter- und Pflanzenextrakten. Das Design dieser Flasche ist durch und durch italienisch. Die Typografie weckt Assoziationen an das alte Rom, während die Blautöne auf die mediterrane Herkunft des Produkts verweisen. Der von Leonardo da Vinci inspirierte vergoldete Verschluss transportiert den Hauch von Luxus, der das Produkt umgibt. Auf einem gesättigten Markt sticht dieses Design sofort ins Auge und verschafft ihm eine herausragende Stellung.

Italicus est une boisson élaborée avec de la bergamote italienne et une sélection méticuleuse d'extraits de plantes. Tout dans cette bouteille représente la quintessence de l'Italie. La typographie évoque des souvenirs de l'*Italia* traditionnelle, tandis que les tons bleus font allusion à ses origines méditerranéennes. Le bouchon doré, inspiré par Léonard de Vinci, traduit le sentiment de luxe que dégage ce produit. Sur un marché saturé, cette bouteille attire immédiatement l'attention et s'avère tout à fait unique.

CACHAREL CATCH-ME

Design: Patrick Veillet
Company: Patrick Veillet
Country: France
Category: Perfumes

BRONZE PENTAWARD 2013

**JEAN-PAUL GAULTIER
KOKORICO**
Design: Hélène Causse, Francesco Moretti
Company: Interbrand
Country: France
Category: Perfumes
SILVER PENTAWARD 2012

PERRY ELLIS
Design: Denis Boudard
Company: QSLD Paris
Country: France
BRONZE PENTAWARD 2009

KILIAN
BLACK PHANTOM
Creative Direction: Franck Basset
Artistic Direction: Dimitri Rastorgoueff
Company: Carré Basset
Country: France
Category: Perfumes
SILVER PENTAWARD 2017

HOMO SAPIENS
Design: Holmes & Marchant team
Company: Holmes & Marchant
Country: China
Category: Perfumes
BRONZE PENTAWARD 2018

YOHJI YAMAMOTO PARFUMS

Packaging Concept and Design: Grisha Serov
Product Development: Anna Zhitareva
Glass Manufacturing: Groupe Pochet
Glass Bottle Finish Manufacturing: Dekorglass
Box Manufacturing: Zfoam
Company: Yohji Yamamoto Parfums
Country: Russia
Category: Perfumes

GOLD PENTAWARD 2019

The bottles for **Yohji Yamamoto Parfums** are clear bullet-shaped containers wrapped with black rings that on closer inspection form his name, Yohji. On the backside of these letters, visible only by peering through the liquid, are phrases associated with each individual fragrance. Mode Zero, for example, reads "Be yourself. You're okay". When it came to packaging, Yamamoto is famous for his love of black, so the team went for a classic approach and opted for an all-black box, unadorned except for an embossed brand logo.

Die Flakons für **Yohji Yamamoto Parfums** sind durchsichtige Behälter in Form von Patronenhülsen mit Streifen aus schwarzem Klebeband, die bei genauem Hinsehen den Namen Yohji bilden. Auf der Rückseite dieser Buchstaben sind Sätze versteckt, die nur sichtbar sind, wenn man durch die Flüssigkeit hindurchsieht. Diese Sätze stehen in Verbindung mit jedem individuellen Duft. Mode Zero zum Beispiel enthält die Worte "Be yourself. You're okay". Wenn es um Verpackung geht, ist Yamamoto für seine Liebe zu Schwarz bekannt, weswegen sich das Team für einen klassischen Ansatz und eine schwarze Schachtel entschied, die bis auf das eingeprägte Markenlogo schmucklos ist.

Le bouteilles pour **Yohji Yamamoto Parfums** sont des flacons transparents de forme ogivale et entourés d'anneaux noirs qui, vus de près, composent le nom Yohji. Derrière les lettres, des phrases associées à chaque parfum ne sont lisibles qu'en regardant à travers le liquide. Par exemple, on peut lire sur la bouteille Mode Zero « Be yourself. You're okay ». Concernant le packaging, connaissant l'amour pour le noir de Yamamoto, l'équipe a suivi une approche classique et opté pour une boite entièrement noire et sans décoration, à l'exception du logo en relief de la marque.

PERFUMED BRACELET

Creative Direction: Sébastien Servaire
Design: Candido Debarros
Technical Direction: Erwann Pivert
Company: Servaire & Co
Country: France
Category: Perfumes

GOLD PENTAWARD 2020

Through the development of its perfumed bracelet, **diptyque** continues its quest for innovation, offering customers consistently inventive and meaningful experiences. The bracelet takes into account the different perspectives of diptyque's three founders – an interior designer, a designer and a painter – with its new technique. The long rolled bracelet is perfumed via microencapsulation, which activates the fragrance by friction when the bracelet is unrolled. When snipped and tied around the wrist, it will provide three days of fragrance.

Durch die Entwicklung seines parfümierten Armbands setzt **diptyque** sein Streben nach Innovation fort und bietet den Kunden durchweg einfallsreiche und bedeutungsvolle Erfahrungen. Das Armband bezieht mit seiner neuen Technik die verschiedenen Perspektiven von diptyques drei Gründern mit ein; einem Innenarchitekt, einem Designer und einem Maler. Das lange aufgerollte Armband ist durch Mikroverkapselung parfümiert, die den Duft durch Reibung aktiviert. Zugeschnitten und um das Handgelenk gebunden, behält es seinen Duft für drei Tage.

En concevant son lien de parfum, **diptyque** poursuit sa quête d'innovation et offre aux clients des expériences invariablement créatives et éloquentes. D'un concept inédit, cet objet de la gamme prêts-à-parfumer intègre les différentes perspectives des trois fondateurs de diptyque, que sont un architecte d'intérieur, un designer et un peintre. Le lien est imprégné de parfum par microencapsulation qu'il diffuse par friction quand il est déroulé. Une fois le lien coupé et attaché au poignet, ses qualités olfactives durent trois jours.

PEPE JEANS

Design: Tailored Perfumes team
Company: Tailored Perfumes
Country: Spain
Category: Perfumes

SILVER PENTAWARD 2019

PEPE JEANS

Design: Tailored Perfumes team
Company: Tailored Perfumes
Country: Spain
Category: Perfumes

SILVER PENTAWARD 2019

ORCHIDÉE IMPÉRIALE

GUERLAIN
PARIS

ORCHIDÉE IMPÉRIALE
CONCENTRÉ DE LONGÉVITÉ
LONGEVITY CONCENTRATE

The result of 10 years of research using **Guerlain**'s orchidarium, this exclusive anti-ageing serum is based on concentrated extracts from orchids. To celebrate this work, a special symbolic casing was conceived: a "capsule-flask", a blue chamber holding the precious ointment as if protecting it from the passage of time. The vial is seamless and appears hermetically sealed, but a ring may be rotated to release a nozzle at one end and a button at the other. The vertical use of this newly-patented concept is unique in cosmetics, and permits the precise dose of cream to be delivered in a manner that feels ritualised and select. The flask rests horizontally in a blue case marked with an orchid symbol.

Das Ergebnis der zehnjährigen Forschung mit dem Orchidarium von **Guerlain** ist dieses exklusive Anti-Aging-Serum, das auf konzentrierten Extrakten von Orchideen basiert. Um diese Arbeit entsprechend zu feiern, entwickelte man ein symbolisches Gehäuse: ein „Kapselflakon", der in seiner blauen Kammer die kostbare Salbe aufnimmt, als bewahre er die Creme vor der verrinnenden Zeit. Die Phiole ist nahtlos und wirkt hermetisch versiegelt, aber durch Drehen eines Rings erscheint am einen Ende ein Röhrchen und am anderen ein Knopf. Die vertikale Verwendung dieses erstmalig patentierten Konzepts ist bei Kosmetika einzigartig und erlaubt die präzise Dosierung der Creme auf eine Weise, die sich sehr ritualisiert und erlesen anfühlt. Die Phiole ruht waagrecht in ihrem blauen, mit einem Orchideensymbol verzierten Behältnis.

Résultat de 10 ans de recherche dans l'orchidarium de **Guerlain**, ce sérum anti-âge luxueux est basé sur des extraits d'orchidée concentrés. Un flacon symbolique spécial a été conçu pour fêter cet accomplissement : une « flasque-capsule », une fiole bleue qui abrite le précieux onguent, comme pour le protéger contre le passage du temps. Elle semble hermétiquement scellée, mais recèle un anneau qui tourne pour laisser apparaître une canule à une extrémité, et un bouton à l'autre. L'utilisation verticale de ce nouveau concept breveté est unique dans le secteur de la cosmétique, et permet de doser la crème précisément en conférant à cette opération une aura de rituel et d'exclusivité. La flasque est couchée dans un coffret bleu marqué d'un symbole d'orchidée.

GUERLAIN
ORCHIDÉE IMPÉRIALE

Art Direction: Sébastien Servaire, Candido de Barros
Photography: Guerlain
Company: R'Pure Studio
Country: France
Category: Make-up, body care, beauty products

GOLD PENTAWARD 2012

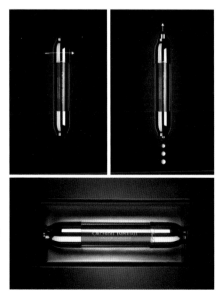

**GIVENCHY
LE PRISME VISAGE PRODUCT**

Design: Elie Papiernik, François Vesin, Marc Venot
Photographer: Eric Sauvage
Company: Centdegrés
Country: France
Category: Make-up, body care, beauty products

BRONZE PENTAWARD 2010

ÍPSA

Art Direction, Creative Direction and Design:
Aoshi Kudo
Company: Communication Design Laboratory
Country: Japan
Category: Make-up, body care, beauty products
BRONZE PENTAWARD 2018

CLÉ DE PEAU BEAUTÉ
Art Direction: Mao Komai
Design: Midori Matsuishi
Company: Shiseido
Country: Japan
Category: Make-up, body care, beauty products
SILVER PENTAWARD 2013

GUERLAIN
SUPER AQUA

Creative Direction: Sébastien Servaire
Art Direction: Candido De Barros
Company: R'Pure Studio/Servaire
Country: France
Category: Make-up, body care, beauty products

SILVER PENTAWARD 2013

POLA
V RESONATIC CREAM

Art Direction: Chiharu Suzuki
Design: Kei Ikehata, Rieko Nakamura
Company: Pola
Country: Japan
Category: Make-up, body care, beauty products
GOLD PENTAWARD 2018

V Resonatic Cream is a revolutionary anti-ageing cream designed to nurture and enhance the face. The concept behind the brand is that beauty in the coming age will mean having a positive influence on our surroundings, and not just on our appearances and inner beings. The package consists of a self-righting jar with a spatula precariously perched on the apex. The gyrating movements of the two convey the impression that they are resonating with one another. The design has been precisely calculated to give the ideal range of movement around the center of gravity. The colorful marble pattern on the outer box hints at something new and previously unseen.

V Resonatic Cream ist eine revolutionäre Anti-Aging-Creme zur Pflege der Gesichtshaut und Verbesserung des Hautbilds. Schönheit wird bedeuten, einen positiven Einfluss auf unsere Umgebung zu haben, statt nur auf unser äußeres und inneres Erscheinungsbild – so das Zukunftsbild der Marke. Der runde Tiegel richtet sich von selbst auf und an seiner Spitze balanciert ein Spatel. Die rotierenden Bewegungen der beiden Elemente erwecken den Eindruck, miteinander im Einklang zu stehen. Das Design ist präzise austariert, um einen idealen Bewegungsradius um den Schwerpunkt herum zu ermöglichen. Das bunt marmorierte Muster der Box verweist auf etwas Neues, nie zuvor Gesehenes.

V Resonatic Cream est une crème anti-âge révolutionnaire conçue pour nourrir et sublimer le visage. Le concept derrière cette marque est que la beauté de demain signifiera avoir une influence positive sur notre environnement, et non seulement sur notre apparence ou notre être intérieur. Le packaging est un pot à redressement automatique coiffé d'une spatule perchée en équilibre précaire. Les mouvements tournoyants de ces deux éléments donnent l'impression qu'ils entrent en résonance l'un avec l'autre. Le design a été calculé précisément pour autoriser une amplitude de mouvement idéale autour du centre de gravité. Le motif marbré de couleurs vives sur la boîte suggère qu'elle contient un objet inédit.

KENDO
MARC JACOBS BEAUTY

Creative Direction: Sam O'Donahue
Company: Established
Country: USA
Category: Make-up, body care, beauty products

SILVER PENTAWARD 2017

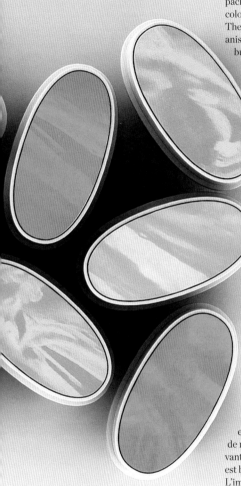

The packaging of make-up products for the skin is typically functional and serious but **Marc Jacobs** opted for a fun and slightly subversive package for **Kendo** to reflect the innovative multi-color formula and the cheekier side of the brand. The basis of the design is a deodorant-style mechanism. The overall appearance is slick and refined but it's infused with an urban and unexpected twist, bringing a sense of humor to an otherwise serious category. Every aspect of the package is meticulously designed, from the overall shape right down to the exact number of ridges in the twisting mechanism.

Die Verpackungen von Make-up-Produkten für den Teint sind meistens funktional und ernst, aber **Marc Jacobs** hat sich hier bei **Kendo** für eine witzige, leicht subversive Variante entschieden, um die innovative Multicolor-Formel und die frechere Seite der Marke hervorzuheben. Grundlage seines Designs ist ein deodorant-ähnlicher Mechanismus. Das allgemeine Erscheinungsbild ist glatt und schnittig, wird jedoch durch einen urbanen, unerwarteten Touch ergänzt, der diese sonst so ernste Produktkategorie mit einem Schuss Humor anreichert. Jeder Aspekt der Verpackung ist sorgfältig durchgestylt, von der allgemeinen Form bis hin zur exakten Anzahl der Rillen im Drehmechanismus.

Le packaging des produits de maquillage sont souvent fonctionnels et sérieux, mais **Marc Jacobs** a choisi pour **Kendo** un emballage ludique et quelque peu subversif afin de mettre en valeur la formule multicolore innovante et le côté insolent de la marque. Le design est basé sur le mécanisme de stick de déodorant. L'impression d'ensemble est élégante et raffinée, mais avec un esprit urbain et inattendu qui injecte de l'humour dans une catégorie plutôt sage. Chaque aspect du packaging est a été pensé dans le moindre détail, de la forme globale jusqu'au nombre exact de rainures dans le mécanisme de rotation.

LA MER
GENAISSANCE DE LA MER

Design: Justin Weinrich
Company: La Mer
Country: USA
Category: Make-up, body care, beauty products
SILVER PENTAWARD 2018

POLA
BA SERIES

Creative Direction: Takashi Matsui
Art Direction: Haruyo Eto
Design: Mai Karin Kamiyama, Rieko Nakamura,
Shingo Isobe
Company: Pola
Country: Japan
Category: Make-up, body care, beauty products

BRONZE PENTAWARD 2018

SOAPSMITH

Design Lead: Alison Mehta
Design Direction: Beth Drummond,
Luke Chawner
Client Direction: Ella McKay
Photography: Carl Bartram
Senior Strategy: Tom Calvert
Illustration: Tom Abbiss-Smith
Company: Bulletproof
Country: UK
Category: Make-up, body care, beauty products

GOLD PENTAWARD 2020

THANMELIN

Creative Direction: Guozheng Jiang, Dan Chen
Strategy Consulting Direction: Yanh Shu
Graphic Design: Fang Li, Qing Li
Product Design: Lexing Xu, Zilei Jiao
Senior Account Executive: Xiangbing Li
Company: Shanghai Nianxiang Brand Design
& Consulting
Country: China
Category: Make-up, body care, beauty products
BRONZE PENTAWARD 2020

CHRISTIAN LOUBOUTIN

Folding carton production: Autajon Group team
Company: Autajon Group
Country: France
Category: Make-up, body care, beauty products
GOLD PENTAWARD 2019

This make-up range for **Christian Louboutin** is a symbol of pure luxury. Reminiscent of Christmas ornaments or gilded icicles, the bottles revel in extravagance and perfectly suit the opulent products contained inside. The cartons are manufactured with a registered Fresnel lens laminated to white board, then printed with gold ink to give a truly eye-catching look. The elegant design is complete with white silk screen printed copy and an embossed logo.

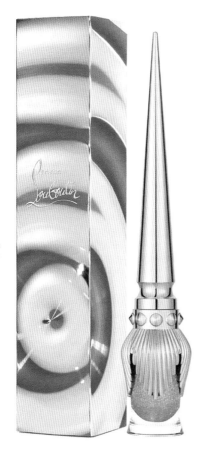

Diese Make-up-Linie für **Christian Louboutin** ist ein Symbol des puren Luxus. An Weihnachtsschmuck oder vergoldete Eiszapfen erinnernd, schwelgen die Flaschen in Extravaganz und passen perfekt zu den opulenten Produkten im Inneren. Um einen richtigen Hingucker zu kreieren, zeigen die Schachteln eine Fresnellinse, die auf Weißkarton laminiert und anschließend mit Goldtinte bedruckt wird. Das elegante Design wird mit weißem Siebdruck und einem geprägten Logo vervollständigt.

Cette gamme de cosmétiques pour **Christian Louboutin** symbolise le luxe dans toute sa splendeur. Les flacons, qui ne sont pas sans faire penser à des décorations de Noël ou des stalactites de glace dorées, sont extravagants et vont comme un gant aux produits luxueux qu'ils renferment. Les boîtes sont recouvertes d'une lentille de Fresnel appliquée sur une surface blanche, puis imprimée à l'encre dorée pour donner un résultat des plus accrocheurs. Le design élégant est complété par une impression en sérigraphie de couleur blanche et un logo en relief.

ONE BY KOSÉ

Creative and Art Direction: Naoko Yokokura
Design: Mami Futagami
Company: Kosé Corporation
Country: Japan
Category: Make-up, body care, beauty products

SILVER PENTAWARD 2019

This luxury lipstick housed in a bespoke, plastic-free aluminium bullet is the debut product for **Juni Cosmetics** whose mission is to "leave a lasting impression, not a lasting problem". The bullet is octagonal, architectural and satisfyingly weighty, so it sits perfectly in your hand and feels substantial. Keen to enhance the raw beauty of aluminium rather than disguise it, they opted for a clear anodise and bead-blast finish that subtly catches the light. Additional design features, such as the bevelled lid and laser-etched "J" logo, add to the visual and tactile experience. The sleek, minimal packaging mirrors the high-tech lipstick formula, which is a make-up/skincare hybrid made of the finest organic and vegan-friendly ingredients.

Dieser luxuriöse Lippenstift, untergebracht in einem kunststofffreien Aluminiumprojektil, ist das Debüt-Produkt von **Juni Cosmetics**, deren Mission es ist, „einen bleibenden Eindruck und nicht ein bleibendes Problem zu hinterlassen". Die achteckige Form ist angenehm schwer und liegt perfekt in der Hand. Die klare Eloxierung und die Perlglanzoberfläche unterstützen die rohe Schönheit des Aluminiums und fangen das Licht ein. Zusätzliche Designmerkmale wie der angeschrägte Deckel und das gelaserte „J"-Logo tragen zum visuellen und haptischen Erleben bei. Die minimalistische Verpackung spiegelt die Hightech-Formel des Lippenstifts wider, der ein Make-up-/Hautpflege-Hybrid aus biologischen und veganen Inhaltsstoffen ist.

Ce rouge à lèvre de luxe logé dans un tube en aluminium sans plastique est le premier produit créé par **Juni Cosmetics**, dont la mission est de « laisser une impression durable, et non un problème durable ». Octogonal, architectural et agréablement lourd, ce tube tient bien dans la main et offre une sensation de solidité. Pour souligner la beauté brute de l'aluminium au lieu de la dissimuler, la marque a opté pour une finition anodisée incolore et microbillée qui capte subtilement la lumière. D'autres caractéristiques, comme le bouchon biseauté et le logo « J » gravé au laser, enrichissent l'expérience visuelle et tactile. Le packaging profilé et minimal est à l'image de la formule high-tech, un hybride entre maquillage et soin à base d'ingrédients bio et vegan.

JUNI COSMETICS

Founder and Direction: Madeleine White
Direction: Suzanne White
Direction and Senior Design: Nick Harvey, Paul Robbins (Product Resolutions)
Logo Design: Carl Gamble
Company: Juni Cosmetics
Country: UK
Category: Make-up, body care, beauty products
SILVER PENTAWARD 2020

JOHN WALKER & SONS ODYSSEY

Creative Direction: Laurent Hainaut
Art Direction: Ann Chen
Visual Strategy/Innovation Direction:
Nicole Duval
Senior Product Design: Loren Kulesus
Product Design: Marco Leone
Design: Alex Boulware
Production Direction: Linda Tseng
Global Design Direction: Jeremy Lindley
Innovation Direction: Regina Galang (Diageo)
POS & Gifting Direction: Jean-Noel Dollet
Invigoration: Steve Wilson (Diageo)
Company: Raison Pure International
Country: USA
Category: Spirits

SILVER PENTAWARD 2013

Commemorating Sir Alexander Walker's epic spirit of adventure and perseverance, the new ultra-premium **Odyssey** is inspired by the original 1932 whisky he brought aboard his voyages on luxury ocean liners. Sensuous and dynamic, the decanter's form captures the emotion of the sea, and with its ability to rock elegantly to and fro when standing, the rolling motion of the waves. When placed in its polyurethane leather-bound cabinet, the bottle is suspended for fluid 360-degree rotation, whilst the design also draws on brass maritime navigational instruments and the precision of highly crafted timepieces. Various elements in the pack nod to an Art Deco past while turning an eye to the future, such as the monogrammed diamond badge and weighty cabinet closure.

Zur Erinnerung an den epischen Abenteurer-geist und die Beharrlichkeit von Sir Alexander Walker ließ sich das neue Ultrapremium **Odyssey** vom originalen Whisky des Jahres 1932 inspirieren, den er auf seine Reisen mit Luxuslinern mitnahm. Sinnlich und dynamisch fängt die Form des Dekanters die Stimmung der See ein. Weil er aufgestellt elegant hin- und herzuschaukeln vermag, lässt er an rollende Wogen denken. Wird die Flasche in ihrem mit PU-Leder bespannten Kästchen platziert, verharrt sie auch bei einer 360-Grad-Rotation in aufrechter Position. Das Design spielt auf maritime Navigationsinstrumente und die Präzision von Chronometern höchster Handwerkskunst an. Verschiedene Elemente der Verpackung zollen ihren Tribut der Art-Deco-Vergangenheit, bleiben aber auch zukunftsgerichtet, z. B. das diamantförmige Emblem mit Monogramm oder der gewichtige Verschluss des Kästchens.

En hommage à l'esprit aventurier et persévérant de Sir Alexander Walker, le nouveau **Odyssey** de qualité supérieure s'inspire du whisky de 1932 qu'il emportait lors de ses voyages sur les luxueux paquebots transatlantiques. Sensuelle et dynamique, la forme de la carafe transmet l'émotion de la mer ; avec son léger balancement, elle évoque le mouvement de roulis des vagues. Logée dans son étui en polyuréthane relié en cuir, la bouteille est suspendue pour permettre la rotation à 360 degrés du liquide. Le design rappelle les instruments de navigation en laiton et les mécanismes d'horlogerie de précision. Plusieurs éléments de l'emballage évoquent le passé Art déco tout en jetant un regard vers le futur, comme le losange monogrammé et la solide fermeture du boîtier.

DEAU COGNAC L.V.O. LA VIE EN OR
Design: Alpha Centauri Design Agency
Gold Decoration: Arthus Bertrand
Company: Distillerie des Moisans
Country: France
Category: Spirits
SILVER PENTAWARD 2014

ABSOLUT VODKA
ELYX

Executive Client Direction: Jonas Andersson
Design Direction: Björn Studt, Henrik Billqvist
Client Management: Britt-Marie Möller
Client Direction: Alfred Alfred (No Picnic)
Industrial Design: Urban Ahlgren,
Thomas Schaad (No Picnic)
Design Engineering/Visualization:
Stefan Wennerström (No Picnic)
Client: The Absolut Company

Global Direction Design Strategy: Anna Kamjou
Global Direction Innovation: Lena Danielsson
Global Marketing Direction: Louise de Fautereau
Global Marketing Management:
Sébastien Borda
Company: The Brand Union
Country: Sweden
Category: Spirits
SILVER PENTAWARD 2013

HILHAVEN LODGE
WHISKEY

Creative Direction: J.B. Hartford
Art Direction: Alex Boulware
Design Direction: Kyle Wessel
Client Service Direction: Megan Bradley
Company: Force Majeure Design
Country: USA
Category: Spirits

BRONZE PENTAWARD 2016

METAXA
ANGELS' TREASURE

Design: Aurélia Jacques, Sébastien Leridon
Company: BETC Design
Country: France
Category: Spirits

BRONZE PENTAWARD 2015

BOND HOUSE No.1

COLLECTION

OUR BOND HOUSE No.1 FINEST MALT
WHISKIES HAVE BEEN CREATED AND
LONG MATURED AT OUR DISTILLERY,
THE BOND WAREHOUSE No.1 WAS THE
LARGEST OF GLENMORANGIE'S TRADITIONAL
18TH CENTURY WAREHOUSES AND UP UNTIL
IT BECAME OUR STILLHOUSE, WAS HEART
OF THE BOND'S CELLARS.

THE EXCLUSIVE GLENMORANGIE RELEASES
FROM BOND HOUSE No.1 ARE EXCEPTIONALLY
SMOOTH, COMPLEX AND ELEGANT.

GLENMORANGIE

HIGHLAND SINGLE MALT
SCOTCH WHISKY

GRAND VINTAGE MALT

1990

GLENMORANGIE

HIGHLAND SINGLE MALT
SCOTCH WHISKY

GRAND VINTAGE MALT

1990

BOTTLED IN 2016

GLENMORANGIE GRAND VINTAGE

Design: Jon Davies, Martyn Wallwork,
Ben Cox, Arron Egan
Company: Butterfly Cannon
Country: UK
Category: Spirits
GOLD PENTAWARD 2017

Glenmorangie Grand Vintage is the first release of a spirit that has been distilled in the current still house, converted in 1990 from the former distillery's Bonded Warehouse No. 1. In its packaging, the traditional craft materials were given a contemporary twist using clean modern geometric lines and a luxurious soft-touch leather-style interior. The graphic elements were etched or applied through a metal decal to give the design both visual and tactile beauty.

Glenmorangie Grand Vintage ist die erste Spirituose, die im derzeitigen Destilleriegebäude der Firma hergestellt wurde. Es entstand 1990 durch Umwandlung des früheren Zolllagers der Distille, dem Bonded Warehouse No. 1. Das Verpackungsdesign verleiht den traditionellen Materialien des Handwerks durch klare, moderne geometrische Linien und eine weiche, luxuriöse Innenauskleidung in Lederoptik einen zeitgenössischen Touch. Die grafischen Elemente wurden radiert oder mit Metallfolie appliziert, wodurch das Design sowohl visuelle als auch taktile Schönheit erhält.

Glenmorangie Grand Vintage est la première version d'un spiritueux qui a été distillé dans l'actuelle salle des alambics, aménagée en 1990 dans l'ancien entrepôt, le Bonded Warehouse No. 1. Pour son packaging, les matériaux artisanaux traditionnels sont réinterprétés dans un esprit contemporain, avec des lignes géométriques modernes et épurées et un intérieur luxueux en faux cuir doux au toucher. Les éléments graphiques ont été gravés ou appliqués par transfert métallisé pour conférer à cet objet une beauté à la fois visuelle et tactile.

MIDLETON
VERY RARE SILENT DISTILLERY

Creative Direction: Mike Parsonson
Structural Design: Stewart Hobbs
Production Direction: Allen Luther
Business Direction: Bernard Gormley
Company: Nude Brand Creation
Country: UK
Category: Spirits
GOLD PENTAWARD 2020

YINXINGYUAN
Creative Direction and Design: XiongBo Deng
Client: Guangxi Yinxingyuan Liquor
Company: Shenzhen Lingyun Creative
Packaging Design
Country: China
Category: Spirits
GOLD PENTAWARD 2019

DYNASTY

*Design, Creative Direction and
Account Direction:* Qingfeng Meng
Company: Shenzhen Qizhi Brand Culture
Country: China
Category: Spirits

BRONZE PENTAWARD 2020

UMESHU THE AMBER

Art Direction: Amano Kazutoshi
Design: Ayana Shirai
Client: Liquor Innovation
Company: P.K.G.Tokyo
Country: Japan
Category: Spirits

SILVER PENTAWARD 2020

CHIVAS REGAL
Illustration: Greg Gossel
Design Finalisation and Range Extension: JDO
Company: Chivas Brothers
Country: UK
Category: Spirits
SILVER PENTAWARD 2020

TIGRE BLANC ALAMBIC EDITION

Glass Bottle and Decoration: Saverglass
Cap: TAPI
Labels: Nacara
Gift Box: Fabrik&Vous
Design and Photography: Tigre Blanc Paris
Company: Tigre Blanc Paris
Country: France
Category: Spirits

BRONZE PENTAWARD 2019

IS VODKA

Design: VGS International Inc. team
Company: VGS International Inc.
Country: USA
Category: Spirits

BRONZE PENTAWARD 2009

ZORE ZALO

Creative Direction: Dimitris Gkazis
Company: Busybuilding
Country: Greece
Category: Spirits

SILVER PENTAWARD 2017

Zore Zalo is a grape-based alcoholic drink, made only on Crete. The name comes from the Cretan dialect and means "difficult step," reflecting the elaborate way it is produced by hand. It is an extremely pure distilled spirit, containing approximately 43 per cent alcohol per volume, and the design aims to express these product features and particularly the full flavor and purity that comes from its organic production, in a modern and minimalistic way, vividly presenting its bold masculine character and clarity.

Zore Zalo ist ein alkoholisches Getränk auf Traubenbasis, das ausschließlich auf Kreta hergestellt wird. Der Name entstammt dem kretischen Dialekt und bedeutet „schwieriger Schritt", eine Anspielung auf die aufwändige Herstellung des Produkts in Handarbeit. Es handelt sich um ein besonders reines Destillat mit einem Alkoholgehalt von etwa 43 Volumenprozent, und das Verpackungsdesign zielt darauf ab, diese Produkteigenschaften, vor allem den intensiven Geschmack und die durch die biologische Herstellung gewährleistete Reinheit, auf moderne, minimalistische Weise hervorzuheben. Gleichzeitig wird der klare, kraftvolle maskuline Charakter lebhaft in Szene gesetzt.

Zore Zalo est une boisson alcoolisée à base de raisin exclusivement fabriquée en Crète. Son nom vient du dialecte crétois et signifie « étape difficile », faisant allusion à son processus de production complexe et manuel. Ce spiritueux distillé est extrêmement pur, avec environ 43 pour cent d'alcool, et la bouteille vise à exprimer ces caractéristiques, plus particulièrement le goût riche et la pureté qui découlent de sa production organique, dans un style moderne et minimaliste qui met en valeur sa masculinité et sa transparence.

L'AMPHORE
Design: Javier Garduño, Israel García
Company: Javier Garduño – Estudio
de Diseño
Country: Spain
Category: Fine wines, champagne
SILVER PENTAWARD 2017

**BLEASDALE
THE IRON DUKE**

Creative Direction: Matthew Remphrey
Design: Kerina West
Company: Parallax Design
Country: Australia
Category: Fine wines, champagne

SILVER PENTAWARD 2014

PERE VENTURA
LA

Design: Josep Maria Morera
Company: Morera Design
Country: Spain
GOLD PENTAWARD 2008

La Pubilla (meaning first daughter born in a family) is part of the Premium range of cavas (sparkling wines) from Pere Ventura Cellars in Sant Sadurní, Catalonia, which is produced using the Champenoise method. Morera Design had to create a unique bottle that would reflect the attributes of the product, a meticulous, elegant, and fresh cava to suit the personality of a young woman. The selection of the unconventional and sleek curves in the bottle's shape, the bottle capsule featuring the profile of the daughter and the story behind "La Pubilla", are all elements chosen to communicate the concept of the product.

La Pubilla (Katalanisch für die erstgeborene Tochter einer Familie) gehört zur Premiumpalette des Cava-Schaumweins vom Weingut Pere Ventura im katalanischen Sant Sadurní. Dieser wird nach der Champagner-Methode produziert. Morera Design wollte eine einzigartige Flasche schaffen, die den Attributen des Produkts entspricht: ein akribischer, eleganter und frischer Cava, der zur Persönlichkeit einer jungen Frau passt. Um das Konzept des Produkts zu vermitteln, entschied man sich für die unkonventionellen und geschmeidigen Linien der Flaschenform, die Korkenhülle mit dem Profil des Mädchens und die „La Pubilla" zugrunde liegende Geschichte.

Le vin **La Pubilla** (terme catalan qui désigne la première fille née dans une famille) fait partie de la gamme premium de cava (vin pétillant) des caves Pere Ventura à Sant Sadurní, en Catalogne, et est produit selon la méthode champenoise. Morera Design devait créer une bouteille originale pour refléter les attributs du produit, un cava soigné, élégant et frais, qui correspond à la personnalité d'une jeune femme. Les courbes originales et épurées de la bouteille, le médaillon décoré du profil de la jeune fille et l'histoire derrière « La Pubilla » sont les éléments choisis pour communiquer sur le concept du produit.

BLUEBERRY

Design: Kuan Fu Wu
Company: Shenzhen Excel Package Co., Ltd.
Country: China
Category: Fine wines, champagne
BRONZE PENTAWARD 2012

MISTINGUETT
TRADITIONAL METHOD

Design: SeriesNemo team
Company: SeriesNemo
Country: Spain
Category: Fine wines, champagne
GOLD PENTAWARD 2017

Mistinguett was one of the greatest French entertainers of all time. Her namesake **Mistinguett Cava** is adorned with feathers to reveal the bottle's suggestive shape and insinuating undulations. The packaging is reminiscent of the sophisticated and festive atmosphere of Parisian high society in the early 20th century. Both pack and product create a balance between seductive strength and coquettish nature. The label, like a silk bow or a piece of jewelry, becomes the essential highlight that every show needs.

Mistinguett war eine der berühmtesten französischen Entertainerinnen aller Zeiten. Ihr Namensvetter **Mistinguett Cava** ist mit Federn geschmückt, um die sinnliche Form der Flasche und die suggestiven Kurven zu betonen. Die Verpackung erinnert an die elegante, festliche Atmosphäre in der Pariser High Society zu Beginn des zwanzigsten Jahrhunderts. Sowohl die Verpackung als auch das Produkt erzeugen ein Gleichgewicht zwischen Koketterie und Verführung. Das Etikett, das einer seidenen Schleife oder einer Schmuckbrosche gleicht, wird zum entscheidenden Highlight, wie es jede gute Show braucht.

Mistinguett a été l'une des plus grandes artistes françaises de tous les temps. **Mistinguett Cava**, baptisé en son honneur, est orné de plumes pour mettre en valeur la forme suggestive de la bouteille et ses ondulations expressives. Le packaging évoque l'atmosphère sophistiquée et festive de la haute société parisienne au début du XXᵉ siècle. Contenant et contenu créent l'équilibre entre force séductrice et nature enjôleuse. L'étiquette, tel un nœud en soie ou un bijou, est la vedette indispensable de tout spectacle.

PERFECCIONISTA

FINCA OFELIA

MADUREZ PARA ALGUNOS,
SENTIDO COMÚN PARA OTROS.
ES CUESTIÓN DE TIEMPO.
LAS IMPERFECCIONES NOS DIFERENCIAN,
NOS HACEN SENTIR ÚNICOS.
VER MÁS ALLÁ DE LO SUPERFICIAL
NOS PERMITE CRECER,
MIRAR CON PROFUNDIDAD
NOS HACE GRANDES.
ES SIMPLE Y COMPLEJO.

VITIVINICULTOR
DAVID ACHA

ENÓLOGO
PABLO ESTÉVEZ

DAVIDE

074/697

PERFE

FI

PERFECCIONISTA

Creative Direction: Roberto Núñez
Client: Bodega Davide
Printing: Avenadecor IPE
Copywriting: Roberto Núñez
Photography: Treviño
Assisting: Ángel Tello
Company: Roberto Núñez
Country: Spain
Category: Fine wines, champagne
PLATINUM PENTAWARD 2019

Perfeccionista is a single-estate limited-production wine, created using "thoughtful viticulture", a considerate and experienced method of winemaking. In order to connect emotionally with the consumer and position the product as a distinctive premium wine, packaging was developed that attaches value to the idea of imperfection, making each piece unique. For each of the 697 exclusive units produced, the wooden tags were broken by hand and individually ink-stamped.

Perfeccionista ist ein Wein aus einer limitierten Produktion, der durch „rücksichtsvollen Weinanbau" entstanden ist. Um eine emotionale Bindung mit dem Konsumenten einzugehen und um das Produkt als herausstechenden Premiumwein zu positionieren, wurde eine Verpackung entwickelt, die einen hohen Wert mit der Idee der Unvollkommenheit verbindet und so jedes Stück einzigartig macht. Für jede der 697 exklusiven Flaschen wurden die Holzschilder von Hand gebrochen und individuell mit Stempeln versehen.

Perfeccionista est un vin qu'un seul domaine viticole produit en quantité limitée par le biais d'une « viticulture consciencieuse », selon une méthode de vinification respectueuse et éprouvée. Afin de nouer un lien émotionnel avec le consommateur et de positionner le produit comme un vin haut de gamme, le packaging conçu donne de la valeur à l'idée d'imperfection, ce qui rend chaque pièce unique. Pour chacune des 697 unités exclusives produites, l'étiquette en bois a été cassée à la main et estampillée individuellement à l'encre.

STERLING VINEYARDS IRIDIUM

Design: Stranger & Stranger team
Company: Stranger & Stranger
Country: UK
Category: Fine wines, champagne

GOLD PENTAWARD 2018

Sterling Vineyards, a unique Napa winery, had lost its way a little over the years and sales were in decline. With such a great brand name, it was an obvious choice to use silver in the rebranding. Each bottle tells a different part of the brand story using silver in different ways, from medals to bling. The iconic Iridium bottle celebrates the silversmiths' craft with a metal sleeve. This strategy caused a surge in sales and the silver bottles appeared on tables at the 2017 Emmy awards.

Sterling Vineyards, ein einzigartiges Weingut im kalifornischen Napa Valley, war im Laufe der Jahre ein wenig vom Kurs abgekommen, und die Verkaufszahlen gingen zurück. Der Markenname lieferte jedoch eine naheliegende und zugleich starke Lösung für das Branding: Silber. Jede Flasche erzählt einen Teil der Firmengeschichte, mit unterschiedlichem Bezug zum Silber, von der Medaille bis hin zum auffälligen Schmuckstück. Das kultige Iridium feiert das Handwerk des Silberschmieds mit einer Metallbanderole. Durch diese Werbestrategie stieg der Absatz sprunghaft an, die silbernen Flaschen standen etwa bei den Emmy Awards 2017 auf den Tischen.

Sterling Vineyards, un domaine viticole unique dans la vallée de Napa, avait un peu perdu sa voie au fil des ans, et les ventes déclinaient. Avec un tel nom, utiliser l'argent dans la stratégie de marque s'est imposé comme une évidence. Chaque bouteille représente un élément différent dans l'histoire de la marque à travers l'argent de diverses façons, sous forme de médailles ou de pure décoration. L'emblématique bouteille Iridium rend hommage au savoir-faire de l'orfèvre avec un manchon en métal. Cette stratégie s'est traduite par une augmentation des ventes, et les bouteilles argentées sont apparues sur les tables de la cérémonie de remise des prix Emmy en 2017.

SAFE POWER

Design: Crystal So, Mavin Ma
Company: Safe Power Printing & Box MFG
Country: Hong Kong
Category: Gourmet food

SILVER PENTAWARD 2019

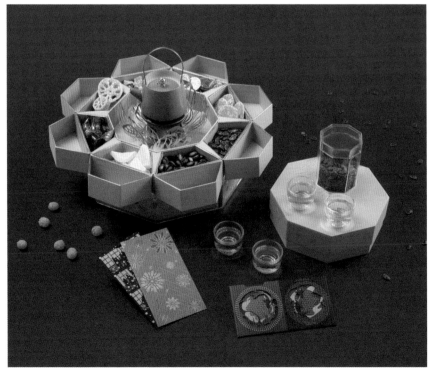

松屋牌原酿山茶油

睡瓜熟

郑山江地的每逢家有一中国藏乡村乡的美景
这里的山茶油都是用本鲜
取自物原壶八百年的山茶树果。经物理压榨而得

PRODUCT of **WUYUAN**   500ml

SONG FENG TSUI
Design: Guiping Nie, Jiao Wang, Yu Zhou
Company: Transmedia Advertising
Country: China
Category: Gourmet food
BRONZE PENTAWARD 2014

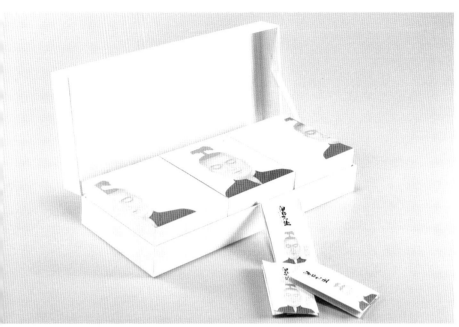

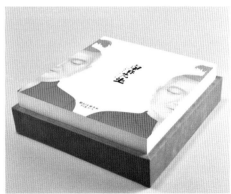

MASTERPIECE DANZHU CHUXIN

Company: Sichuan Guge Dynasty Brand Design Consultant
Country: China
Category: Gourmet food

SILVER PENTAWARD 2016

SONG YAN TEA

Design: Li Zhiming
Company: ZhiMing Design
Country: China
Category: Gourmet food
SILVER PENTAWARD 2018

S&B FOODS

Art Direction: Kazutoshi Amanod
Manufacture: Fukunaga-Print
Company: P.K.G.Tokyo
Country: Japan
Category: Gourmet food
BRONZE PENTAWARD 2018

T HOUSE TIME

Design: OCD, Liuwen Design Studio
Company: Shenzhen Oracle Creative Design
Country: China
Category: Gourmet food
BRONZE PENTAWARD 2017

CINCO JOTAS

Industrial Design: Marta Zabala
Art Direction: Clara De Sousa
Industrial Design Direction: Pep Trias
Craftsmanship Direction: Xavi Cuixart
Client Management: Mario González
Direction: Ignacio Muguiro
Company: Morillas Brand Design
Country: Spain
Category: Gourmet food

GOLD PENTAWARD 2019

Cinco Jotas acorn-fed Ibérico ham is Spain's national treasure, and such an authentic delicacy deserves extraordinary and unique packaging. Breaking with traditional packaging codes, this unconventional box has an unexpected shape that fits perfectly with the geometry of the product that it contains. The iconic hexagonal box holds one Cinco Jotas 100% Ibérico ham leg and a half piece of Cinco Jotas 100% Ibérico presa. Adorning the box are several birds of the Dehesa, the forest where the pigs live and feed from holm oak acorns. These birds have an important role in the life cycle of the acorn, which is essential to creating the flavour of the authentic 100% Ibérico Cinco Jotas Bellota ham.

Cinco Jotas iberischer Schinken vom Eichel-schwein ist Spaniens Nationalschatz und eine so authentische Delikatesse verdient eine einzigartige Verpackung. Diese unkonventionelle Box bricht mit allen Verpackungscodes und hat eine unerwar-tete Form, die sich perfekt an die Geometrie des darin enthaltenen Produkts anpasst. Die sechs-eckige Box enthält eine Cinco Jotas 100 % Ibérico Schinkenkeule und ein halbes Stück des Cinco Jotas 100 % Ibérico presa. Die Box wird mit einigen Vögeln aus der Dehesa geschmückt, den Wäldern, in denen die Schweine leben und sich von den Eicheln der Steineiche ernähren. Diese Vögel spielen eine wichtige Rolle im Lebenszyklus der Eichel, die essenziell für den authentischen Geschmack des 100 % Ibérico Cinco Jotas Schinkens sind.

En Espagne, le jambon de porc ibérique nourri aux glands **Cinco Jotas** est un trésor national, un mets fin qui mérite un emballage unique et exceptionnel. Son packaging rompt avec les codes traditionnels et se présente dans une forme inédite qui épouse parfaitement la géométrie du produit qu'il renferme. La boîte hexagonale emblématique abrite un jambon Cinco Jotas 100 % ibérique et une demi-presa Cinco Jotas 100 % ibérique. Elle est décorée d'oiseaux de la dehesa, la forêt où les porcs vivent et s'alimentent des glands de chênes verts. Ces oiseaux jouent un rôle important dans le cycle de vie des glands, essentiels pour donner tout son goût au jambon de bellota Cinco Jotas 100 % ibérique.

27+ UMF MANUKA HONEY

Client: P.A. & S.C. Steens
Design: David Trubridge
Cardboard Engineering: Think Packaging
Manufacturing: Wrapology International Ltd
Photography: Emirali Photography
Art Direction Photography and Editing: Ssaalltt
Company: Think Packaging
Country: New Zealand
Category: Gourmet food

SILVER PENTAWARD 2019

PENHALIGON'S
CHRISTMAS GIFT COLLECTION

Design: jkr design team
Company: jkr
Country: UK
Category: Limited editions, limited series,
event creations

SILVER PENTAWARD 2014

MANDOM
THE 80ᵀᴴ ANNIVERSARY
FRAGRANCE

Box Design: Forme Design Office Inc.
Design: Hirai Yuko, Imahori Atsuko
Bottle: Able Design Planning
Art Director: Hanamura Kenji
Designer: Shigeta Motoe
Company: Forme Design Office Inc.
Country: Japan
Category: Limited editions, limited series,
event creations

SILVER PENTAWARD 2009

PALMER CASK 150

Design: SeriesNemo team
Company: SeriesNemo
Country: Spain
Category: Limited editions, limited series, event creations

GOLD PENTAWARD 2018

Palmer Cask 150 dates back to 1867, the year when Alfred Nobel patented the invention of dynamite and the first submarine cable was laid between Portugal and England. The story of this 150-year-old tawny port is printed in gold on the glass of the limited-edition bottle. On the outside, the label tells the history we all know about while the rest of the story is hidden inside. Only those who own one of the 1,000 bottles produced will be able to read it. The bottle has a double-height base and a transparent top that lets you see through to the cork, for centuries at the heart of Portugal's wine production.

HENNESSY XO

Design: Marc Savary, Julien Zylbermann
Companies: Appartement 103, Hennessy
Country: France
Category: Limited editions, limited series, event creations

SILVER PENTAWARD 2017

Palmer Cask 150 geht bis ins Jahr 1867 zurück, als Alfred Nobel die Erfindung des Dynamits patentieren ließ und zwischen Portugal und England das erste Unterseekabel verlegt wurde. Die Geschichte des 150 Jahre alten Tawny Port steht in goldenen Buchstaben auf dem Glas dieser Sondereditionsflasche. Auf der Außenseite erzählt das Etikett die Geschichte, die wir alle kennen, während der restliche Teil sich innen verbirgt. Nur diejenigen, die eine der 1 000 produzierten Flaschen besitzen, können ihn lesen. Der Flaschenboden ist doppelt so hoch wie üblich, und der Hals ist transparent, sodass man den Korken sehen kann – seit Jahrhunderten das Herzstück der portugiesischen Produkte für den weltweiten Weinmarkt.

Palmer Cask 150 date de 1867, l'année où Alfred Nobel a breveté l'invention de la dynamite et où le premier câble sous-marin a été posé entre le Portugal et l'Angleterre. L'histoire de ce porto tawny vieux de 150 ans est imprimée en lettres dorées sur le verre de la bouteille en édition limitée. À l'extérieur, l'étiquette raconte l'histoire que nous connaissons tous, mais le reste de cette histoire est caché à l'intérieur. Seuls les propriétaires des 1 000 bouteilles produites peuvent donc le lire. La bouteille a une base à double hauteur et le haut est transparent afin de laisser voir le bouchon en liège, qui se trouve au cœur de la production de vin du Portugal depuis des siècles.

HENNESSY

Creative Direction: Julien Zylbermann,
Marc Savary
Client: Hennessy V.S.
Artwork: Felipe Pantone
Company: Felipe Pantone – Appartement 103
Country: France
Category: Limited editions, limited series,
event creations

PLATINUM PENTAWARD 2020

Released globally at a limited quantity of 70 pieces, this Collector's Edition from **Hennessy** was created in partnership with the world-renowned and pioneering street artist Felipe Pantone. The result of this collaboration is a super clean, shiny white PET box that once opened reveals the whole world of Felipe Pantone through a prism of graphical elements and textures. At the centre of the experience, the consumer is invited to build their own art sculpture around a customized Hennessy V.S bottle which is printed with the latest cutting-edge digital technologies in CMYK. The exclusive carafe stands on a pedestal in the centre of a grid of moiré-finished rods that consumers themselves can place, move and interchange to alter the bottle's optics.

Diese Collector's Edition von **Hennessy** wurde mit einer weltweit limitierten Stückzahl von 70 Flaschen in Partnerschaft mit dem Straßenkünstler Felipe Pantone entworfen. Das Ergebnis dieser Zusammenarbeit war eine glänzend weiße PET-Box, die nach dem Öffnen die Welt von Felipe Pantone durch ein Prisma von grafischen Elementen und Texturen offenbart. Im Zentrum des Erlebnisses steht der Verbraucher, der eingeladen ist, seine eigene Kunstskulptur um die Hennessy V.S-Flasche zu bauen, die mit den neuesten digitalen Technologien in CMYK gedruckt wurde. Die exklusive Karaffe steht auf einem Sockel in der Mitte eines Gitters aus Stäben mit Moiré-Muster, die der Kunde selbst positionieren, bewegen und verändern kann, um die Optik der Flasche zu verändern.

Avec un lancement mondial limité à 70 unités, cette édition Collector de **Hennessy** a été créée en collaboration avec Felipe Pantone, artiste de rue innovateur et de notoriété mondiale. Le fruit de ce travail est une boîte PET d'un blanc immaculé qui, une fois ouverte, révèle tout l'univers de Felipe Pantone à travers un prisme d'éléments graphiques et de textures. Au cours de l'expérience, le consommateur est invité à construire sa propre sculpture artistique autour d'une bouteille Hennessy V.S personnalisée et imprimée en quadrichromie à l'aide de technologies numériques de pointe. La carafe de luxe repose sur un piédestal au centre d'une grille de tiges moirées que le consommateur peut insérer, déplacer et permuter pour changer le visuel de la bouteille.

The brief was to create new gift set packaging which would encourage the (re)discovery of **Hennessy XO**'s greatness and reach a new generation of luxury drinkers. With the knowledge that ice-cold water is a taste enhancer, the limited-edition box was made with a perfectly symmetrical diamond cut design carved out of a single injection-moulded block, giving the effect of a block of ice. When closed, the box seems to encase the fire of XO cognac, but when open, it becomes an elegant ice bucket to use on special occasions. Under the light, the facets make the block sparkle like real glass or diamonds, creating an enchanting and festive atmosphere for a new luxury ritual of cognac tasting.

Die Vorgabe war es, ein neues Geschenkset zu entwerfen, das die (Wieder-)Entdeckung von **Hennessy XO**s Profil fördern und eine neue Generation von Kunden erreichen sollte. Mit dem Wissen, das eiskaltes Wasser ein Geschmacksverstärker ist, wurde die in limitierter Auflage hergestellte Box mit einem perfekt symmetrischen Diamantenschnitt-Design aus einem einzelnen Spritzgussblock herausgearbeitet, der den Effekt eines Eisblocks nachstellt. Wenn sie geschlossen wird, scheint die Box das Feuer des XO-Cognacs zu umschließen, wenn sie geöffnet ist, wird sie zu einem eleganten Eiskühler, den man zu besonderen Anlässen nutzen kann. Im Licht lassen die Facetten den Block glitzern wie echtes Glas oder Diamanten und schaffen damit eine bezaubernde, feierliche Atmosphäre für ein neues luxuriöses Ritual der Cognac-Verkostung.

Le brief créatif portait sur l'invention d'un coffret-cadeau afin de faire (re)découvrir toute la grandeur de **Hennessy XO** et atteindre une nouvelle génération d'amateurs de boissons de luxe. L'eau glacée étant un exhausteur de goût, le design de la boîte en édition limitée a été conçu comme un diamant taillé parfaitement symétrique à partir d'un bloc moulé en une seule injection ; l'effet obtenu est celui d'un bloc de glace. Quand la boîte est fermée, elle semble renfermer le feu du cognac XO ; ouverte, elle devient un élégant seau à glace à utiliser lors d'occasions spéciales. Sous une lumière, les facettes font étinceler le bloc tel du verre véritable ou des diamants, ce qui crée une atmosphère festive et féérique pour un luxueux rituel de dégustation de cognac.

HENNESSY XO

Global Creative Direction and CEO:
Sébastien Servaire
Design Creative Direction: Candido de Barros
Design: Thomas Chouvaeff
Product Design Development Management:
Erwann Pivert
Account Direction: Anne Pilliard
Film Artistic Direction: Sébastien Servaire,
Marie Galanti
Photography: Claude Badée
Company: Servaire & Co
Country: France
Category: Limited editions, limited series,
event creations
GOLD PENTAWARD 2019

ACQUA DI PARMA

CEO: Thierry Cazaux
Creative Strategy Direction:
Marine Forlini-Crouzet
Art Direction: Damine Escaravage
Product Development and Innovation Direction:
Paola Paganini (Acqua di Parma)
Senior Product Management: Ginetta Rizzi
(Acqua di Parma)
Company: Chic
Country: France
Category: Limited editions, limited series,
event creations
GOLD PENTAWARD 2020

With advent calendars gaining popularity in the luxury market, **Acqua di Parma** took this as an opportunity to offer renewed value to the customer in an innovative way. Staying true to the brand DNA and building on its iconic cylinder, an ingenious folding structure was developed to hold 25 Acqua di Parma products of 11 different shapes and dimensions. The structure invites the consumer to take part in a smart, dynamic and delightful ritual. The luxury of the project is encapsulated in the elegance of the unfolding calendar, the delicacy of the magnetic opening and the high-quality of the product's manufacturing.

Da Adventskalender auf dem Luxusmarkt immer beliebter werden, sah **Acqua di Parma** dies als Möglichkeit, seinen Kunden auf innovative Weise neue Wertigkeit zu bieten. Um der Marken-DNA treu zu bleiben und auf dessen bekannte Zylinder aufzubauen, wurde eine geniale Faltstruktur entwickelt, die 25 Produkte von Acqua di Parma mit elf verschiedenen Formen und Dimensionen aufnehmen kann. Die Struktur lädt den Kunden dazu ein, an einem intelligenten, dynamischen und freudvollen Ritual teilzunehmen. Der Luxus dieses Projekts wird durch die Eleganz des aufklappbaren Kalenders, die Feinheit der magnetischen Öffnung und die hohe Qualität der Produktherstellung verkörpert.

Les calendriers de l'avent sont en vogue sur le marché des produits de luxe, et **Acqua di Parma** a saisi cette occasion pour se revaloriser auprès de ses clients de façon innovante. Fidèle à l'ADN de la marque et partant de son emblématique cylindre, une ingénieuse structure articulée a été conçue pour accueillir 25 produits Acqua di Parma de 11 formes et dimensions différentes et pour inviter le consommateur à suivre un rituel exquis. Le luxe de ce projet réside dans l'élégance du calendrier qui s'ouvre, dans la finesse de l'ouverture aimantée et dans la qualité supérieure des produits.

QUINTA DO CRASTO

Design: Omdesign team
Company: Omdesign
Country: Portugal
Category: Limited editions, limited series,
event creations

SILVER PENTAWARD 2019

CLÉ DE PEAU BEAUTÉ

Creative Direction: Taisuke Kikuchi
Art Direction and Design: Kaori Nagata
Photography: Masato Kanazawa, Taihei Iino
Artwork: Ayana Otake
Kimono Making: Tachibana
Kimono Coordination: Katsumi Hayashi, SACRA
Company: Shiseido
Country: Japan
Category: Limited editions, limited series, event creations

SILVER PENTAWARD 2020

CINCO JOTAS

Industrial Design: Albert Pérez
Art Direction: Clara De Sousa
Industrial Design Direction: Pep Trias
Craftsmanship Direction: Xavi Cuixart
Client Management: Mario González
Direction: Ignacio Muguiro
Company: Morillas Brand Design
Country: Spain
Category: Limited editions, limited series, event creations

SILVER PENTAWARD 2019

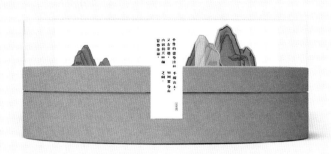

YAN TU

Creative Direction: Jonny Wang
Design: Jerry Liu
Company: East Orange
Country: China
Category: Distributors'/retailers' own brands, private labels

SILVER PENTAWARD 2019

VEUVE CLICQUOT ROSÉ VALENTINE'S DAY MEGAPHONE

Creative Direction: Jean-Sébastien Blanc, Vincent Baranger
Design: Martin Lefèvre
Company: 5.5 designstudio
Country: France
Category: Casks, cases, gift boxes, etc.

BRONZE PENTAWARD 2015

JOHNNIE WALKER PLATINUM LABEL

Design: Denis Boudard
Photography: Studio Eric Jacquet
Company: QSLD Paris
Country: France
Category: Casks, cases, gift boxes, etc.

BRONZE PENTAWARD 2012

DOM PÉRIGNON

Creative Direction: Joseph Hascoet
Company: Atelier Casanova
Country: France
Category: Casks, cases, gift boxes, etc.

GOLD PENTAWARD 2017

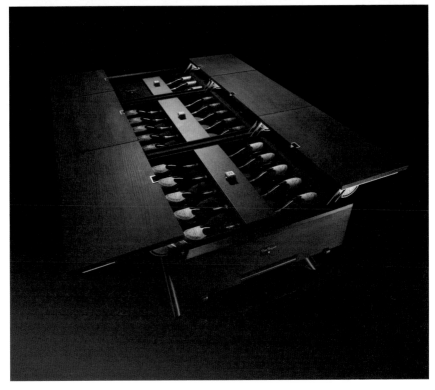

PERNOD RICARD ABSOLUT

Design: ButterflyCanon
Company: Dapy – DO International
Country: France
Category: Casks, cases, gift boxes, etc.
SILVER PENTAWARD 2017

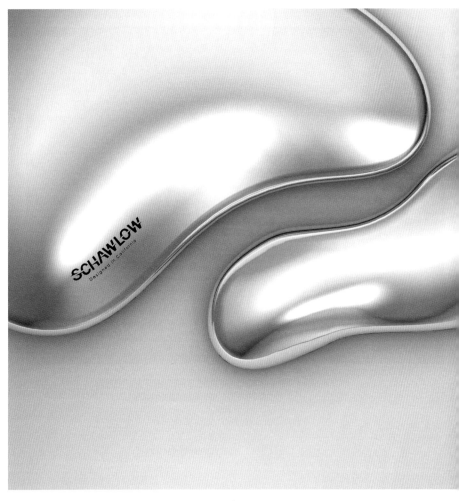

SCHAWLOW JEWELLERY

Design: Andy Liu, Xiechen Lu, Liu Wen
Company: Oracle Creative Design
Country: China
Category: Casks, cases, gift boxes, etc.
GOLD PENTAWARD 2018

The unique boxes in which **Schawlow Jewellery** is packaged represent the three different states of silver, from solid to liquid. In the necklace packaging, it is as if the temperature has been increased to melting point so that the silver block resembles a molten mass. For the bracelet packaging, the silver has become a liquid that flows downhill. For the ring, it is as if the temperature has continuously increased, causing the silver to appear like a drop of water as it collides with hot metal. The silver flows gently, like water, but is indestructible, like gold. The creative nature of the packaging makes it a precious artwork in itself.

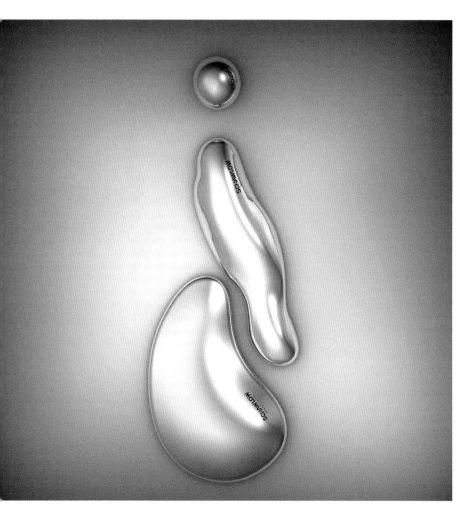

Die ungewöhnlichen Behältnisse, in denen der Schmuck von **Schawlow Jewellery** verkauft wird, repräsentieren die drei Aggregatzustände des Silbers, von fest bis flüssig. Bei der Halskettenschachtel scheint das Silber eine zähe Masse zu sein. Für das Armband wurde das Silber verflüssigt und scheint abwärts zu fließen. Beim Ringdöschen wirkt es wie ein Tropfen, der auf heißes Metall fällt und sogleich verdampfen wird. Das Silber fließt sachte wie Wasser, ist aber so unzerstörbar wie Gold. Kreative Verpackungen, die selbst zu Kunstwerken werden.

Les singuliers écrins à bijoux de **Schawlow Jewellery** représentent les trois états de l'argent, de solide à liquide. Pour l'écrin à collier, c'est comme si la température avait été augmentée jusqu'au point de fusion, afin que le bloc d'argent se transforme en masse fondue. Pour l'écrin à bracelet, l'argent est devenu un liquide qui s'écoule. Pour l'écrin à bague, la température est encore plus élevée, et l'argent ressemble à une goutte d'eau s'écrasant sur du métal brûlant. L'argent coule comme de l'eau, mais est indestructible comme l'or. La créativité de ce packaging en fait une véritable œuvre d'art.

DUVAL-LEROY

Creative Direction: Jean-Sébastien Blanc,
Vincent Baranger
Design: Anne-Dorothée Schultz,
Max Berthois
Company: 5.5 designstudio
Country: France
Category: Casks, cases, gift boxes, etc.
BRONZE PENTAWARD 2017

VEUVE CLICQUOT

Design: CHIC team
Creative Lead: Loic Le Bihan
Product Design: Bastien Renard
Manufacture: Virojanglor
Company: Virojanglor
Country: France
Category: Casks, cases, gift boxes, etc.
SILVER PENTAWARD 2018

VEUVE CLICQUOT

Design: Servaire & Co team
Manufacturer: Virojanglor
Company: Virojanglor
Country: France
Category: Casks, cases, gift boxes, etc.

SILVER PENTAWARD 2018

TANQUERAY NO. TEN

Design: Jon Davies, Martyn Wallwork, Ben Cox
Production: Virojanglor
Company: Butterfly Cannon
Country: France, UK
Category: Casks, cases, gift boxes, etc.

SILVER PENTAWARD 2017

The art-deco-inspired gift packaging of **Tanqueray No. Ten** is reminiscent of the Roaring Twenties, the heyday of the cocktail. The wire-framed cage gives a special feel to the bottle and is also useful for holding cocktail garnishes. The clever design makes the packaging an item that need never be thrown away but can be used as an ornament in the home.

Die vom Art déco inspirierte Geschenkver-packung von **Tanqueray No. Ten** erinnert an die Wilden Zwanziger, die Blütezeit des Cocktails schlechthin. Der Drahtkorb verleiht der Flasche ein besonderes Flair und erweist sich zudem als nützliches Gefäß für die Cocktail-Zutaten. Das clevere Design macht die Verpackung zu einem Gegenstand, den man nicht wegwirft, sondern im Haushalt als Deko-Artikel benutzen kann.

Tanqueray No. Ten s'est doté d'un packaging cadeau d'inspiration Art déco qui évoque les Années folles, l'âge d'or des cocktails. Cette cage en fil de fer donne une personnalité unique à la bouteille, et est aussi très pratique pour y loger des ingrédients à cocktail. Cette idée astucieuse trans-forme le packaging en objet que l'on ne jette pas, et que l'on utilise au contraire comme élément de décoration.

JOHNNIE WALKER
BLUE LABEL

Design: Tom Dixon
Manufacture: Virojanglor
Company: Virojanglor
Country: France
Category: Casks, cases,
gift boxes, etc.

BRONZE PENTAWARD 2018

VALE D. MARIA PORT 1969

Design and Creative Direction: Pedro Roque
Company: RitaRivotti® Premium Packaging Design
Country: Portugal
Category: Fine wines, champagne

SILVER PENTAWARD 2020

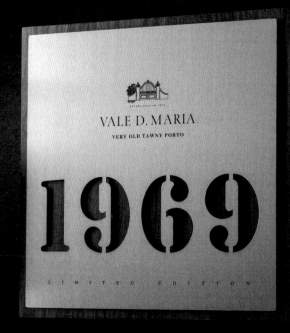

Cîroc Vodka's Halo table server has been an icon of the brand's on-trade experience and popular in nightclubs for several years, but it needed a refresh. The solution was a deceptively simple structure inspired by contemporary luxury yacht design. With crisp, flowing curves it glows in an uninterrupted circle of light, a literal halo around Cîroc's distinctive bottle. The new design also incorporates two styles of illumination via one simple button, with a choice of either a constant light or multicoloured LEDs pulsing in sequence. The Halo itself is covered in Cîroc iridescent blue chrome, with a mirror finish that reflects light as well as the energy and vibrancy of night or daytime partygoers, whilst the Cîroc logo remains boldly visible, even when not illuminated.

Der **Halo** von **Cîroc Vodka** ist schon lange eine Ikone im Handel und in Nachtclubs beliebt, sein Design musste aber trotzdem aufgefrischt werden. Die Lösung war eine täuschend einfache Struktur, inspiriert von dem Look einer Luxusjacht. Ein leuchtender Kreis bildet buchstäblich ein Halo, einen Heiligenschein, um Cîrocs unverwechselbare Flasche. Das neue Design vereint zwei Beleuchtungsstile in einem Knopf, durch den man die Wahl zwischen konstantem Licht oder verschiedenfarbigen LEDs hat. Der Halo ist mit blauen Cîroc-Chrom überzogen, dessen Hochglanz-Finish sowohl das Licht als auch die Energie und die Lebendigkeit der Partygänger reflektiert, während das Cîroc-Logo auch im unbeleuchteten Zustand deutlich sichtbar bleibt.

Après des années de popularité dans les discothèques et à symboliser l'expérience de la marque **Cîroc Vodka**, le présentoir **Halo** avait besoin d'un coup de fraîcheur. La solution trouvée est une création d'apparence simple, inspirée du design contemporain des yachts de luxe. Ses courbes nettes et gracieuses font rayonner un cercle lumineux ininterrompu, tel un véritable halo autour de la bouteille originale de Cîroc. Un bouton permet de choisir entre deux modes d'éclairage : une lumière permanente ou des LED multicolores qui s'allument tour à tour. Le présentoir est recouvert de chrome bleu irisé Cîroc, avec un fini miroir réfléchissant la lumière ambiante et la vitalité des fêtards nocturnes ou en journée. Pour sa part, le logo Cîroc reste à tout moment très visible, même sans éclairage.

CÎROC VODKA

Creative Direction: Arron Egan, Jon Davies
Design: Martyn Wallwork
Supplier: Dapy Paris
Company: Butterfly Cannon
Country: UK
Category: Casks, cases, gift boxes, etc.

GOLD PENTAWARD 2019

THE DALMORE

Photography: Studio 5•5
Creative Direction: Vincent Baranger
Design: Martin Lefèvre, Georges Diant,
Clément Nambot, César Potel
Company: Studio 5•5
Country: France
Category: Casks, cases, gift boxes, etc.

GOLD PENTAWARD 2020

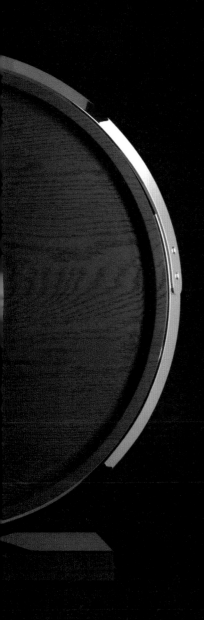

In celebration of their 180th anniversary, **The Dalmore** decided to mark the occasion with the release of an extremely old whisky (aged 60 years). To present this exceptional whisky made from two very old casks that were long stored at the Highland distillery, the designers created a unique bottle artwork and glorifier. The design intention was to embody the legacy of the distillery and symbolise the twin casks that came together to create this extremely limited-edition whisky. This resulted in a glorifier made of two casks covers joined together, and lead the concept and shape for the logo.

Anlässlich der Feier ihres 180. Jubiläums beschlossen **The Dalmore** einen extrem alten Whisky (60 Jahre gealtert) auf den Markt zu bringen. Um diesen außergewöhnlichen Whisky zu präsentieren, der aus zwei sehr alten Fässern stammt, die lange in der Highland-Distillery gelagert wurden, kreierten die Designer ein einzigartiges Flaschenkunstwerk und einen Hingucker. Das Design sollte das Vermächtnis der Brennerei verkörpern und die identischen Fässer symbolisieren, die bei der Herstellung dieses Whiskys in limitierter Auflage zusammengebracht wurden. Das Ergebnis war eine Trophäe, die aus zwei verschiedenen Fassabdeckungen besteht, die zu einer zusammengefügt wurden und so das Konzept und die Form des Logos vorgeben.

Pour commémorer son 180ᵉ anniversaire, **The Dalmore** a décidé de marquer l'occasion en proposant un whisky très âgé, de 60 ans. Pour présenter cette eau-de-vie d'exception vieillie dans d'anciens fûts longtemps conservés à la distillerie dans les Highlands, les designers ont conçu une bouteille unique glorifiant son contenu. L'intention était que cette œuvre d'art incarne l'héritage de la distillerie et symbolise les deux fûts ayant servi à l'élaboration de ce whisky en édition hautement limitée. Le résultat est un écrin composé de deux couvercles de fûts qui se chevauchent et définissent le concept et la forme du logo.

CHAMPAGNE TAITTINGER

Creative Direction: Vitalie Taittinger,
Jérémy Malabre, Justine Baillette,
David Jankowski
Design: Jonathan Allègre, Mathieu Bourel,
Laura Kiritzé Topor
Product Development: Boris Pommeret
Company: Makao
Country: France
Category: Casks, cases, gift boxes, etc.

SILVER PENTAWARD 2019

WU

Design Guidance: Bosom
Photography: Hello Ogata
Company: 7654321 Studio
Country: China
Category: Casks, cases, gift boxes, etc.
SILVER PENTAWARD 2020

THE SOUL OF MAOTAI-FLAVOUR

Creative Direction and Design: Li Zuo
Company: Guangzhou Wendao Advertising
Country: China
Category: Casks, cases, gift boxes, etc.

SILVER PENTAWARD 2020

**SHISEIDO
CALLA LUCENT**
Design: Ping Mu
School: Shanghai Institute of Visual Art
Country: China
Category: Packaging concept (student)
BRONZE PENTAWARD 2017

IN'PRESSIVE NAILS
Design: Elie Papiernik, Sophie Robbe,
Lucas Dumon, Prisca Renoux, Marion Perret
Company: Centdegrés
Country: France
Category: Packaging concept
SILVER PENTAWARD 2017

A TIME BOTTLE

Art Direction and Design: Anna Sakaguchi,
Miki Kawamura
Company: Anna Sakaguchi / Miki Kawamura
Country: Germany
Category: Packaging concept
GOLD PENTAWARD 2019

A Time Bottle is a perfume bottle made of
reused ocean plastic which becomes unique over
the years through everyday use. It's like beach
glass, shaped slowly after being gently ground and
shaped by the waves. In recent years plastic has
been strongly associated with terms like mass
production, but if it is turned into a material that
can be used over a long time, not just mass produced then thrown away, it can also reduce the
amount of plastic created. The idea behind A Time
Bottle is to give plastic new value by becoming
a long-term usable material, creating "antique
plastic" which sees its value grow with the passage
of time.

A Time Bottle ist ein Parfümflakon aus recyceltem Plastik aus dem Meer, das im Laufe der Zeit und durch den täglichen Gebrauch einzigartig wird – wie ein Stück Glas, das sanft von Meereswellen geschliffen und geformt wurde. In den vergangenen Jahren wurde Kunststoff stark mit Begriffen wie Massenproduktion in Verbindung gebracht, dabei kann man es über eine lange Zeit verwenden, anstatt es in rauen Mengen wegzuwerfen. So lässt sich die Herstellung von Plastik reduzieren. Die Idee hinter A Time Bottle ist, Plastik aufzuwerten, es als langfristig verwendbares Material zu nutzen und in „antikes Plastik" zu verwandeln, dessen Wert mit den Jahren steigt.

A Time Bottle est un flacon de parfum fabriqué à base de plastique récupéré des océans et dont l'aspect évolue avec le temps par son utilisation quotidienne. Il s'apparente aux tessons de verre trouvés sur les plages, lentement taillés et polis par les vagues. Ces dernières années, le plastique est surtout associé à la production de masse, mais s'il devient un matériau avec une longue durée de vie au lieu d'être simplement produit puis jeté, il peut aussi réduire la quantité de plastique générée. L'idée derrière A Time Bottle est de revaloriser le plastique en le convertissant en un matériau utile à long terme, créant ainsi du « plastique antique » dont la valeur augmente avec le passage du temps.

NIGHT BEASTS ABSINTHE

3D: Jing Lin
Company: Leandro Crispim
Country: Singapore
Category: Packaging concept

SILVER PENTAWARD 2020

FAUST OLIVE OIL

Creative Direction: Pedro Vareta
Product Design, 3D Modelling and Rendering:
Ricardo Ribeiro
Graphic Design: Rui Magalhães
Project Management: Lourenço Neves
Company: VOLTA Brand Shaping Studio
Country: Portugal
Category: Packaging concept

SILVER PENTAWARD 2019

MYAIR

Creative Direction and Design: Anna Rufova
3D Visualisation: Nikita Bulgakov
Company: Anna Rufova
Country: Russia
Category: Packaging concept
BRONZE PENTAWARD 2019

COLUMNA

Design: Sara Faulkner
Company: JDO
Country: UK
Category: Packaging concept
BRONZE PENTAWARD 2020

BRABANT WHISKY

Design and 3D Visualisation: Untactil team
Company: Untactil
Country: Spain
Category: Packaging concept

SILVER PENTAWARD 2019

SALUTE

Design: Yanlong Zhou
Supervision: Gu Chuan-Xi
School: Shanghai Institute of Visual Arts (SIVA)
Country: China
Category: Packaging concept (student)

GOLD PENTAWARD 2020

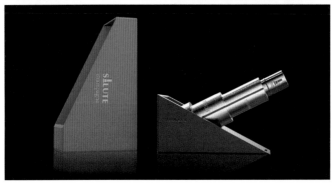

MING

Design: Kong Haoru
Visual Consultation: Liu Yuxin
School: North China University of Science
and Technology
Country: China
Category: Packaging concept (student)

GOLD PENTAWARD 2019

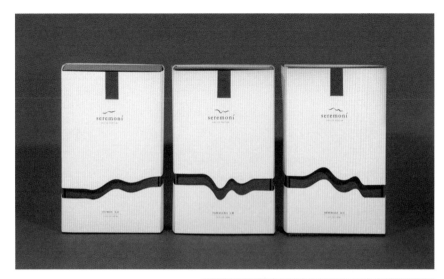

SEREMONI PERFUME PACKAGING

Fabrication Assisting: Xinda Wang
School: School of the Art Institute of Chicago
Country: USA
Category: Packaging concept (student)
SILVER PENTAWARD 2019

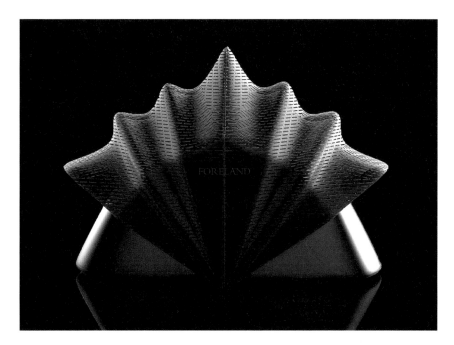

FORELAND

Design: Dai Dong
Supervision: Hu Jijun
School: Shanghai Institute of Visual Arts (SIVA)
Country: China
Category: Packaging concept (student)
SILVER PENTAWARD 2019

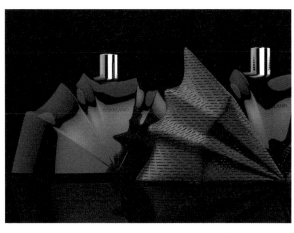

SHOW TAIL

Design: Liu Yuanzhuo
Supervision: Gu Chuanxi
School: Shanghai Institute of Visual Arts (SIVA)
Country: China
Category: Packaging concept (student)

BRONZE PENTAWARD 2019

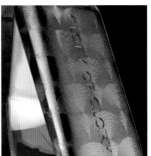

RAY

Design: Pei Ziwen
Supervision: Hu Jijun
School: Shanghai Institute of Visual Arts (SIVA)
Country: China
Category: Packaging concept (student)
BRONZE PENTAWARD 2019

Conscious hugs
for curious kids

Conscious hugs
for curious kids

Best of the category
Household maintenance / Home improvement
Electronic / Non-electronic / Entertainment
Baby products / Pet products
Tobacco products

other markets

Self-promotion
Distributors'/retailers' own brands, private labels
Sustainable design
B2B products / Brand identity programs
Packaging concept

CS LIGHT BULBS

Concept and Design: Angelina Pischikova
Photography: Rodion Kovenkin
Country: Belarus
Category: Best of the category
PLATINUM PENTAWARD 2017

Der weißrussische Elektrofachhandel **CS** versorgt den heimischen Markt mit über 5 000 Produkten. Für diese Produktpalette ließ sich die Verpackungsdesignerin Angelina Pischikova von einer Geschichte über Thomas Edison inspirieren, der die Glühbirne angeblich erfand, nachdem er Glühwürmchen beim Erzeugen von Licht beobachtet hatte. In ihren detailreichen Entwürfen stellt Pischikova Parallelen zwischen der Gestalt verschiedener Insekten und der Form der jeweiligen Glühbirnen her. Die Verpackung zeigt ein Insekt, das Licht abstrahlt, genau wie Edison es beobachtet hatte. Die Illustrationen auf den Verpackungen erregen Aufmerksamkeit und wecken die Neugier.

The electrical supplier **CS** provides over 5,000 products to its domestic market in Belarus. For this product range, packaging designer Angelina Pischikova was inspired by a story that Thomas Edison created the first light bulb after watching fireflies creating light. Her detailed creation matches the shapes of different insects to the shapes of the light bulbs in the product range. This packaging shows an insect creating light, just as Edison is reported to have seen. The illustrations on the packaging capture the attention and inspire curiosity, making the product stand out.

CS propose plus de 5 000 produits électriques sur son marché national en Biélorussie. Pour cette gamme de produits, la designer de packaging Angelina Pischikova s'est inspirée d'une histoire selon laquelle Thomas Edison aurait créé la première ampoule après avoir regardé des lucioles faire de la lumière. Sa création toute en détails fusionne la forme de différents insectes et celle des ampoules de la gamme. Elle montre un insecte faisant de la lumière, tout comme dans l'histoire sur Edison. Les illustrations du packaging attirent l'attention et attisent la curiosité pour démarquer le produit.

GAUSS

Design: Alexey Lavrentiev, Max Tushakaev,
Vasily Gubin, Ilya Soloviov
Company: Fastway. Ideas that rock!
Country: Russia
Category: Household maintenance

SILVER PENTAWARD 2009

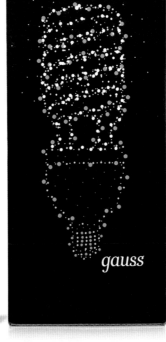

STIIK

Art Direction: Kazutoshi Amano
Design: P.K.G.Tokyo / kad ltd.
Product Design: Eiji Sumi
Concept: Kenji Wada
Client: Ko Design Concept
Company: P.K.G.Tokyo
Country: Japan
Category: Household maintenance
GOLD PENTAWARD 2019

SILVER CROSS
UK LIMITED

Design: Emma Morton, Adam Rix, Simon Griffin
Company: Love
Country: UK
Category: Home improvement

GOLD PENTAWARD 2008

SEEPJE

Design: FLEX/design team
Company: FLEX/design
Country: Netherlands
Category: Household maintenance

SILVER PENTAWARD 2017

**RESESH
NATURAL STONE**
Art Direction: Emi Isemura
Design: Rie Nakai
Company: Kao Corporation
Country: Japan
Category: Household maintenance
SILVER PENTAWARD 2016

MEDICI THREAD

Design: Elena Zaitseva
Country: Russia
Category: Household maintenance
SILVER PENTAWARD 2020

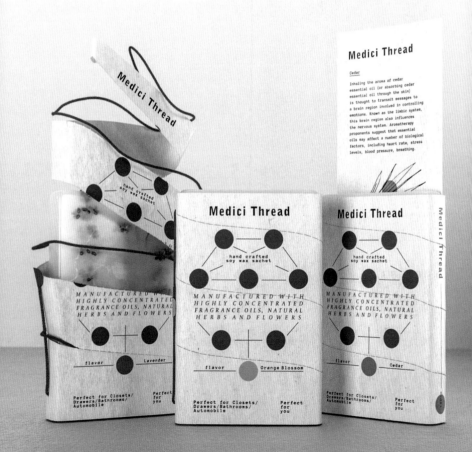

METHOD
Industrial Design: Sean McGreevy
Senior Brand Design: Tammy Dyer
Senior Digital Design: Cat Oshiro
Company: Method Products PBC
Country: UK
Category: Home improvement
GOLD PENTAWARD 2019

ABUNAYYAN ELECTRIC LUMI
Creative Management: Jonathan Ford
Creative Direction: Sarah Cattle
Design Direction: Dan Gladden
Senior Creative Strategy: Jack Hart
Company: Pearlfisher London
Country: UK
Category: Household maintenance
SILVER PENTAWARD 2015

YIN SHANG YIN

Creative Direction: Yu Guang
Design: Wu Chang Fei
Company: Shenzhen Greensong Design
Country: China
Category: Home improvement

SILVER PENTAWARD 2019

RECYCLING FOR EVER

Design: Fabrice Peltier
Company: P'référence
Country: France
Category: Home improvement

BRONZE PENTAWARD 2011

BRÜKEN

Creative Direction: Gregory Tsaknakis
Design: Aris Pasouris
Company: Mousegraphics
Country: Greece
Category: Home improvement

SILVER PENTAWARD 2011

INSTAX

General Management: Kazuhisa Horikiri
Design: Akihiko Ikegami
Company: Fujifilm Corporation
Country: Japan
Category: Electronic

GOLD PENTAWARD 2020

XBOX

Packaging Design: Mark Weiser
Creative Direction: Kevin Marshall
Company: Microsoft
Country: USA
Category: Electronic
DIAMOND PENTAWARD 2019

What made this Diamond winning piece stand out was its unique customer experience. Designed for gamers with limited mobility, the **Xbox Adaptive Controller** perfected the out-of-box experience with its accessible packaging. Using insights gleaned from beta testers and UX respondents, each element of the packaging and unboxing had accessibility first in mind. Key elements that were incorporated include loops, which are highly proven to assist in accessibility, and an open area under the controller, making it easier to remove it from the box. This packaging design was a milestone for accessible packaging, one which Microsoft should be proud of.

Dieser Diamant-Gewinner stach vor allem durch seine einzigartige Verbrauchernähe heraus. Entworfen für Gamer mit eingeschränkter Beweglichkeit bietet der **Xbox Adaptive Controller** mit seiner barrierefreien Verpackung ein ganzheitliches Auspackerlebnis. Die Erfahrungen von Beta-Testern und Erkenntnisse aus einer Verbraucherumfrage flossen in das Design ein, damit jedes Element der Verpackung in der Praxis funktioniert. Schlüsselelemente, sind Schlaufen, die sich gut greifen lassen, sowie ein offener Bereich unterhalb des Controllers, der das Herausnehmen aus der Box erleichtert. Das Verpackungsdesign ist ein Meilenstein für barrierefreie Verpackung, auf das Microsoft stolz sein sollte.

La raison pour laquelle cette création lauréate d'un Diamond s'est distinguée est l'expérience unique qu'elle garantit au consommateur. Conçue pour les joueurs à mobilité réduite, la manette **Xbox Adaptive Controller** atteint la perfection de l'expérience immédiate grâce à son packaging accessible. À partir des informations obtenues de testeurs bêta et de personnes interrogées sur l'UX, chaque élément de l'emballage et son unboxing privilégient l'accessibilité. Des aspects clés ont été incorporés, comme des anses à l'utilité prouvée en matière d'accessibilité et un espace ouvert sous la manette pour en simplifier l'extraction de la boîte. Le design de ce packaging a fait date dans l'histoire des emballages accessibles, et Microsoft peut en être fier.

OKAERI

Client: Yamachiku Co., Ltd.
Creative Direction: Katsuaki Sato
Art Direction and Design: Takenori Sugimura
Package Design: Yoichi Yoshinaga
Company: Katsuaki
Country: Japan
Category: Non-electronic

SILVER PENTAWARD 2020

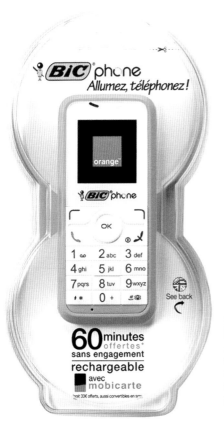

BIC/ORANGE
BIC PHONE

Design: Didier Cosson, Benoit Pean
Company: P'référence
Country: France
Category: Electronic

BRONZE PENTAWARD 2009

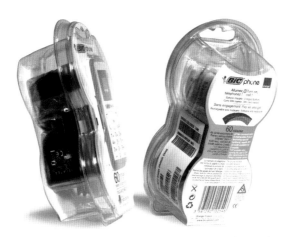

SAKURA SHIMIZU

Art Direction: Nobuya Hayasaka
Creative Direction: Hitoshi Kobayashi
Design: Nobuya Hayasak
Production: arica design
Client: Sakura Shimizu
Company: arica design
Country: Japan
Category: Non-electronic

GOLD PENTAWARD 2020

NEUDIES

Client: Nuedies
Product Design, Graphic Design, Illustration,
Photography and Art Direction:
Enrique Diaz Rato
Company: Enrique Diaz Rato
Country: USA
Category: Entertainment
BRONZE PENTAWARD 2019

HEMA

Concept and Design: Richard Mooij (Magnet Design), Hema design team
Packaging Management: Kirsten Wiarda (Hema)
Project Management: Laura Vermeer (Hema)
Company: Magnet Design
Country: Netherlands
Category: Entertainment

PLATINUM PENTAWARD 2020

This packaging for Dutch retailer **Hema** encloses a range of inflatables for summer fun. The design concept was to show a variety of summer products that look like they have been dropped into mini swimming pools, and there's even a typical ladder that leads into the pool visible on the box, bringing the image to life. All the toys have been designed exclusively by Hema and represent the retailer's most famous icons, like a smoked sausage, Takkie the dog, a tompouce pastry and an ice cream cone. Hema's overall ambition is to stop putting plastic products into plastic packaging, so cardboard boxes were chosen to package and protect the products inside.

Die Verpackung für den niederländischen Einzelhändler **Hema** betrifft eine Reihe von aufblasbaren Spielzeugen für den Sommerspaß. Das Designkonzept zeigt eine Vielfalt an Produkten, die aussehen, als ob sie in Minischwimmbecken fallen gelassen wurden. Es gibt sogar eine Leiter, die in das auf der Schachtel sichtbare Schwimmbecken führt und die das Bild zum Leben erweckt. Alle Spielzeuge wurden exklusiv von Hema entworfen und repräsentieren die bekanntesten Symbole des Einzelhändlers, wie die gebratene Wurst, Takkie den Hund, einen niederländischen Tompouce-Kuchen und eine Eistüte. Hema hat es sich zum Ziel gesetzt, Plastikprodukte nicht mehr in Plastik zu hüllen, daher wurden Kartonagen gewählt, um die Produkte darin zu verpacken und zu schützen.

Ce packaging pour la chaîne de magasins néerlandaise **Hema** renferme une collection d'objets gonflables pour les activités estivales. L'idée du design était de montrer un éventail de produits semblant avoir été jetés dans des mini-piscines : on y voit même la typique échelle à emprunter pour entrer dans l'eau pour une image plus réaliste. Tous les jouets ont été exclusivement conçus par Hema et représentent les icônes de la chaîne, comme une saucisse fumée, le chien Takkie, un mini-gâteau et un cône de glace. L'objectif d'Hema est d'arrêter de vendre des produits en plastique dans des emballages en plastique, d'où le choix de boîtes en carton pour emballer et protéger les produits.

SINCE 1958

COLLECTION
TREASURES

[珍]藏[珍]品[

SEAGULL CAMERA

Design: Zhihao Zhang
Company: KHT Brand
Country: China
Category: Entertainment

GOLD PENTAWARD 2019

Out of nostalgia for **Seagull Camera**, a famous camera brand founded in 1958, Shanghai Seagull Digital Camera Co., Ltd. decided to restart the product line and remanufacture this iconic product. It is not only a digital camera but also a time machine that can capture every special moment, place and event. The use of copper and brown leather in the packaging are characteristic of Chinese industry of the 1950s, whilst the exquisite bronzing and lock add to the collectability of the product.

Aus Nostalgie für die **Seagull Camera**, entschied die Kameramarke Shanghai Seagull Digital Camera Co., Ltd., die 1958 gegründet wurde, sein beliebtes Produkt neu aufzulegen. Dabei handelt es sich nicht nur um eine Digitalkamera, sondern auch um eine Zeitmaschine, die besondere Momente, Orte und jedes Ereignis aufzeichnen kann. Die Verwendung von Kupfer und braunem Leder für die Verpackung sind charakteristisch für die chinesische Industrie der 1950er-Jahre, während die exquisite Bronzefarbe und der Verschluss jedes Sammlerherz höher schlagen lässt.

C'est par nostalgie pour **Seagull Camera**, la célèbre marque d'appareils photo fondée en 1958, que Shanghai Seagull Digital Camera Co., Ltd. a décidé de relancer la gamme et de refabriquer ce produit emblématique. Plus qu'un appareil numérique, cette machine à remonter le temps capture les moments, les lieux et les événements spéciaux. Pour le packaging, le recours au cuivre et au cuir brun est caractéristique de l'industrie chinoise dans les années 1950, alors que le superbe brunissement et le mode de fermeture font du produit un objet de collection.

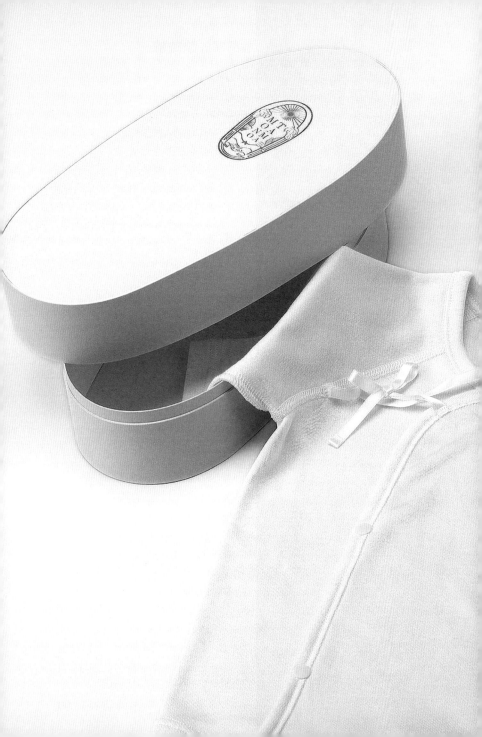

TAMAMONO
Art Direction and Design: Keiko Akatsuka
Box Artisan: Suzuki Shofudo
Client: Elegrance
Company: Keiko Akatsuka & Associates
Country: Japan
Category: Baby products
GOLD PENTAWARD 2017

ORCHID VALLEY PET CASKETS

Design: Leanne Balen
Company: Dessein
Country: Australia
Category: Pet products

BRONZE PENTAWARD 2016

**TAHWA
BRUCE LI**

Design: Tiger Pan
Company: Tigerpan packaging
design studio
Country: China
Category: Tobacco products

SILVER PENTAWARD 2014

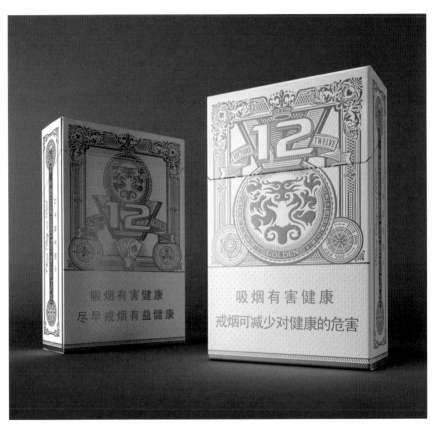

**PHOENIX
V12**
Design: Tiger Pan
Company: Tigerpan packaging
design studio
Country: China
Category: Tobacco products
SILVER PENTAWARD 2014

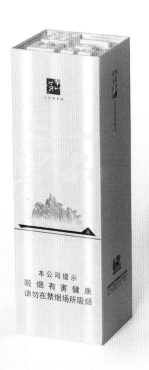

HUANG SHAN

Art Direction: Chen Yingsong
Graphic Design: Cheng Wenbin, Tang Zhong
Company: Shenzhen Yuto Packaging Technology
Country: China
Category: Tobacco products

GOLD PENTAWARD 2019

STRANGER & STRANGER
ULTIMATE DECK

Creative Direction: Kevin Shaw
Design: Cosimo Surace, Ewa Oliver,
Francesco Graziani
Company: Stranger & Stranger
Country: UK
Category: Self-promotion
GOLD PENTAWARD 2013

Every year Stranger & Stranger creates a
limited-edition product to mark the festive season
and celebrate success with the people who make
it happen. Taking a decisive break from the cus-
tomary Christmas bottle, on this occasion the
agency elected to give out the **Ultimate Deck**, a
pack of 54 picture cards from Dan and Dave. This
departure commemorated the breaking-out from
their comfort zone in 2012 to dabbling in fine
foods, cosmetics and luxury luggage. For the first
year, the agency also had a second limited batch
produced, of just 100, and offered to the public
for sale.

Jedes Jahr schaffen Stranger & Stranger als
Sonderauflage ein Produkt, um die Feiertage am
Jahresende zu betonen und mit jenen Menschen
den Erfolg zu feiern, die ihn verdient haben. Man
beschloss, sich deutlich von der üblichen Ge-
schenkflasche zu Weihnachten abzusetzen: Die
Agentur wählte für diese Gelegenheit das **Ultimate Deck**, ein Kartenspiel mit 54 Karten von
Dan and Dave. Dieses Ausscheren feierte auch den
Ausbruch von 2012 aus der Komfortzone: Seitdem
versucht man sich in Feinkost, Kosmetik und
luxuriösem Reisegepäck. Die Agentur hat in diesem Jahr auch zum ersten Mal eine zweite Auflage
von insgesamt nur 100 Stück produzieren lassen,
die in den öffentlichen Handel ging.

Chaque année, Stranger & Stranger sort un
produit en édition limitée pour marquer le début
des fêtes de fin d'année et célébrer les réussites avec
les personnes y ayant contribué. Pour rompre avec
la coutume de la typique bouteille pour Noël,
l'agence a pour cette occasion choisi d'offrir
Ultimate Deck, un jeu de 54 cartes illustrées par
Dan et Dave. Ce choix est venu marquer leur sortie
de leur zone de confort en 2012 pour se lancer
dans les produits gourmets, les cosmétiques et les
bagages de luxe. La première année, l'agence a
produit une seconde édition limitée de 100 unités
seulement qu'elle a mises en vente.

ORIGINALITY AND IMAGINATION

Design: Stocks Taylor Benson Design team
Company: Stocks Taylor Benson
Country: UK
Category: Self-promotion

SILVER PENTAWARD 2019

DESIGN

CREATE

DISTIL

CLAY FIGURE

General Management: Kazuhisa Horikiri
Design: Daisuke Sato
Company: Fujifilm Corporation
Country: Japan
Category: Self-promotion

SILVER PENTAWARD 2019

Omdesign created this wood and cork package as a symbol of their strong commitment to sustainability. It contains an LBV 2012 port wine, a classic Portuguese product, as well as an envelope containing an acorn that can be planted to create a new cork oak tree. The seedling can either be propagated within the original packaging or planted outdoors, where the planting area can be marked by a wooden ring contained within. In this way, the raw materials used to create the packaging are returned directly to nature. The casket material is produced without the use of any oil derivatives. The "98/89" printed on the label refers to the year the company was founded (1998) and the 89 awards they received during 2016.

Omdesign hat diese Verpackung aus Holz und Kork als Symbol ihres großen Engagements für Nachhaltigkeit entworfen. Sie enthält einen LBV Portwein von 2012, ein klassisches portugiesisches Produkt, sowie einen Umschlag mit einer Eichel, die man einpflanzen kann, um eine neue Korkeiche heranzuziehen. Der Sämling kann entweder in der Originalverpackung heranwachsen oder im Freien eingesetzt werden, wo sich die Stelle mit dem beigefügten Holzring markieren lässt. Auf diese Weise werden die für die Verpackung verwendeten Rohstoffe direkt in die Natur zurückgeführt. Zur Herstellung der Umhüllung werden keinerlei Ölderivate benutzt. Die Aufschrift 98/89 bezieht sich auf das Gründungsjahr der Agentur (1998) und die 89 Auszeichnungen, die sie im Jahr 2016 erhalten hat.

Omdesign a créé ce coffret en bois et liège pour symboliser son engagement envers la préservation de l'environnement. Il contient un vin de Porto LBV 2012, un grand classique parmi les produits portugais, ainsi qu'une enveloppe contenant un gland qui peut être planté pour faire pousser un chêne-liège. Le semis peut se faire dans le coffret d'origine ou en extérieur, où l'emplacement peut être marqué par l'anneau en bois fourni. Ainsi, les matières premières utilisées pour créer le packaging retournent directement à la nature. Le coffret est produit sans utiliser aucun produit dérivé du pétrole. La mention « 98/89 » imprimée sur l'étiquette fait référence à l'année de création de l'entreprise (1998) et aux 89 récompenses qu'elle a reçues en 2016.

OMDESIGN

Design: Diogo Gama Rocha
Company: Omdesign
Country: Portugal
Category: Self-promotion

GOLD PENTAWARD 2017

LRXD

Creative Direction: Kelly Reedy, Jamie Reedy
Design: Drew Bentley
Copywriting: Ashley Rutstein
Production: Valerie Hawks
Senior Producer: Jamie Sharp
Production Company: Method & Madness
Company: LRXD
Country: USA
Category: Self-promotion
BRONZE PENTAWARD 2018

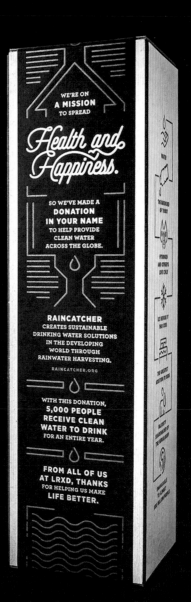

LE LOGIS
GREY GOOSE SINCEREMENT

Design: Linea team
Company: Linea – The Spirit Valley Designers
Country: France
Category: Self-promotion
SILVER PENTAWARD 2017

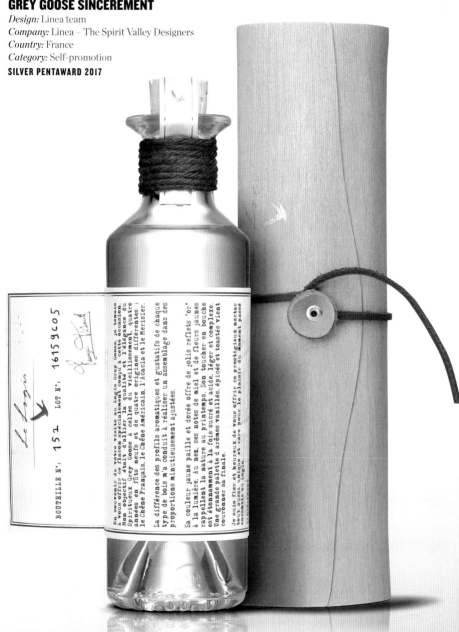

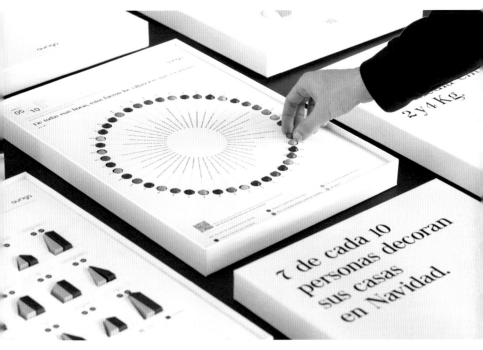

AURIGA

Creative Direction: Javier Bidezabal
Art Direction: Johana Dueñas,
Eduardo España, Javier Bidezabal
Copywriting: Eduardo España
Design: Carmina Escudero, Carmen Cuadrado
Photography: Pedro Maìrnez,
Agustín Escámez (Q&Cumber)
Production: Tamar Valdenebro
General Account Direction: Cristina Hernández,
Raquel Guerrero
CEO: Balba González Camino
Client: Auriga
Company: Auriga
Country: Spain
Category: Self-promotion
PLATINUM PENTAWARD 2019

This self-promotional piece by **Auriga** features a set of four chocolate boxes with edible infographics. To create a standout seasonal gift for their clients, they turned Christmas data into a design which was simple to understand and interactive. Using premium materials, each box is designed to be an experience allowing users to take a tour through all the data and information whilst enjoying a delicious treat. Different shapes and flavours of chocolate represent different kinds of information, creating something pleasing both to the eyes and to the taste buds.

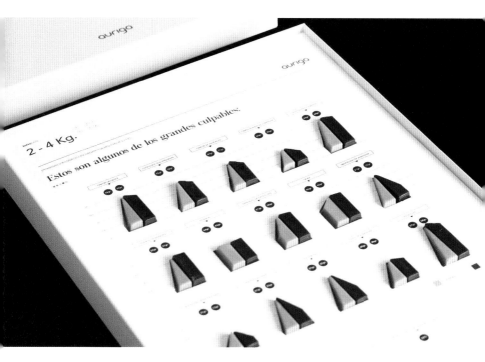

Dieses Selbstvermarktungsstück von **Auriga** beinhaltet ein Set aus vier Schokoladenschachteln mit essbaren Infografiken. Um ein herausstechendes Geschenk zu schaffen, wurden Weihnachtsdaten in ein Design verwandelt, das einfach zu verstehen, und interaktiv ist. Mit hochwertigen Materialien entworfen, erläutert jede Grafik Fakten, während die Käufer einen Leckerbissen genießen können. Die unterschiedlichen Formen und Sorten der Schokolade repräsentieren verschiedene Informationsarten und sind sowohl bekömmlich für die Augen als auch für den Magen.

Cette création d'autopromotion par **Auriga** se compose d'un lot de quatre boîtes de chocolats aux infographies comestibles. En vue d'offrir à ses clients un cadeau d'exception pour les fêtes, la marque a converti des données sur Noël en un design intuitif et interactif. Chaque boîte est fabriquée à l'aide de matériaux haut de gamme et pensée comme une expérience : les destinataires découvrent ainsi les informations tout en savourant une délicieuse gâterie. Les formes et les goûts des chocolats correspondent à divers types d'informations, ce qui donne une composition plaisante tant visuellement que pour les papilles.

RAT APPLE CIDER

Creative Direction: Andrey Kugaevskikh
Design: Anastasia Ushnurtseva
Company: Svoe Mnenie
Country: Russia
Category: Self-promotion
SILVER PENTAWARD 2020

This company-issued **Rat Apple Cider** was presented as a New Year's gift to the partners of Svoe Mnenie branding agency. The ordinary bottle was made to look like a rat – the symbol of the year according to the Chinese calendar. A cork covered with red sealing wax forms the rat's nose, the whiskers are made of twine and the red eyes and ears are printed on the paper package of the bottle. On the bottle label, an apple-shaped brain holds keywords related to the agency's work and symbolises the taste of the drink itself. It is also worth mentioning that the stem of the fruit takes the shape of a rat, happily leaving the maze of tasks completed in the passing year.

Dieser **Rat Apple Cider** wurde den Partnern der Svoe Mnenie Branding Agentur als Neujahrsgeschenk überreicht. Handelsübliche Flaschen wurden dafür in Ratten verwandelt – laut dem chinesischen Kalender das Tierkreiszeichen des Jahres. Ein Korken, bedeckt mit rotem Siegelwachs, formt die Nase der Ratte, Fäden um den Flaschenhals bilden die Schnurrhaare und rote Augen sowie die Ohren sind auf einen Papierumschlag gedruckt. Es ist noch erwähnenswert, dass das Etikett, ein apfelförmiges Gehirn, die Mottos der Agentur führt und gleichzeitig den Geschmack des Getränks symbolisiert. Der Stiel der Frucht formt eine Ratte, die das Labyrinth aus erledigten Aufgaben des Jahres glücklich hinter sich lässt.

Le cidre **Rat Apple Cider** a été produit comme cadeau de Nouvel An aux partenaires de l'agence de branding Svoe Mnenie. La bouteille a été pensée pour ressembler à un rat, signe de l'année selon le calendrier chinois. Recouvert de cire à cacheter rouge, le bouchon représente le nez de l'animal, alors que ses moustaches sont faites de ficelle et ses yeux rouges et ses oreilles sont imprimés sur l'emballage papier de la bouteille. Sur l'étiquette, un cerveau en forme de pomme contient des mots clés liés au travail de l'agence et symbolise le goût de la boisson ; sans compter la tige du fruit en forme de rat heureux de sortir du labyrinthe de projets accomplis l'année passée.

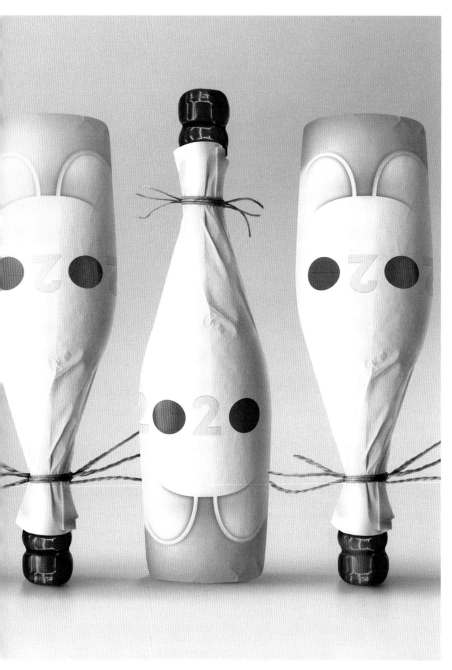

SUSHI VESLA

Art Direction: Ermek Cherkesov
Creative Direction: Oleg Barinboim
Agency Production: Sevda Jalal
Case Direction: Dmitry Kostuchenko
Account Management: Anna Dzhandoeva
Executive Creative Direction: Dmitry Tutkov
Company: TUTKOVBUDKOV
Country: Russia
Category: Distributors'/retailers' own brands, private labels
SILVER PENTAWARD 2019

LOVING HOME CUTTING BOARDS

Creative Direction: Hyunjoo Choi
Design: Seungje Choi, Eunjin Oh
Company: Emart
Country: South Korea
Category: Distributors'/retailers' own brands, private labels
SILVER PENTAWARD 2013

JIAN WO

Creative Direction: Jeff Wu
Graphic Design: Qiong Wu, Juan Ying Zheng
Client: Womai, COFCO
Company: Beijing Perfect Point Design
Country: China
Category: Distributors'/ retailers' own brands,
private labels

BRONZE PENTAWARD 2019

WILDLY CRAFTED BOTTLES

Design: Seriesnemo industrial and graphic team
Company: SeriesNemo
Country: Spain
Category: Sustainable design
GOLD PENTAWARD 2020

The glass in **Wildly Crafted Bottles** comes from an industrial oven with the highest percentage of PCR (post-consumer recycled) glass in the market. All types of recycled glass are accepted, meaning that slight variations occur, but this is seen to reflect the authenticity and exclusivity of the products. NºT REGULAR Spirits embraces imperfections, thereby reducing waste. The inevitable defects that appear during production are integrated and not considered errors but values of differentiation, creating a unique product.

Das Glas der **Wildly Crafted Bottles** stammt aus einem Industrieofen mit dem auf dem Markt höchsten Prozentanteil von PCR-Glas (Post-Consumer-Recycled, also nach der Nutzung durch den Konsumenten recyceltes Glas). Alle Arten von Glas werden genutzt, was bedeutet, dass kleine Farbunterschiede entstehen können, wodurch aber die Authentizität und Exklusivität widergespiegelt wird. NºT REGULAR Spirits nimmt Unvollkommenheit an und reduziert so Abfall. Kleine Fehler, die während der Produktion entstehen, werden integriert und kreieren ein einzigartiges Produkt.

Les bouteilles **Wildly Crafted Bottles** sont fabriquées dans un four industriel avec du verre contenant le pourcentage PCR (recyclé post-consommation) le plus élevé du marché. Tous les types de verre recyclé sont acceptés, ce qui entraîne de légères variations et rend les produits authentiques et exclusifs. NºT REGULAR Spirits se saisit de ces imperfections en vue de réduire le gaspillage. Ces défauts inévitables apparaissent en cours de production sont conservés et ne sont pas considérés comme des erreurs, mais comme une marque de différenciation au résultat unique.

ZËRNA

Creative Direction: Farrukh Sharipov
Client Service Direction: Alina mirzaeva
Account Management: Anna Pak
Art Direction: Timur Aitov
Copywriting: Aleksandra Khalimon
Design: Tamilla Mirzaeva, Kristina Popova
Company: Synthesis creative lab
Country: Uzbekistan
Category: Sustainable design

SILVER PENTAWARD 2020

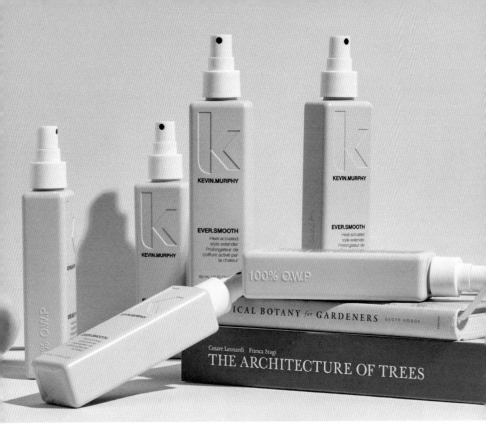

KEVIN.MURPHY

Founder and Creative Direction: Kevin Murphy
Managing Direction: Christian Jensen
(Pack Tech A/S)
Company: Kevin.Murphy
Country: USA
Category: Sustainable design
BRONZE PENTAWARD 2020

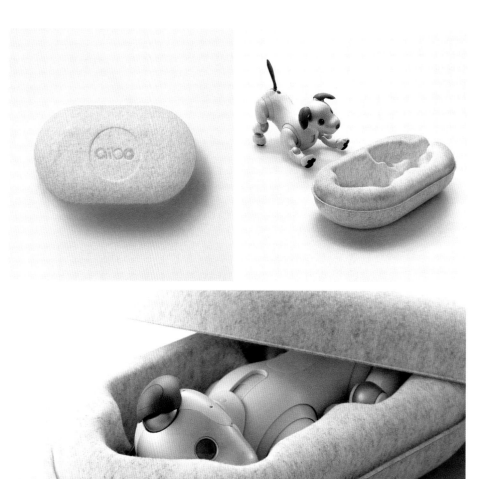

AIBO
Design: Kenichi Hirose, Daigo Maesaka,
Tetsuro Tsuji
Company: Sony Corporation
Country: Japan
Category: Sustainable design
SILVER PENTAWARD 2019

O-I VORTEX BOTTLE

Design: O-I research and development team,
O-I product innovation team
Company: O-I North America Glass
Country: USA
Category: B2B products
GOLD PENTAWARD 2011

Die innovative Flasche *O-I Vortex* schafft anhand einer speziellen Designtechnologie eingeprägte Rillen im Inneren des Flaschenhalses. Der so entstehende auffällige Look soll den Konsumenten vor dem Regal faszinieren. Diese neue Form der Glasverpackung galt bei der 0,3-Standard-Langhalsbierflasche als Pionierstück. Hier setzte man auf die erfolgreiche Entwicklung eines inneren Designs von miteinander verschlungenen Spiralen — deutlich genug, um von außen sichtbar zu sein, und auch bei hoher Produktionsrate leicht replizierbar. Um das Etikett einfach aufbringen zu können, ließ man das Äußere der Flasche glatt. Die Flasche erschien zum ersten Mal 2010 in der Öffentlichkeit, als sie von Miller Lite vorgestellt wurde.

The innovative *O-I Vortex* bottle uses special design technology to create internally embossed grooves inside the bottle's neck for a distinctive look intended to intrigue consumers at point-of-purchase. This new form of glass packaging was pioneered for the standard 12-ounce, long-neck beer bottle and relied on the successful development of an internal design of intertwining spirals substantial enough to be seen on the outside of the bottle and able to be replicated at a high rate of production. The exterior was left smooth for ease of label application. The bottle was first seen by the public in 2010 when it was taken up by Miller Lite.

Le tourbillon en relief dans le col de la bouteille *O-I Vortex* a été créé à l'aide d'une technologie spéciale, et il lui confère un aspect caractéristique qui vise à intriguer les consommateurs sur le lieu d'achat. Ce nouveau genre de conditionnement en verre a été testé pour la bouteille de bière standard de 35 cl à long col. Son succès dépendait de la mise au point d'un motif interne de spirales entrelacées suffisamment prononcé pour être visible de l'extérieur, et pouvant se prêter à une cadence de production élevée. L'extérieur est lisse pour faciliter l'application des étiquettes. Le public a pu voir la bouteille pour la première fois en 2010, lorsque Miller Lite a décidé de l'utiliser.

DRIPP COFFEE SHOP

Creative Direction: David Turner,
Bruce Duckworth, Sarah Moffat
Design: Chris Garvey, Rebecca Au Williams
Design Direction: Chris Garvey
Illustration: Chris Garvey
Company: Turner Duckworth: London
& San Francisco
Country: UK, USA
Category: Brand identity programs
GOLD PENTAWARD 2013

ENJOY *Budweiser* FREELY.

Prohibition Brew

When **Budweiser** launched a non-alcoholic beer called Prohibition Brew, they were referencing the company's prominent role in 1920s America. The design team JKR drew inspiration from a 1920s label found in the firm's archives, picking up heritage elements to tell the story of the beer's origins. The brand was an immediate success, with its tagline "Enjoy Freely" changing perceptions of what a non-alcoholic beer could be.

Als **Budweiser** ein alkoholfreies Bier namens Prohibition Brew herausbrachte, bezog man sich damit auf die prominente Rolle der Firma im Amerika der 1920er-Jahre. Das Designerteam JKR holte sich Inspiration von einem in den Firmenarchiven entdeckten Etikett aus der damaligen Zeit und griff traditionelle Elemente auf, um die Ursprungsgeschichte des Biers zu erzählen. Die Marke wurde sofort ein großer Erfolg mit dem Slogan „Enjoy Freely", der das Image von alkoholfreiem Bier grundlegend veränderte.

La bière sans alcool Prohibition Brew de
Budweiser fait référence au rôle important que
la marque a joué dans l'Amérique des années 1920.
L'équipe de design JKR s'est inspirée d'une étiquette de l'époque trouvée dans les archives de
Budweiser, et a repris des éléments de son patri-
moine pour raconter l'histoire des origines de
cette bière. Le succès a été immédiat, et le slogan
« Enjoy Freely » (Dégustez en toute liberté)
a changé la façon dont le public perçoit la bière
sans alcool.

BUDWEISER PROHIBITION BREW

Executive Creative Direction: Tosh Hall
Design Direction: Paul Sieka
Copywriting: Jen Chandler
Photography: Martin Wonnacott
Illustration: Filip Yip
Typography: Ian Brignell
Account Direction: Phil Buhagiar
Account Management: Josh Griffin
Company: Jones Knowles Ritchie
Country: UK
Category: Brand identity programs
GOLD PENTAWARD 2017

SONG HE

Art Direction: Zhang Xiaoming
Company: Unidea Bank
Country: China
Category: Brand identity programs
GOLD PENTAWARD 2020

Aimed at a younger audience, **Song He** whiskey is a blended grain whiskey contained in four fun, stylish and easy-to-carry bottles. The design uses four animal characters, one for each bottle, to represent four different energies for gift giving: the squirrel representing Kindness, the monkey Justice, the rabbit Wisdom and the bear Power.

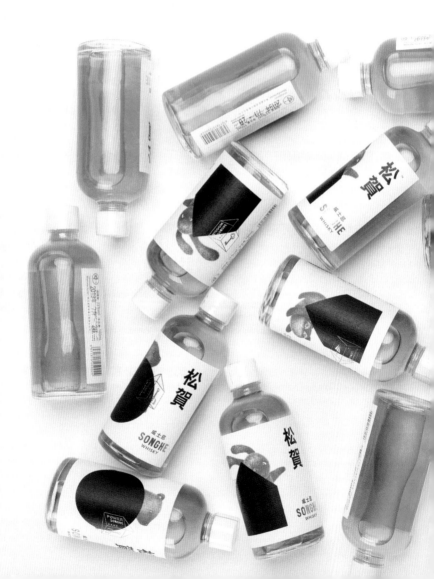

Auf eine jüngere Kundschaft zugeschnitten, ist der **Song He** Whiskey, der aus verschiedenen Getreidesorten besteht und in vier stylishen, leicht zu tragenden Flaschen erhältlich ist. Das Design nutzt Tierfiguren, eine für jede Flasche, um die vier verschiedenen Dynamiken des Verschenkens zu repräsentieren: das Eichhörnchen für Freundlichkeit, den Affen für Gerechtigkeit, den Hasen für Weisheit und den Bären für Stärke.

S'adressant à un public jeune, le whisky de grain blended **Song He** est proposé dans quatre bouteilles élégantes et faciles à transporter. Sur chacune d'elles se trouve un personnage animal représentant l'une des quatre motivations pour faire un cadeau : l'écureuil symbolise la bonté, le singe la justice, le lapin la sagesse et l'ours le pouvoir.

BUD LIGHT

Executive Creative Direction: Tosh Hall
Managing Direction: Sara Hyman
Design Direction: Andy Baron
Design: Adam Howard, Augustus Cook,
Robert Medkeff, Izgi Yapici, Daniel Díarcy
Account Direction: Phil Buhagiar
Account Management: Caitlin Cross
Visualization: Justin Sottile, Matthew Coluccio
Company: Jones Knowles Ritchie
Country: UK
Category: Brand identity programs
BRONZE PENTAWARD 2017

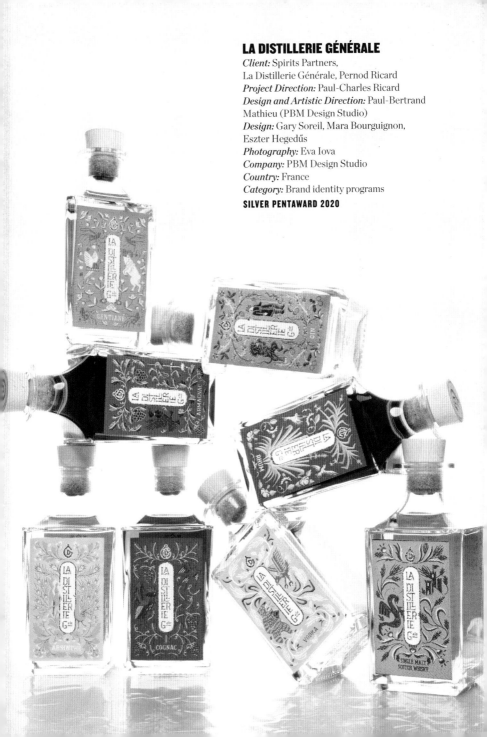

LA DISTILLERIE GÉNÉRALE

Client: Spirits Partners,
La Distillerie Générale, Pernod Ricard
Project Direction: Paul-Charles Ricard
Design and Artistic Direction: Paul-Bertrand
Mathieu (PBM Design Studio)
Design: Gary Soreil, Mara Bourguignon,
Eszter Hegedűs
Photography: Eva Iova
Company: PBM Design Studio
Country: France
Category: Brand identity programs
SILVER PENTAWARD 2020

GASTROPOLIS FOOD MARKET

Client: Collective LLC
Creative Direction: Armenak Grigoryan
Art Direction and Design: Karen Gevorgyan
Copywriting: Ani Gevorgyan
Company: formascope design
Country: Armenia
Category: Brand identity
programs
SILVER PENTAWARD 2019

HACEB

Creative Direction: David Freyre
Art Direction and Graphic Design:
Oscar Gutiérrez
Company: Grupo ImasD
Country: Colombia
Category: Packaging concept

SILVER PENTAWARD 2017

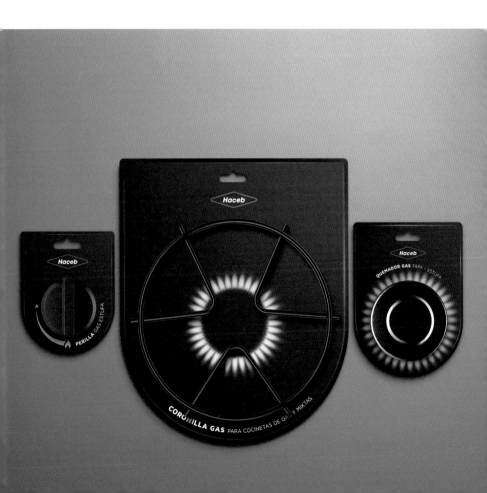

THE LIFE LAUNDRY

Design: Sara Jones
Company: Anthem Benelux
Country: Netherlands
Category: Packaging concept
GOLD PENTAWARD 2017

Primarily led by advances in performance and cleaning power, the language and designs used for most detergents focus on disinfecting the clothing we wear – clothing that for the majority of us doesn't get very dirty. Fragrance is an emotionally powerful driver for purchasers, but the scents used are mostly synthetic and brashly described on the pack. Fabric is a delicate material that we wear next to our skin but the laundry room itself is usually a rather unloved space in the home. **The Life Laundry**'s design represents a future vision of superior fabric care. Designed for the home as well as the shelf, the clever handle, use of natural fragrance, and premium packaging create a desirable brand that cares for and prolongs the life of your clothing. The Life Laundry aspirational lifestyle concept was awarded Gold in the 2017 Pentaward Worldwide Packaging Design Competition.

Bei Waschmittelverpackungen zielen Text und Design meist auf die Fortschritte in der Waschleistung ab und konzentrieren sich auf die Desinfektion unserer Kleidung – die in den meisten Fällen gar nicht mehr sehr schmutzig wird. Der Duft ist beim Kauf ein emotional wichtiger Faktor, doch sind die verwendeten Duftstoffe überwiegend synthetisch und werden auf der Packung nur nachlässig beschrieben. Stoffe sind ein empfindliches Material, das wir direkt auf der Haut tragen, aber die Waschküche ist für gewöhnlich ein eher ungeliebter Raum in unserem Zuhause. Das Design von **The Life Laundry** entwirft die Zukunftsvision einer besseren Stoff-Pflege. Das für zuhause ebenso wie fürs Verkaufsregal zugeschnittene Design mit dem cleveren Griff, die Verwendung natürlicher Duftstoffe und die edle Verpackung erzeugen eine attraktive Marke, die unsere Kleidung pflegt und ihre Lebensdauer verlängert. Das ehrgeizige Lifestyle-Konzept von The Life Laundry wurde bei der Pentaward Worldwide Packaging Design Competition 2017 mit Gold ausgezeichnet.

Le langage et les visuels employés pour la plupart des détergents se basent avant tout sur les progrès réalisés dans le domaine du pouvoir nettoyant, et s'intéressent à l'hygiène des vêtements que nous portons, alors que la majorité d'entre nous ne se salit généralement que très peu. Les odeurs sont un moteur émotionnel puissant pour les acheteurs, mais les parfums utilisés sont souvent synthétiques et décrits de façon tape-à-l'œil sur l'emballage. Le tissu est un matériau délicat que nous portons contre la peau, mais la buanderie est souvent une pièce à laquelle on prête peu d'attention. Le design de **The Life Laundry** représente une vision futuriste de l'entretien du linge. Conçus pour la maison ainsi que pour les rayonnages, la poignée intelligente, le parfum naturel et le packaging haut de gamme créent une marque séduisante qui prend soin de votre linge et prolonge sa durée de vie. Le concept d'art de vivre ambitieux de The Life Laundry a remporté le Gold Pentaward lors de l'édition 2017 de cette compétition mondiale de design de packaging.

ＤＲＹ

ＬＩ

ＳＳ

THE LIFE LAUNDRY

WITH ESSENTIAL OILS OF
BERGAMOT & NEROLI
NON BIOLOGICAL
POWDER

30 LOADS OF LUXURIOUS FRESHNESS

BRIGHT MEN

Creative Direction: Yoshio Kato
Art Direction: Yoshio Kato, Eijiro Kuniyoshi
Design and Illustration: Takaaki Hashimoto
Company: Kotobuki Seihan Printing
Country: Japan
Category: Packaging concept
GOLD PENTAWARD 2019

BEAN PLAYING TENNIS

Owner and Creative Direction:
Kyanne Bückmann, Kevin Davis
Company: Bowler & Kimchi
Country: Netherlands
Category: Packaging concept
GOLD PENTAWARD 2020

Bean Playing Tennis is a packaging concept
that not only stands out but helps motivate kids to
get outside and have fun. Inspired by the green
bean, this tennis ball pack takes the shape of a
massive bean pod and holds four green bean tennis
balls. With a semi-matt finish the hard plastic pod
clamps the balls in place but is soft enough to allow
the balls to be pulled out of it. A hook extends from
the top of the bean pod in an organic shape, allowing it to be hung in shop displays or on the mesh
fence at a tennis court.

Bean Playing Tennis ist ein Verpackungskon-
zept, das nicht nur heraussticht, sondern auch
dazu beiträgt, Kinder zu motivieren, nach draußen
zu gehen und Spaß zu haben. Inspiriert von grünen
Bohnen, hat dieses Paket mit Tennisbällen die
Form einer Bohnenhülse, die vier grüne Bohnen-
Tennisbälle enthält. Mit einer halbmatten Oberfläche klemmt die harte Kunststoffschale die Bälle
fest ein, ist aber weich genug, dass man die Bälle
gut herausziehen kann. An der Oberseite der Bohnenhülse ist ein Haken angebracht, an dem man
sie sowohl im Schaufenster als auch am Maschen-
drahtzaun auf dem Tennisplatz aufhängen kann.

Bean Playing Tennis est un concept d'emballage qui ne passe pas inaperçu et motive les enfants
à sortir et s'amuser. Imitant un haricot vert, cet
étui pour balles de tennis ressemble à une énorme
cosse et peut contenir quatre balles-graines. De
finition semi-mate, cette cosse en plastique dur
retient les balles mais est suffisamment souple
pour pouvoir les retirer. La partie supérieure se
termine par un crochet de forme organique per-
mettant de pendre la cosse dans une vitrine ou
au filet du court de tennis.

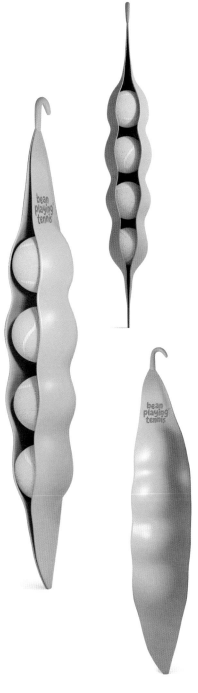

NO
BUGS
IN MY
BOX

GREEN
FINGER
FOOD

natural food for plants

Box Plants
6 meals for your greens

250ml

I'M
FEELING
HYDRA
BLUE

GREEN
FINGER
FOOD

natural food for plants

Blue Hydrangeas
6 meals for your greens

250ml

GREEN FINGER FOOD

Senior Design: Sandra Wiggers
Company: SGK Anthem – Amsterdam
Country: Netherlands
Category: Packaging concept

BRONZE PENTAWARD 2019

THE BROOMS

Creative Direction: Yoshio Kato
Art Direction: Yoshio Kato,
Eijiro Kuniyoshi
Design and Illustration:
Yasunori Wakabayashi
Company: Kotobuki Seihan Printing
Country: Japan
Category: Packaging concept
SILVER PENTAWARD 2020

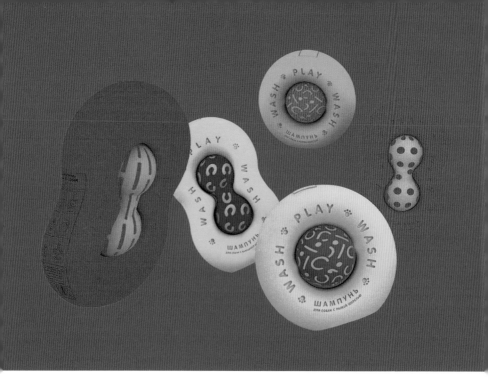

WASH&PLAY

Design: Anna Kondratova, Natalia Radnaeva
Curation: Oksana Paley
School: HSE Art & Design School
Country: Russia
Category: Packaging concept (student)
NXT-GEN PENTAWARD 2019

Wash&Play is a shampoo for dogs that turns the ordinary process of washing your pet into an exciting game. The concept is based on the similarity dogs can have to children, as both are cute and love toys. The packaging for Wash&Play attracts attention thanks to its expressive shape and bright colour palette, which also allows the user to identify the shampoo type by the attached dog toy and the pattern on the product.

Wash&Play ist ein Hundeshampoo, das den alltäglichen Prozess des Haustierwaschens in ein aufregendes Spiel verwandelt. Das Konzept basiert auf der Idee, dass Hunde, genau wie Kinder, Spielzeug lieben. Die Verpackung von Wash&Play erregt dank seiner ausdrucksstarken Form und der leuchtenden Farben Aufmerksamkeit und der Käufer erkennt die unterschiedlichen Shampoos anhand der Spielzeugs und der Muster auf dem Produkt.

Wash&Play est un shampooing pour chiens qui convertit le nettoyage de votre animal en un moment ludique. Le concept part de la similarité entre les chiens et les enfants, qui comme eux sont attendrissants et aiment les jouets. Le packaging de Wash&Play attire l'attention par sa forme et par sa palette de couleurs vives. Le consommateur peut identifier le type de shampooing grâce au jouet qu'il intègre et aux dessins sur le produit.

LIL'LAMB

Tutoring: Leonid Slavin, Evgeni Razumov,
Denis Shlesberg
Illustration: inspired by artworks of
Stacie Bloomfield
3D Visualisation: Pavel Gubin
Product, Packaging Concept and Art Direction:
Kate Zakharova
School: British Higher School of Art and Design
Country: Russia
Category: Packaging concept (student)
GOLD PENTAWARD 2020

The **LIL'LAMB** brand reflects the idea of a newborn's innocence. It offers granulated and concentrated 0+ detergent based on Marseille soap's 17th-century formula composed of three natural ingredients: olive oil, spring water and wood ash. This soft and gentle soap can be used as a universal cleanser for hand and machine laundry, toys, fruit and surfaces, and as a stain remover or softener – one product instead of six. Cardboard boxes for refills, durable ceramic accessories and reusable dispensers help save plastic, money and the planet.

Die Marke **LIL'LAMB** spiegelt die Unschuld eines Neugeborenen wider. Sie bietet granulierte und konzentrierte 0+-Waschmittel auf Basis der aus dem 17. Jahrhundert stammenden Formel der Marseiller Seife an, die aus drei Inhaltsstoffen besteht: Olivenöl, Quellwasser und Holzasche. Diese sanfte und schonende Seife kann als universeller Reiniger für Hand- und Maschinenwäsche, Spielzeuge, Obst und Oberflächen sowie als Fleckenentferner oder Weichspüler verwendet werden – ein Produkt, statt sechs verschiedener. Pappkartons zum Nachfüllen, langlebiges Keramikzubehör und wiederverwendbare Spender helfen, Plastik und Geld zu sparen und den Planeten zu retten.

La marque **LIL'LAMB** transmet toute la candeur du nouveau-né. Sa gamme 0+ de lessives concentrées en poudre est élaborée à partir de la formule datant du XVIIe siècle du savon de Marseille, qui compte trois ingrédients : huile d'olive, eau de source et cendre de bois. Ce savon doux et délicat peut être employé comme nettoyant universel pour le lavage du linge à la main ou en machine, le nettoyage de jouets, de fruits ou de surfaces, mais aussi comme détachant et adoucissant, soit six produits en un. Les boîtes en carton pour les recharges, les accessoires durables en céramique et les distributeurs réutilisables supposent une économie de plastique et d'argent, ainsi qu'une bonne action pour la planète.

INDEX

100 Illustrators

The Package Design Book

Logo Design. Global Brands

D&AD. The Copy Book

Modern Art

Bookworm's delight: never bore, always excite!

TASCHEN
Bibliotheca Universalis

Design of the 20th Century

1000 Chairs

1000 Lights

Industrial Design A–Z

Bauhaus

1000 Record Covers

20th Century Photography

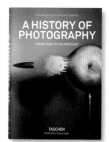

A History of Photography

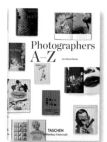

Photographers A–Z

Eugène Atget. Paris

Photo Icons

New Deal Photography

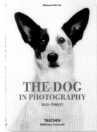

The Dog in Photography

Curtis. The North
American Indian

Stieglitz.
Camera Work

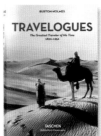

Burton Holmes.
Travelogues

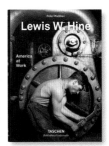

Lewis W. Hine

Film Noir

Horror Cinema

100 All-Time
Favorite Movies

The Stanley Kubrick
Archives

20th Century Fashion

Fashion History

1000 Tattoos

Tiki Pop

IMPRINT

© 2023 TASCHEN GmbH
Hohenzollernring 53, D–50672 Köln
www.taschen.com

Editor
Julius Wiedemann

English Translation
Isabel Varea Riley for Grapevine Publishing
Services, London

German Translation
Ulrike Becker, Berlin; Lea Buseck for
Delivering iBooks & Design, Barcelona;
Jürgen Dubau, Freiburg

French Translation
Aurélie Daniel and Valérie Lavoyer
for Delivering iBooks & Design, Barcelona

Printed in Slovenia
ISBN 978–3–8365–9099–0